Indra

Utkarsh Patel is a lecturer of comparative mythology at the University of Mumbai and is a guest faculty in many other academic institutions across the country. He is an author of mythological fiction. He is also a founder member of 'The Mythology Project' (www.themythologyproject.com), which explores our rich cultural heritage through archival collections and by researching living myths and traditions.

Utkarsh regularly conducts workshops on various world mythologies—Greek, Mesopotamian and Norse—in addition to the epics of India, particularly the Ramayana and its myriad versions. Utkarsh is a TEDx speaker. He is also regularly invited to speak on various mythological subjects, with an emphasis on the interpretation of mythological characters and incidents, feminism, management and other topics, at various literary forums and festivals, organizations, etc.

For more on his work, visit www.utkarshmp.com

Also by the author

Shakuntala: The Woman Wronged

Indra

The Rise and Fall of a Hero

UTKARSH PATEL

Published by
Rupa Publications India Pvt. Ltd 2022
7/16, Ansari Road, Daryaganj
New Delhi 110002

Sales centres:
Allahabad Bengaluru Chennai
Hyderabad Jaipur Kathmandu
Kolkata Mumbai

Copyright © Utkarsh Patel 2022

All rights reserved.

No part of this publication may be reproduced, transmitted,
or stored in a retrieval system, in any form or by any means,
electronic, mechanical, photocopying, recording or otherwise,
without the prior permission of the publisher.

This is a work of fiction. Names, characters, places and incidents are either the
product of the author's imagination or are used fictitiously and any resemblance
to any actual person, living or dead, events or locales is entirely coincidental.

ISBN: 978-93-5520-540-7

First impression 2022

10 9 8 7 6 5 4 3 2 1

The moral right of the author has been asserted.

Printed in India

This book is sold subject to the condition that it shall not, by way of trade or
otherwise, be lent, resold, hired out, or otherwise circulated,
without the publisher's prior consent, in any form of binding
or cover other than that in which it is published.

To Viki,
For being there...always!

Contents

Introduction   *xi*

PART 1: THE BIRTH

1. Birth of a Hero — 3
2. Indra — 8
3. The Family — 11
4. Varuna — 14
5. Mitra — 19
6. Youth — 25
7. Conflict — 29
8. Separation — 33
9. Rishi Gautama — 39
10. Ahalya — 45
11. 'My Name Is Indra' — 50
12. The Call — 53

PART 2: THE RISE

13. The Enemy — 59
14. Vala — 66
15. The Slaying — 74
16. The Battle — 79
17. The Release — 83
18. The Father — 88
19. Apala — 90
20. Namuchi — 96
21. The Ashwins — 102

22. Saraswati	109
23. Battle with Namuchi	115
24. Indra: The Warrior	118
25. The First Signs of Danger	121
26. Ahibhanava	125
27. Vritra	128
28. Vishnu	134
29. At Vritra's Lair	137
30. The War	143
31. The War Plan	147
32. An Unusual Attack	151
33. Sage Dadhichi	153
34. Vajra	158
35. Vritra Awakens	161
36. The Battle Royale	163
37. The Aftermath	169
38. The Homecoming	172
39. A New Era Begins	175
40. Who Is Vishnu?	181
41. Vishnu Speaks	183
42. The Day After	194
43. Indra and Ahalya	196
44. The Curse	199
45. Stony Inertness	204
46. The Heartbreak	207
47. Indra after Ahalya	214
48. Shachi: The Indrani	218
49. Elsewhere in the World	222

PART 3: THE FALL

50. Indrotsav	229
51. Brahma-hatya	235
52. The Replacement	240
53. Nahush	244
54. Nahush's Demand	247
55. Nahush's Wedding	251
56. Rumours About the Dark Boy	256
57. Change of Lifestyle	260
58. Far Away in Vrindavan	262
59. Krishna Asserts	267
60. The Wrath of Lord Indra	272
61. The Unimaginable	275
62. Back in Vrindavan	279
Epilogue	283
Acknowledgements	294
Bibliography	295

Introduction

It is often found that people judge a person or phenomenon based on a single aspect that is visible about them. What is seen is perceived, as it is witnessed and is subject to one's own understanding or what one is prone to understanding. Much the same happens or has happened with gods and deities too. Certain gods are eulogized, often at the cost of the others, while certain gods are vilified and, in due course, marginalized. However, matters are not as simple as they sound and a perfect example of this complexity is Indra.

The Rig Veda has close to 250 hymns dedicated to Indra and about 300 hymns refer to him in association with other gods. Indra is also mentioned in other texts, like the Atharva Veda, the *Satapatha Brahmana* and, of course, the epics Ramayana and Mahabharata. His constant presence in the post-Vedic period, though in stark contrast to his Vedic glory, necessitates an important study of Indra. Scholars, both Indian and international, have studied the intriguing phenomenon called Indra.

A school of thought believes that Indra was not originally a god but a human hero who was deified in due course of time due to his seemingly unachievable feats. He even superseded the other existing gods of the day. His mortal connect is often found in many of his essentially human characteristics that the Vedic poets have referred to as his 'weaknesses', the most important of which was his fondness for soma. His indulgence in drinking is a theme for many of the hymns in the Rig Veda.

Indra, along with his warrior persona, was also a deity

of fertility in the Vedic times. There are many hymns which invoke Indra to grant fertility and virility. A deity who granted the boon of children to women, he was also associated with bringing rains. Often, his many associations or rendezvous with women, both married and unmarried, were metaphors for his fertility, be it Apala, who invoked Indra, or Ahalya, who is the anthropomorphized form of 'the yet unploughed land'. However, these associations were later targeted as his wayward ways, which merited punishment or ridicule.

The Vedic texts, thus, present an interesting combination of human and superhuman qualities and it is this combination that makes the character of Indra so attractive. However, this same humanness leads to his forced downfall in the post-Vedic times.

Indra's decline is narrated in the Ramayana, through his tryst with Ahalya and subsequent punishment by Sage Gautama. He then lost in combat with Meghnad, the son of Ravana. This earned Meghnad the epithet of Indrajeet—the one who vanquished Indra. Following this incident, Indra was in a state of constant insecurity and was reduced to a shadow of his former self. The episode of Govardhan Parvat, where he is made to kneel and apologize to a child-Krishna is nothing short of complete annihilation of the former greatness of Indra.

Indra: The Rise and Fall of a Hero is an effort to novelize this brief theory about Indra's life. It depicts the greatness of a Vedic hero and his fall in the Puranic times. Creative liberties have been taken to put the journey of Indra in a sequential form, as there is no serialized mention of his story in any of the texts—from the Rig Veda, which refers to Indra the most to elsewhere in the epics or Puranic texts. Several scholarly works in the form of academic papers, books and opinions have been referred to in the making of this novel. Many episodes, especially from the epic Mahabharata have been avoided, to ensure that this account doesn't end up being just an amalgamation of all the myths and stories related to Indra.

The purpose of this novel is to highlight the theory behind the rise and fall of Indra. It is a small effort to uplift the image of an erstwhile hero, who has been much maligned, often out of ignorance about how the wheel of time spares none, not even the gods!

Part I

The Birth

Birth of a Hero

There was something unusual in the air. There was no sound, no breeze and time seemed to have stopped as the world waited with bated breath. The eerie silence was unnerving and unsettling. Just what was this in anticipation of? What was the world waiting for?

In the stillness of the infinite silence, the Mother was waiting in anticipation of giving the world its elements. She knew that she was overdue in giving the world its hero, its saviour, its nature, without which there would be no life, no sustenance, no nourishment—nothing at all. But she had been putting it off for too long now...rather she didn't even remember how long it had been. She feared delivering this child. Why? There was an uncertainty about this child. She knew...she knew that this was an extraordinary child, a child who would rule over the worlds, a child who would be so famous that his father would be hidden in his shadow! The child's father feared this moment of being forgotten. The world had not yet witnessed the moment where fathers took pride in their sons' achievements. This was the beginning of the world and such feelings were not the norm yet. The siblings were concerned about their status once he came into being. Would he challenge the existing order?

Change in the world is inevitable, irrespective of its relevance or method. Times were changing and the world was waiting for someone who could herald this change. The universe was craving for its saviour. The birth of this child was not just desirable, it was a necessity. The world needed someone to allow it to function with order, save it from undesirable elements and bring balance. This birth would be a moment whose significance could not be described in words—she could only feel it. She knew it because she was the Mother.

She could feel rumblings in her womb, much like the earth realizing the tremors of an earthquake. She knew that she had held the child in the womb for too long and it wasn't going to be easy to do so any longer.

She could feel her conscience questioning her from deep within her: *Why? Why aren't you allowing him to come out?* I am not sure the world is ready for my child, thought the Mother. *There is no better time than this, woman. What will be, will be. Please allow him to emerge, the universe is waiting for him and he has work…that which none but he must accomplish…that which none but he can do.*

The Mother knew that she couldn't hold him within her for long. Considering the stage the society was in, conflicts and changes were going to be the norm. Could she resist these changes and conflicts? Even if she could, then for how long and at the cost of what personal trauma? She could see that she was only postponing the inevitable. She needed to end her trauma because it was unbearable and, of course, futile. She decided to let her child emerge and breathed slowly. She tried to relax and let things take their course.

But what was this? Now the child seemed to be unwilling. What had happened? The child suddenly seemed reluctant.

No, woman, no! He cannot emerge the normal way. He will emerge from your sides. But how is that possible? That is unnatural! *He is unusual, woman, and the usual emergence is not for him. He is different and he will not be debased by emerging the usual way!* But won't that kill me? *No, it will not. Sons don't harm mothers.*

Not him, woman, you can rest assured! His emergence from your side will be the normal, woman!

The Mother was confused. She was much overdue and her conscience was forcing her to deliver this child. While it was unnatural for her to feel such a dilemma, a mother is seldom wrong about her offspring. She knows her child even before the child understands anything about itself. Who is this child going to be? Why does the path of his emergence have to be unnatural? She could sense a storm brewing inside her, making her feel very uneasy and uncomfortable. She knew this wasn't going to be easy. She might not be able to contain him within herself any more. He was determined to emerge. She could tell that he would only emerge from her sides, as she was beginning to feel uneasy.

Unnatural are the ways of the great. While she knew that this child was different—she had always felt it within her—she could sense it at that moment. Something was bothering her. Would the world understand his difference? In the world of gods that she had been establishing and among the ones yet to come, would he be the natural leader?

The Mother was thinking myriad thoughts that seemed to be rushing through her. The emotions elicited by these thoughts were beyond her. She knew that what she was going through was not just anxiety about an impending birth. This was beyond all that. But right then, she couldn't handle the sudden surge... it was time to release him. She could no longer hold him in. These months of carrying him had to end. A child is born with its destiny and this one, too, would have it etched in him. She had done what she could, but it had to end. In his case, though, she didn't know how it would end.

She was unsure of the outcome, once the child was out of her. She had never delivered a child from her sides and she didn't know how it would work. While this had never happened before, she seemed to have no choice. She also knew that she wouldn't be able to resist it any longer. Even if she was not sure why she had resisted giving him to the world, she knew it was time that she did. Not because she wanted to but because she seemed to be losing the reason or ability to hold him in any longer. He seemed unwilling to stay confined within the safety of her womb.

Suddenly, the entire universe seemed to be convulsing in the throes of birth. A strong wind started to blow, the trees were unable to bear the brunt of the wind and the smaller ones started getting uprooted. It seemed as if the mountains would topple and crush all that was underneath them. The rivers started flowing uncontained, their waters overflowing their banks. Was this turmoil heralding the arrival of a hero or the beginning of the end? The Mother was heaving and panting. She wasn't sure if she wanted the time to pass faster or to not come at all. She had neither experienced anything like this and nor had she ever wanted to.

She could feel her sides tear apart. It felt like the earth breaking open to reveal its innards. She was scared that she would not see another day in her life. She was worried about whether she would even get to see her newborn. At that moment, she was bundle of nerves—thoughts were racing through her and shooting in and out of her like arrows. Each arrow pierced her with pain and left a wound, oozing blood. Profusely sweating, writhing in seemingly never-ending pain and agony, she passed out.

The birds and animals had all hidden wherever they could. The father, who had been in a slumber all this while, emerged from his hideout to see what was ailing his beloved, but couldn't find her. The shaking ground made it even worse. He felt that his love needed him more than ever and that he must go be with her. But where was she?

The Mother had passed out under a tree in her sacred grove. Right next to her was the most handsome child the world would ever see. His roving eyes seemed to be taking in the sights of the world around him. It seemed as if he was seeing all that would soon be his and he would be the master of it all. He looked at his Mother, who had passed out. He knew that it hadn't been easy for her, for she had done what no one had ever done and would ever do. He had emerged from her sides. She would never forget this experience but would cherish it when she opened her eyes and saw him. He smiled and waited for her to wake up.

Indra

The chaos had settled and in hindsight, there was not much destruction. No mountain had toppled over and no river had overflown. While the large trees were firmly held by their roots, some small and weak ones had been uprooted. The storm had passed and there was joy in the air—it suddenly seemed like spring. The clouds seemed to be whispering something to the skies, while the breeze was heralding the arrival of the saviour. The buds couldn't wait to flower and the flowers were blushing. Fruits ripened as if they couldn't wait to be of service to the newborn.

The Mother had hidden herself in a grove, wanting to deliver the child in silence but nature had something else in mind. What she wanted to hide was out in the open. The entire universe was aware that an extraordinary child had been birthed. He was one of the most handsome children ever born. His enigmatic smile announced his first victory at having his way in how he had been birthed. The child had a yellowish-brown complexion and some light orange-coloured strands of hair were visible on his otherwise bald head.

Everyone, including the father, was out in search of the Mother and her child. The Mother, exhausted from the experience, had not been able to open her eyes. She had not even realized that the moment had passed, even if it had been the most harrowing moment of her life. She was still in a state of shock and her exhaustion was laced with the fear of the unknown.

When she opened her eyes after what seemed like ages to her, she saw a tawny-coloured child smiling at her and tugging at her breasts. In that moment, she forgot all her exhaustion, fears and dilemmas. She pulled the child to her and nourished him. When he had been fed, she felt fulfilled and a sense of motherhood swept over her like never before. She had mothered sons before but never had she felt like she did that day. This sure was different. The child had rattled all her senses; he was Indra—he who rattled all her senses!

Just then she heard a commotion of people approaching. She looked around and realized that her child's birth seemed to have been preceded by some unrest and destruction. She was scared and worried for the child. She collected herself, picked up the child and hid behind a large tree. She saw her husband and others pass by. She let them go and stepped out from behind the thick tree trunk only when she could no longer hear the group of people looking for her. She tiptoed out of the grove and headed home, unsure of the repercussions of this childbirth.

On the way home, the Mother was amazed at the sense of calm in the air. An unexpected spring seemed to have set in and the sky was clear. The birds were singing and there was a sense of expectation in the air. Expectation of what? Why was there radiance without light? Why was there music in the air when no one was playing an instrument? Why did she feel that the plants and trees were dancing to a tune that she could not hear? What was all this joy about when she wasn't even sure if the child would be welcomed into her family?

Something was not clear; she knew not what it was. But she was happy that there was joy around. She wanted to take her mind off the ominousness that had preceded the birth of her child. She was keen for the child to be accepted by all—his brothers and, above all, his father. While the tribe also had to accept him, she knew that they would, as would the family. The tribe was a lesser concern for her at that moment.

The Family

There had been an uncanny quietness in the household ever since the tawny child had been born. The young brothers were curious but cautious about the newborn. The father was glad to see the Mother well but was hesitant to show his emotions towards the child. There were mixed emotions about the newborn.

All of the tribe's men and women came to celebrate the birth, as was the tradition. Every birth was a cause for celebration and everyone, without discrimination, was allowed to participate in the joyous moment of the family. These were also the moments when everyone came together to celebrate and enjoy. A small feast was due and the Mother got busy with the preparations. A large bonfire was lit at night and the merrymaking commenced around it, as was the norm. The Mother was beaming at the birth of her hero, though she could sense uneasiness about him. Among the people around her, she found herself alone in her joy. The children had not been even slightly curious about the child, except for the youngest—Agni. He seemed to be getting curious but something was holding him back. The eldest, more reserved one, Varuna, was aloof, unattached and had not even bothered to keep his coldness private. The other siblings were more or less following Varuna's footsteps.

The father was missing from the festivities around the bonfire, as he had to urgently deliver some tools. While the urgency was real, and the tribe was aware of it, the Mother somewhere felt that the work could have waited and he could have spent some time at the gathering. However, she also was kind of glad that he wasn't around. As the chief of the tribe, he had his responsibilities and there was no doubt that he executed them with utmost dedication. The Mother resolved that time was the best healer and she didn't want to make too much out of the present coldness and leave it to each of their destinies.

The celebratory dance was over and so was the barrel of soma. No celebration was complete without soma, the juice of the climber, which had few leaves and bore lovely white flowers on its stem. The tribesmen took these climbers and pressed them between stones to extract the juice. While the men juiced the stems, the women hummed:

O soma, give us thy juice.
Thy juice which heals the wounds
of the heart and mind
and kills sorrow and sadness.
O soma, give us thy juice.
Thy juice which cheers our
hearts and limbs
and nights of darkness.
O soma, give us thy juice.
Thy juice which inspires our bards
to praise and sing
songs of the night, songs of the day and songs of joy.
O soma, give us thy juice,
for you are our muse and we sing because of you.
O soma, give us thy juice.

The tribesmen were leaving one by one, taking their tired and sleepy children with them. At last, the Mother was alone with her child, who just never stopped smiling! Strangely, the child had not cried all through the celebration, despite all the noise around. He had seemed to be part of the celebration! No one had failed to observe and mention this to her.

She noticed that Agni was keen to come close to the child. She knew she had to win them over one by one. She offered her hand to him and he reacted immediately. He came closer, took a look at the baby and smiled. The Mother felt relieved. She knew that one of them had been converted.

Agni was staring at the child, who seemed very happy to play with Agni. No one used to play with Agni because he was too young but now he had found someone who was smiling at him and knew that they would soon play together. The Mother noticed a sense of satisfaction on Agni's face.

It was late by the time the father arrived, exhausted. The Mother had dozed off and the fire was still burning. The father came close to the Mother and noticed the child sleeping peacefully. He had never seen such a beautiful child. He was happy but wondered what was making him hold back his emotions. Why was he unable to express his happiness? Why was he hesitating to pick up the child and embrace him as he would usually do? Some things cannot be explained and one should allow them to pass.

The father went out and sat next to the dying embers of the bonfire. He needed rest and a good night's sleep. Things would change, and change for good, he was sure. This was some passing phase, which need not be understood, like many things in the world.

Varuna

Varuna had seen Indra grow up in the last few years and found Indra a lot different from him and the others. Indra had a mind of his own and had too many questions about a lot of existing practices. Varuna was close to his father and had his way of looking at things. He preferred order rather than chaos, which seemed to be Indra's hunting ground. It was not surprising to find Indra wherever something had gone wrong, though it seldom seemed to be his fault!

In the short time when Indra was growing up, Varuna was beginning to get increasingly worried about him, especially the way his 'digression' from the norms seemed to be acceptable to people. Indra's complete disdain for order and norms was something that didn't sit well with Varuna. He couldn't remember anybody else at Indra's age behaving this way. Mother often told Varuna to ignore Indra, as he was just a child. Varuna never argued with his Mother and gave in to her cajoling, but he could feel the beginning of the waves of change.

Varuna lived in a uniquely magnificent palace. It had a thousand doors that were open to anyone who wanted to meet with or speak to him. Although he did not sit on a throne, as he believed that all were equal, his authority was unmistakable. He seemed to have only one purpose—ensuring that nothing was wrong anywhere in the world. Maintaining order in nature was all that mattered to him.

Indra found him very boring. The few times that he had spoken to Varuna, Indra did not like his serious demeanour and his penetrating gaze. Just why was he so serious? Indra wondered, often aloud! Varuna seemed to exist for others and orderliness was all that he cared for. Nothing other than norms, rules, etc. moved him. Indra felt that Varuna disapproved of some of his behaviour and often went to the Mother to air his 'concerns' about Indra's ways.

So, what were Indra's ways? Well, Indra had no ways. Indra lived in the moment and did what was right or rather what seemed to be right in the moment. Too many norms, rules and orderliness were not something that impressed him.

Mitra, Varuna's constant companion and a friend of the family, was much more reasonable and often intervened with Varuna in favour of Indra. Mitra found Indra different and interesting and would often laugh away Indra's 'disorderliness'. Indra, too, found Mitra more amenable and natural and preferred his manner of discussing matters. On the contrary, Varuna would often end discussions by announcing, with an air of finality, 'You are too young to understand this!' Somewhere Indra knew that this assertion was less about ending the discussion and more about Varuna's inability to take the conversation further.

This was more than visible in the issue of King Harishchandra. This matter had been discussed and debated so much that everyone ended up being involved in it, and Indra also had an opinion on it. The poor king had no children and had promised Varuna that if he was blessed with a son, then he would offer the son as a sacrifice! This was particularly strange for a man who had wished for a son not just for the joys of parenthood but also to ensure safe passage into the afterlife. Indra had called the King selfish. Varuna had initially objected to the King's request because he felt that his objection would help maintain order.

Later, the King was blessed with a son but when he grew

older, he refused to be sacrificed. Indra felt that the prince had a right to live his life and make his decision and that he should not be made a pawn in the 'dealings' of the King and Varuna. Needless to say, Varuna was upset with the way Indra described his 'deal' with the King and even doubted that Indra had something to do with the prince's decision. Varuna, in his anger, cursed the King with dropsy, which severely affected the King's health and functioning. Meanwhile, the prince decided to leave his palace for the forest.

After many years in the forest, the prince met a starving Brahmin, who had three sons. He offered a hundred cows to the Brahmin in exchange for one of his sons, who could be offered as a sacrifice to Varuna in his place. The Brahmin agreed. When he reached home, he realized he loved his eldest son too much for him to be sacrificed. Meanwhile, the mother loved the youngest son too much for him to be sacrificed. So, it was decided that the middle son, Shunahshepa, would be offered as a sacrifice. Indra found this odd and felt sad for Shunahshepa, especially when he thought about how he must have felt when he learnt that he had been offered as a sacrifice because he was neither his mother's nor his father's favourite child.

The Brahmin and Shunahshepa reached the court along with the prince and Varuna agreed to accept Shunahshepa as the sacrifice. Soon, everything was organized for the sacrifice but just before the event, Shunahshepa decided to offer his last prayers. His hymns touched a few gods and they intervened on his behalf with Varuna and he was allowed to live. The King was also cured of his illness. However, Shunahshepa refused to go back with his father, who had traded him for a hundred cows, and when none of the attending sages had wanted to sacrifice him, his father had offered another hundred cows for the ritual to be completed.

Indra appreciated Shunahshepa's decision and later argued with Varuna about his stubborn insistence on the sacrifice. Varuna felt that if a commitment had been made, it must be honoured, while Indra felt that such commitments should not even be accepted in the first place. 'Why would a man want a child, if he must kill him later?'

Varuna corrected Indra, 'The word is not "kill", it is "sacrifice"!'

A surprised Indra asked, 'Would the change of the word change the destiny of the child? Would he go on to live, if he was "sacrificed" instead of "killed"?' Indra found this kind of a debate very superfluous, where the semantics of a word seemed to be more important than the real meanings of actions. While many sensed logic in the young Indra's arguments, Varuna was upset with the growing acceptance of Indra's logic by others. In the end, one wasn't sure if Varuna was more upset with King Harishchandra and his son who had refused to be sacrificed, or with Indra for airing his disapproval of the whole thing and that too in public.

Indra had never thought of criticizing something in private, rather he never did *think*—something his Mother always cautioned him about. Mother was sensing the difference in his behaviour and was beginning to get worried, especially because more and more people were beginning to find more reason in Indra's approach than Varuna's, which had never happened before. Varuna had been the unopposed ruler so far and no one had questioned his moves since he had taken over from the father. Well, at least no one had until that time.

Besides, Indra was too direct with his opinion but often used to get overlooked because of his age. Lately, though, the opposition and difference between him and Varuna had become a matter of hush-hush discussions.

Before things went out of hand, the Mother wanted to ensure that there was no clash of opinions and values, which definitely seemed to be happening. Indra's better relationship with his sibling, Agni, was the saving grace for the Mother. Varuna, however, had always been a serious kind, much like his preference for the silent and still waters of the seas and ocean. Once in a while, though, she did notice the strong underlying currents that could turn into powerful and destructive waves.

Mitra

Mitra was smiling, as usual, when he walked into the cottage. As soon as he entered, he noticed one of Varuna's spies whispering something in his ear. There was nothing unusual about this, as the numerous, unknown spies under Varuna's charge used to keep a tab of everything for him. While Mitra didn't quite like the idea of spies, Varuna had always rationalized it by saying that there was no way one could rule with just two eyes—these spies were his eyes all over the world and enabled him to dispense justice and punishment where needed.

'Something sure seems to be amusing you!' exclaimed Varuna in a not-so-happy voice. Mitra continued to smile and said, 'Isn't that just me?' Varuna couldn't dispute that, as Mitra was known to smile all the time. Varuna wrapped his golden mantle around him and came towards Mitra, not before indicating to his spies to leave them alone. Mitra could sense some tension in the air but decided to ignore it, as Varuna was prone to being worried, often over trivial things. Well, they were trivial to others, not to Varuna. For him, everything was important and relevant. He never separated matters into degrees of right and wrong, something was either right or wrong.

Mitra knew that Varuna would say what he wanted when he wanted to—there was no need to probe. Varuna finally said, 'So, have you heard what my younger brother was up to?'

So, Indra was the subject of concern, thought Mitra. This further amused him, as he found this younger brother of Varuna quite interesting, especially when he contradicted Varuna, and often found his arguments sensible, though challenging.

'Now what has he done?' asked Mitra, not quite sure if he wanted to know.

'He has made friends with the Maruts, the mischievous sons of Rudra, and has been gallivanting all around!'

'And how is that wrong?' asked Mitra, wondering what he was missing.

'I didn't say anything was wrong, but the Maruts?' questioned Varuna.

'While I do agree that the Maruts are a bit mischievous and often loud, you can't deny that they are brave and ferocious too. If your brother has befriended them, I see no harm in that,' reasoned Mitra.

'That's not the point,' said Varuna, 'you are not getting what I am saying. He anyway has a different mindset and now the friendship with the Maruts is simply going to make him more unreasonable.'

'Unreasonable? Why do you say that?' wondered Mitra.

'Don't you see?' asked Varuna. 'He argues out of context, challenges every norm and the order of nature and questions everything that I have taken pains to establish over time. He seems to have no regard for rules and principles. His disdain for ethical behaviour is visible. How come you can't see all this?'

Mitra smiled and responded, 'I think you are overreacting. He is young and youth is impulsive. Give him time and he will mellow down.'

'Would you take the same stand with someone else?' asked Varuna.

'He is not someone else,' replied Mitra matter-of-factly.

'What's so special about him? For me, all are the same, sons of my Mother or sons of others. I don't believe in separate rules,' replied Varuna sternly.

Mitra could sense the looming tension, going beyond the usual worry of Varuna. He knew he had to intervene before matters went out of hand. 'Why don't you speak to him and try to understand him?' suggested Mitra.

'Why? Why would I do that? I haven't done that with anybody so far!' objected Varuna.

'Well, so far, no one had managed to get you this worried either,' replied Mitra.

Varuna was quiet. There was no denying that no one before Indra had ever managed to bother him so much. Needless to say, Varuna didn't quite have a direct charge against Indra. So, what was bothering him? The open disregard for the norms that he had laid down? The disdain for what was of utmost significance to him? The disregard for ethical practices that he thought were sacrosanct?

Mitra noticed that Varuna was quiet. He decided to leave it at that. Mitra knew better than to probe beyond a point. This young brother of Varuna was different and challenged the status quo, which upset Varuna a bit and Mitra could see that some of the things Indra said were quite logical. Mitra could sense a breeze of change and somehow, he wasn't feeling perturbed about it; he couldn't say the same about Varuna though!

'If Indra's friendship with the Maruts is the only thing bothering you, then I feel that there isn't anything to it. He will soon outgrow them,' said Mitra, trying to get to the bottom of Varuna's concern.

'Yesterday, they were bothering the sages in the ashram by blowing strong winds and extinguishing their ritualistic flames,' replied Varuna, looking really concerned.

'So, did the sages complain to you?'

'No, not as yet.'

'Then why are you bothered?' wondered Mitra, and suddenly added, 'And how did you find out about it?'

Before Varuna could respond, Mitra asked, rather surprised, 'Are you spying on your brother?'

Varuna tried to reason with him, 'Well, not on him, but then, it was reported to me by... Yes, by my spies, as they do everything else.'

'Please, Varuna, they are young and these are nothing but youthful indulgences and till matters are not brought up, I don't think you should bother,' Mitra replied concernedly.

'So, according to you, one should wait for rules to be completely broken before one addresses an issue? Is that what you are suggesting?' asked a worried Varuna.

'Where are you taking this?' asked Mitra.

'You are missing something, my dear friend,' said Varuna, 'He has to uphold the norms of nature and anything that goes against the set rules is not tolerable... I will not tolerate such behaviour from anyone. In fact, I am rather surprised that you don't find anything wrong with this. This was not how you thought earlier.'

Mitra couldn't deny Varuna's observation. Once, when the Maruts had uprooted a tree during the yajna of a sage, he had spoken up on behalf of the sages. But that day, he was feeling much more tolerant towards the mischief of the same Maruts. Was it because they were now associated with Indra? Mitra smiled to himself.

'So, you do realize that you seem to be a bit more partial towards Indra?' asked Varuna, as if reading Mitra's thoughts.

'I am more partial to the changing times, my dear friend,' reasoned Mitra, 'I think you need to realize that the rules and the norms laid down by you are being challenged. Either you have a justification for your norms or you don't. If you don't, then that means that they are outdated.'

'Outdated!' exclaimed Varuna, rather loudly, 'Outdated? Rules and norms can never be outdated! What has been relevant will always be relevant. I will not let anybody challenge my norms. They are for the well-being of the society at large. If anybody and everybody challenges them every now and then, that's a sure recipe for disaster. I will not let that happen. I am the upholder of ethics and principles and nobody, I repeat, nobody—not even Indra—can upset the established norms.'

Varuna left the hall in anger, sweeping his mantle around him. Mitra was worried. He knew Varuna too well to think that he would change his stance, but he also felt that Indra was the face of the changing times. Mitra found Indra's arguments quite reasonable. Although, a few did contradict the established norms, some of which, Mitra felt, were not entirely justifiable. The growing acceptability of Indra's views couldn't be undermined, not that he was whipping up support for what he thought. It's strange how his views were being accepted without him even making any effort to enlist support for them. There was something natural about him, his deeds and his thoughts. To be fair to him, it wasn't only his charm and demeanour, which was quite attractive to say the least! Mitra had noticed how people often forgot what he was saying and kept staring at him. There were strange things he had heard about Indra that were simply attributed to his youth!

Besides, Mitra liked this young man, who had grown quite fast and seemed to be maturing quickly. However, he was worried about this simmering conflict with Varuna and he felt that something ought to be done before the matter came out in the open.

'You seem worried,' Mother's voice jolted Mitra out of his reverie. He stood up in reverence when he noticed her standing in front of him. She gestured him to sit. Mother took a seat next to him.

'Is it Indra?' asked the Mother, reading his thoughts, 'Or is it Varuna and Indra?'

Mitra was not surprised that Mother had an inkling of his worries.

'It's both, Mother,' said Mitra.

Mother looked down, her worries validated. She had been sensing the growing conflict between her sons. Why just her, even her attendants had been discussing this. She was rather surprised to learn that her attendants had good things to say about Indra, when none of them had even dared to speak about Varuna, ever. Indra would often stop by and speak to them, smile at them and even ask about their well-being, which was so unnatural. They liked it and she couldn't quite fathom what was wrong with it, if at all. But then, nobody had ever done this before... So...

'Something needs to be done about this, Mother,' she heard Mitra say, 'before it blows out of proportion.'

'Yes,' murmured Mother, deep in thought. 'I wonder what can be done...'

Youth

There was something in the air, which was making everything seem very different. The fragrance of the flowers and the different colours just added to the confusion that had been brewing in the air. The new-found roots of a plant were so rejuvenating that one just couldn't have enough of them! What did they call it? Ah, yes, the soma plant!

Indra noticed a few of the Maruts chewing on them. When he enquired about it, they gave him some. At first, it tasted odd and, for a moment, Indra wondered what was in there but even before the thought was out of his mind, he felt different. He tried some more and started liking it. It did make him a tad restless, which the Maruts noticed, some of whom had started running around by then. They asked him to follow them.

The Maruts were a group of young boys. There was something about them—it was tough to say if people hated the Maruts more or were scared of them. Either way, Indra felt that people were biased against them. Besides their penchant for mischief, they were simpletons who were often associated with their father, Rudra. Needless to say, the Marut boys did have a wild side but then what is youth if it does not have a wild side!

Indra had lately begun enjoying the company of the boys, who lived high in the mountains and were known to be brave while also enjoying life. Of course, Indra had seen a few of them get angry, which did not end well, with a couple of trees being uprooted and a few huts being ravaged, but besides this, they were fun to be with. One good thing about them was that they never got into the good and bad of life, about which Varuna constantly talked to him. Varuna talked of nothing other than right and wrong and laws and rules! The Maruts, on the contrary, enjoyed their life and never felt bad about it. They were literally a band of merrymakers.

The root that they had given him to taste had been exhilarating, to say the least, and he was glad he had tasted it. While there was something that was making him restless, he felt a sudden urge to move the mountain ahead of him or maybe uproot a tree at that very moment. It was a great feeling and Indra wanted to try some more of the root, but the Maruts had left in a hurry and he was left wandering around the forest. Indra decided to sit under a tree and enjoy the breeze and the sights and sounds around him.

He closed his eyes, trying to absorb the feeling, when he suddenly heard some music floating in from far away. He opened his eyes and looked around but could not see anybody. The music was lilting enough for him to get up and look around. Without realizing it, Indra started to walk towards the sound. He did not know what it was, but it sure was worth following. He soon came across a small pond surrounded by bushes, which were in full bloom. Some lovely girls were frolicking in the water. One of them was sitting on a small rock next to the pond and playing a string instrument. Indra didn't know where to look, at the girl playing the music or at the ones splashing around in the water or at the ones who were basking under the bright sunlight on the side.

He crouched behind a shrub and watched them quietly. Something stirred within him; he had never felt like this before. He wanted to go close to them and...and maybe speak to them. They were so beautiful; suddenly the flowers had lost their meaning to him. The sound of the breeze seemed to be fading against the music being played by the damsel, whose long hair was romancing the breeze. The girls were in a world of their own, the sun shining on their glistening bodies. Seeing so many of them in the water excited him. He had never felt like this before. Was it the soma roots or was it the weather or was it the girls?

Indra couldn't resist walking up to them from his hiding spot in the bushes. The girls suddenly noticed him, shrieked and ran out of the water, clutching onto whatever they could lay their hands on. That moment of them running helter-skelter was a moment to die for, thought Indra! He might want to witness it every day! Just then, he noticed the girl on the rock; she was staring at him, with no change in her demeanour and the music had not stopped even for a moment. Indra felt as if she was playing just for him and nothing had changed for her.

The other girls, too, had noticed this and while some of them had managed to regain their composure, they were quite surprised to see the two of them staring at each other. It was then that they noticed that the intruder was a handsome young man. His long, orange-coloured curls were held back by the band on his forehead. His piercing eyes had a look that could disarm the most powerful adversary, and these were just lovely girls! The tawny-coloured beard barely managed to hide his defined jawline, which clearly displayed his youth. There was something magnetic about him. His muscular body was visible and soon, it wasn't just the girl playing the instrument, but the others, too, were quiet and had forgotten the discomfort they had felt some time back.

Indra moved closer to touch the girl sitting on the distant rock, unaware that he was walking right into the pond. Even the silent ripples on the water seemed to desire to touch him and soon, Indra swam up to the girl. The others gasped at the unexpected turn of events wondering how he could come so close and that too in the women's pond; needless to say, each one of them was wishing that he would come towards her!

Soon, Indra had reached the rock and was sitting next to the girl, who had stopped playing the instrument but the music continued as a koel started cooing in the distance. Indra looked at the girl and her fingers, which had been playing the music. He touched her fingers and was about to move the strands of hair from her face to get a better look at her, when the other girls shrieked in horror. They had spotted someone behind the hedges. Their shrieks brought Indra and the girl back to their surroundings, but, by then, the person had vanished. The girl with the instrument slipped past Indra, and soon, all the girls left; not before each of them stole a final glance at Indra.

Indra was left alone, angry and irritated at the sudden turn of events. He just slipped down the rock into the pond but even the water did not cool him. What was this? Why was he feeling restless? Who was the intruder that had come in the way of him and the girl? What had he been planning to do anyway, when he came close to her? What was this feeling and why was it disturbing him so much?

Indra didn't know how long he was in the water, immersed in the thoughts of the girl and the others. He kept on recounting the series of events in his mind and lived that last moment over and over again. Tired, he decided to go back—he was beginning to feel hungry...there was something in those soma roots, though!

Conflict

It was close to sunset when Indra reached home to rest, except something seemed amiss. He was greeted by a stern Varuna, with Mitra beside him along with Mother and a few others. Indra's first reaction was—*now what?*

He had hardly crossed the threshold when he heard Varuna thunder, 'Were you at the *kanya-kund*?'

Indra had never heard that before, 'Was I *where*?'

'Kanya-kund!' bellowed Varuna, with Mitra trying to cool him down.

'What is kanya-kund?' Indra asked, puzzled.

'It's the place where young girls bathe and it is *prohibited* for any male to be there!'

'*Rules,*' Indra muttered under his breath, then said, 'Oh, that! Well, I didn't know that no male was supposed to go there. I was thirsty...Wait, who told you about it?'

'You don't ask me questions and I am aware of—' Varuna had barely finished his statement, when Indra cut him off angrily. 'Are you sending your goons after me?' He looked at Mother accusatorially.

'They are not goons, they are my spies and they are everywhere,' said Varuna.

'Mother!' yelled Indra, 'This is not fair! He is tailing me.' He looked at Varuna, 'Do you do that with everybody or is it just me?'

Mitra was expecting this. He tried to intervene, but Indra raised his hand and asked insistently, 'I want this answer from

Varuna: is it just me or do you have your goons tailing others, like Mitra or even Mother?'

'Shut up, Indra! I know who needs to be kept an eye upon! And you dare not speak about Mother like that,' Varuna warned.

Indra looked at Mother, who looked worried. While he did feel bad for her, he knew that this had to be resolved. He was getting frustrated by the rules and Varuna's spies tailing him. He knew that the commotion at the pond had been created by one of Varuna's spies. 'So what was your goon doing at the kanya-kund? Isn't that against your rules since I am told all your goons are males?' Indra continued questioning.

'They can go anywhere! And stop questioning me. You haven't answered me yet!' yelled Varuna.

'I am not answerable to anyone! Besides, I didn't know that males were not allowed in certain places. By the way, may I add that I was following your goon when I saw him heading to this place.'

'That's not true!' yelled out one of the attendants standing aside.

Indra turned sharply and rushed towards him while exclaiming, 'So you are the one!'

'Stop right there!' shouted Varuna, but Mitra had already managed to get hold of the charging Indra.

'You are lying!' said Varuna.

'My word against your goon's! You trust your servants more than your brother! Well, that speaks volumes about you,' Indra said, looking at Mother.

'First of all—' began Varuna, when Indra interrupted again. 'Fair enough, let's say, I did. I didn't know that men are not supposed to go there. So, what next? I suppose you will punish me for this, for I can't imagine that you can do anything else!

But let me tell you one thing, you and your rules are obnoxious and soon there will be new rules!'

'And who will write them? You? You who has such disdain for rules?' retorted the angry Varuna.

Mitra looked at Mother and gestured for her to intervene—he thought that things were starting to go out of hand. While Mitra was aware that a rule had been breached, he also felt that there had been no complaint as such and Varuna was being harsh on the young Indra. It is possible that he really didn't know that the place was not meant for men.

'I think we need to leave the matter here,' said Mother, taking Mitra's hint. Varuna tried to say something but kept quiet when he saw her raising her hand to keep him quiet. 'Leave it to me. I will speak to Indra about it and he won't do it again,' she stated with an air of finality.

The angry Indra hated that his Mother was giving a word on his behalf, but Mitra, who was holding him, pressed his arm, indicating him to keep quiet and let the matter rest there.

Varuna left the cottage in a huff, followed by his attendants. Indra was angry. 'He sends his goons after me! He has something against me, I know he hates me!'

Mother walked up to Indra, who had dropped to the floor in exasperation. She sat next to him and said, 'He has a responsibility and is just ensuring that the rules are being followed by all, my son.'

'Rules! That's all he cares for! Who made these rules and for whom? Has anybody told him that these rules of his are meaningless and stifling?'

Mother looked at Mitra, who was smiling. He walked to one end of the cottage and sat on a wooden stump and looked at Indra. Mother was trying to console him, 'Don't talk like that!

It is because of him that everything is in order. It is not an easy task and that's why he has no friends.'

'He has no friends because he loves his power and is reveling in it. He needs to be thrown out—'

'Indra!' shouted Mother. 'Don't speak like that!' she was both angry and worried.

Mitra rose from his place and took Indra out of the cottage, to the grove, and made him sit under a tree. Indra was in a rage and Mitra knew that it would be best to just keep quiet for the time being. They sat there quietly. Indra glowered at the ground while Mitra looked at him.

After a long silence, Mitra noticed Mother's shadow in the distance. He looked at her and walked up to Indra. He kept his hands on Indra's shoulder and ruffled his hair. Indra looked up at a smiling Mitra. Mitra gestured towards Mother and said, 'I don't know about you, but she is hungry!' and left.

Indra looked in the distance and saw Mother's silhouette. He got up and went towards the cottage.

'Anger and hunger are very poor friends!' said Mother.

'I haven't had anything since morning,' said Indra. 'I was famished when I walked in but then I was fed "rules" as soon as I walked in,' he complained bitterly.

'Now, now, my son...let's leave it at that for the day,' said Mother with a sense of finality before they sat down to eat.

That night, Indra slept fitfully. He knew that he couldn't stay at home while his brother was ruling. Something had to be done. But what—that was the question.

Separation

'I have thought over it, son. This is the best for everyone,' said Mother.

Mitra was not sure if this was the case. 'Have you spoken to him?' asked Mitra.

'No, not yet. Just wanted to discuss it with you, as I think you tend to understand him better than many of us.'

Mitra smiled, 'I don't know why or what it is, but there is something about him, Mother. He is too restless to be left doing nothing. His restlessness, his energy and his anger, I feel, can be utilized for the betterment of the people. While his actions do sometimes go against the established code, nobody is complaining about it. This raises a very important question: who is upset with the breach of code? This is creating a bit of confusion: if nobody is upset with the breach, then is it a breach at all?'

Mother looked up at the ruminating Mitra. 'You seem to be speaking his language! Your friend will not be very happy to hear your words!'

Mitra smiled. 'I know, Mother, but I have been thinking. Indra is raising questions through his actions, some of which just can't be evaded. Who knows, maybe he is ushering in a wave of change.'

'You have a point, Mitra,' said Mother. She had never seen it this way. She had been so busy pacifying one or the other son that she had missed this important point that Mitra had raised.

'I wanted you to be around when I speak to him. He tends to behave better with you around than with Varuna. Besides, I don't want him to think that Varuna had anything to do with my decision,' added Mother.

'That's going to be tough to manage, Mother,' muttered Mitra.

'But he really didn't, this is my decision,' Mother.

'I understand, Mother,' said Mitra, 'but that doesn't mean Indra will agree with you. He doesn't take anything at face value. He is sure to see Varuna's hand in it.'

Mother looked worried, not that the thought had not crossed her mind. She was hoping that her actions wouldn't be seen this way. 'You will help me, won't you? If matters reach that level?' asked Mother.

'Of course, Mother, you can count on me,' Mitra replied eagerly.

'Did you call me?' Indra asked as he entered the room. His voice trailed off when he saw Mother and Mitra together. 'What have I done now?' he asked, seeming dejected. He knew that he had been called in for some purpose.

'Nothing, my son, just sit next to me,' said Mother, trying to sound as normal as she could.

Indra could see through the effort but decided not to force it out of her. He looked at Mitra, who was also trying his best to seem normal. Indra decided to ignore his instincts and wait to hear them out.

'I know you are upset with what happened the other day...' began Mother. He wasn't surprised that it had to do with Varuna. What wasn't?

'Please, Mother, don't expect me to apologize! I have made no mistake and I am not going to feel sorry, much less say it to him!' retorted Indra.

'Why don't you listen to what Mother has to say?' urged Mitra.

Indra considered his intervention and knew that there was something beyond what he was thinking. He realized that it would be best to wait it out. He nodded and looked at Mother.

'Look, my son,' began Mother, 'I am not saying you are wrong, but yes, things were not seen the way you were seeing them. Maybe, what you do is not incorrect in general, but it is also not appropriate by the established standards of our world. When such differences occur—when both options seem to be correct—my wisdom says that it's time to change and move on.' Mother paused before continuing, 'But also remember that such changes do not creep in quietly without bothering anybody. Some get affected by such changes. Before you usher in any changes,' Mother advised sagely, 'I think you need to know what changes you are making, as opposed to the existing system. To do so, there is something called education that must be undertaken.'

Education? Indra wondered, *what was Mother referring to?* He decided to listen.

'Unfortunately, we have been too busy with a lot of things, but I feel you are at the right age and this is an appropriate time to begin your education; besides, it's never too late to learn,' Mother concluded.

'Learn? Education? Just what are you saying, Mother?' said Indra, losing his patience. 'Can you come to the point?'

Mother looked at Mitra and then at Indra, 'Rishi Gautama is a renowned sage who runs a gurukul, and I am planning to send you there.'

'Send? What do you mean, send me there?' Indra was perplexed.

'Mother wants you to spend some time at the ashram of Rishi Gautama,' added Mitra helpfully.

'Ashram? Rishi Gautama? Just what is going on? Will someone

please explain who this man is and what does he teach?' Indra nearly yelled.

'Calm down, son.' Mother began, 'Rishi Gautama is a renowned guru who runs an ashram, where students learn the art of life and other valuable lessons. I wish for you to go there and spend some time with him.'

'Spend time with him? Why? Why must I go there?' Indra was beginning to understand what was happening.

'You have to go there, son, because gurus teach in an ashram. Besides, he is a renowned sage and is well-versed with all that you need to know,' Mother explained.

'Are you sending me away from here?' Indra looked straight at Mother and then at Mitra.

'My son, whatever made you say that? Why would I do that?' pleaded Mother, not that she hadn't expected this.

'Indra—' Mitra began, but was abruptly interrupted by Indra's raised hand, who asked, looking straight at Mother, 'Why else did this come up so suddenly now?'

'I was awaiting word from Rishi Gautama, as he doesn't take too many students. I have just heard from him and he wants to admit you in his ashram now,' Mother said her well-rehearsed lines.

Indra looked at Mitra, who was smiling, as usual.

'Did Varuna go there too?' asked Indra.

That was a question that neither of them had expected.

'No, he didn't,' replied Mitra. 'Nor did I. But that is because Rishi Gautama was not a guru when we were your age. Besides, there had been no gurukuls then. But now, Rishi Gautama and his gurukul are well known and we feel that the place will do you good and prepare you for the future, especially in a world that is changing.'

Mother heaved a sigh of relief for the timely intervention by Mitra.

'Did Varuna have anything to do with this?' asked Indra.

'No, no, my son, this is entirely my decision,' replied Mother.

'I don't believe it...' Indra said as he stormed out of the cottage.

Mother looked at Mitra helplessly, who immediately followed Indra. Indra sat under the shade of a tree, sulking, as he knew that he wouldn't be able to say no to Mother and at the same time, was disappointed that he would have to give in to Varuna's machinations, as he was sure that Varuna was behind this.

Indra felt a hand on his shoulder. He looked up at Mitra, 'So you, too, are a part of this, right?'

'Part of what, Indra?' asked Mitra mildly.

'This conspiracy by Varuna to get rid of me.'

'And then?' asked Mitra.

'What do you mean by "and then"?' asked a puzzled Indra.

'Get rid of you for how long? Did Mother say that you will be gone forever? Is she sending you there forever? How is this a conspiracy? Besides, what if I tell you that Varuna doesn't even know about this?'

Indra hesitatingly replied, 'I am not sure I would believe you.'

'I know,' said Mitra, 'that's exactly why I didn't say that. But if you believe me, let me assure you that Varuna is not even aware of this. Unfortunately, Rishi Gautama's message came at a time when you and Varuna had a difference of opinion, but the news had to be broken nonetheless. Could Mother have waited for more time? Yes, she could have, but would you have stopped doubting her then? Besides, what was the guarantee that you two wouldn't have gotten into another conflict by then?' smiled Mitra. After a lull for some time, he added, 'You are brave, Indra, but that's not all that one needs to learn. In such dynamic times, one has to be equipped with knowledge of all kinds and there isn't anybody here who is equipped to teach. You need to see the world outside this place and learn. Learning is not just limited to some scriptures; education is not a few texts. The more you see outside your limited world, the more you learn and the more you learn, the better you are at handling people and situations. The world is changing, and in this changing world, education at a gurukul will only be an advantage.' Mitra was looking far into the horizon.

Indra stared at Mitra. He seemed to make sense, as always. 'I wonder why you are not the head of our tribe, Mitra. You are so reasonable, unlike...' Indra trailed off.

Mitra smiled, 'Imposition of rules is always an unenviable task, my dear. You feel so, as I don't tell you, don't do this or don't do that. The day that responsibility falls on me, you will not like me either.' He continued, 'Today you dislike Varuna because he has this task of running things properly, and in an unbiased manner. Such people are seldom loved, and if they are loved by all, that means that they are not doing their job well! There cannot be different rules for different people, and to judge is the worst job ever. Trust me, Indra, Varuna means no harm to you. It's just that he has a responsibility and he is executing it well. This is not to say that you are wrong. However, your methods are more impulsive and often emotional, which, of course, doesn't make them wrong. It does often make them questionable in the larger scheme of things.'

Indra was listening to every word Mitra had to say. Mitra always managed to make sense and, as always, had a calming effect on him. They sat there, staring at the horizon. The sun was taking a dip in the distant sea. Mitra was lost in thought and Indra was wondering what life at the ashram would be like.

Rishi Gautama

Life at the ashram was very different from what Indra's life had been back home. Everything was regulated—the wake-up time, time for ablutions, time for collecting firewood, time for meditation—everything had a schedule. Rishi Gautama was a stickler for discipline and Indra definitely had an issue with this. However, Mother had made him promise that he would never give the Rishi a reason to complain or regret taking him as a student. The rules of the ashram had been told to him before he started living there and it was made abundantly clear that there would never be any scope for arbitration between the sage and him—Rishi Gautama would prevail in every case!

While this unilateral judgement in case of a dispute was unacceptable to Indra, he also understood that this was only a matter of a few years. Besides, the old man did possess a sense of authority, which seemed well earned to Indra. Also, the Rishi seemed to be more reasonable and not dogged about his thoughts—he welcomed debates, which was such a far cry from back home! Indra found it extremely strange that the sage was constantly composed and seldom got angry or happy, though it was nice to see him smile occasionally.

One day, Indra was late in the morning and, thus, his ablutions took longer than usual. That day had been earmarked for collecting firewood, which had to be done before noon. As a rule, the sage wanted all the students to go together to collect firewood and if there was one thing that Indra found tough to cope with it was the early morning routine. Vishnu, one of his mates, did wake him up a couple of times, but Indra was just not able to wake up.

When the sage noticed that all those who had been deputed to collect firewood were present, except Indra, he asked them to wait. After some time, the others wondered if they should go and wake Indra up, which the sage quietly declined. The boys were waiting under a tree. They were beginning to feel upset, as they could neither leave nor wake him up. They were also aware that they had run out of firewood, so, this would have severe repercussions.

By the time Indra woke up, it was indeed late and he rushed through his ablutions and hurried to the cottage, where the others were waiting for him. He found it odd and wondered aloud why they hadn't left without him if he was late one day. The sage heard him and came out of the cottage to say that this was the work of a team and it needed all of them to do it together. Indra was irritated at this and asked, 'What if I was unwell?'

'Were you? If you were not, let's not debate about it,' was the sage's calm and firm response.

'Enough time has been wasted; now please go and get the sticks,' he ordered before retiring to his cottage.

The other students were already upset and angry. Even his new-found friend Vishnu was upset. It was quite late and the sun was beating down on the earth. While the ground heated up, the sunrays from the heavens were only sapping the energy out of the group. It was impossible to sustain the heat. All the other students felt that they had to undergo the trouble only because of Indra and he could see hatred in everybody's eyes, though none of them said anything.

While the heat was taking its toll on Indra, too, he just couldn't understand the big deal about oversleeping a little.

Besides, making everyone wait till he woke up was a bit too much. Indra decided to ignore such silly norms of the ashram. Because of the heat, they couldn't collect much firewood and returned to the ashram. The students who were supposed to prepare meals were waiting for the wood. They only started their work after they had gotten the wood for the day, which, unfortunately, was not much. Seeing such few sticks, they complained. Everyone just looked at Indra, who had decided not to meet anybody's gaze. It is alright to err once in a while, he thought to himself.

The day went by as usual, but the dinner was very frugal. Since limited firewood had been collected that day, by the time dinner was cooked, it was almost over, which led to the frugal meal. Indra could sense seething anger among everybody, but Rishi Gautama did not say a word. Indra was wondering when he would get angry and say what he had to. Indra had rehearsed an effective rebuttal to every statement that the sage might utter. He was prepared.

The day ended without any further development. Indra found one of the students whisper something to Vishnu and then both of them looked at him. Indra decided to ignore them, as he had gotten used to such behaviour during the day. Something told him that this conversation was different. Vishnu walked up to him and said, 'While I don't want to rake up the matter, as Guruji has asked all of us to keep it to ourselves, you need to know something.'

Indra gave him a questioning look.

Vishnu explained, 'Guruji has not had his meal tonight.'

'Why?'

'There wasn't much left, as only a little food was cooked.'

'Then all of us could have eaten a little less and left some for him; we wouldn't have died if we ate one morsel less, would we?' asked Indra, finding it odd that he was being blamed for an old man starving.

'That was what he said,' said Vishnu, pointing at the boy who left the kitchen last. 'But Guruji said that everything should be served to the boys, who needed the nutrition more than him.'

Indra was upset. He felt that this one aspect was being taken a bit too far and he was being made to feel guilty for something as inane as oversleeping.

Indra impulsively got up and headed towards the Rishi's cottage. He was working on something outside the cottage. Seeing Indra, he looked up. 'You haven't slept yet, my son?'

'Is it true that you have not had dinner today?' Indra was not used to pleasantries.

'Who told you?' the Rishi asked calmly.

'That's not the answer to my question. Besides, everyone knows and I am being held responsible for it,' retorted Indra.

'First,' said the sage, 'even if I was hungry, I would not speak to my guruji that rudely. However, I will overlook that, as I feel you, too, have not had a full meal and an empty stomach is known to cause irritation or rage. Second, I did not tell anybody to make you feel guilty and third, it is not important what they feel; what is important is what you feel—do you feel guilty?'

'Not for oversleeping, no,' Indra asserted firmly.

'Then there is nothing to worry about. Go to sleep,' said the sage.

'But that's not fair,' Indra tried to reason. 'Everyone is making me feel guilty.'

'No one can make you feel guilty if you don't want to.'

'I am not guilty about oversleeping, but I do feel bad about you not having your meal, as there wasn't enough.'

'They are connected, but if it's your will to separate them, so be it. As far as I am concerned, I am not blaming you for anything.'

Indra stood there, seething at the situation, not knowing what to do. There was some cold water in front of the sage. He offered the glass to Indra, 'Here, have this, it will cool you down.'

Indra did not take it and kept staring at the floor.

The sage came closer to Indra, placed his arm around Indra's shoulders and walked towards the trunk of a huge tree. Indra allowed himself to be taken there. Both of them sat down but neither spoke for a very long time.

Finally, Rishi Gautama calmly said, 'I don't blame you for anything, but I want you to remember that some tasks must be done as decided. The sun can't decide to go slow or be late, just as the flowers can't decide not to bloom when they must. The others could have gone without you, but this was a team task and you all had to do it together. No one person should get all the credit and no one should get less. We have five fingers and each is of a different size, but our hand only performs well when they are together. Try working without the thumb and you will realize that it's a job not done well. You are the thumb of your group and, thus, the team could not leave without you.'

Indra looked up at the old man. 'Missing one meal at my age is not a huge loss, but less food for any one of you means a lot to me, as you boys do all the hard work and depriving all of you of a full meal makes me feel guilty. I am being selfish. I am taking care of my guilt!' the Rishi said, smiling.

Indra was rather amazed.

The sage continued, 'As a leader of your team, lead from the front. Be an example and set high standards. That's the easiest way to earn respect. Breaking rules is the easiest option, but sticking to them is tough.'

Indra's long hair ruffled in the breeze. For a while, there was silence, until the sage said, 'Go, my son, tomorrow is a long day and I am sure you don't want to wake up late tomorrow, do you?' He was smiling.

Indra felt his eyes go moist—his Guruji's face grew hazy. He avoided the Rishi's gaze and rushed to his cottage. On his way, he wiped the tear that had escaped his eye and entered his cottage to find the lamps blown off and everyone fast asleep. Much to his relief, nobody noticed him enter the cottage. He couldn't take Rishi Gautama's words off his mind till late into the night.

Ahalya

The morning was bright and Indra was feeling a lot better after having slept over the incident of the previous day. He was the first to wake up and realized that early morning was indeed lovely. Being alone with nature while it wakes up was a unique experience. There was music in the air, dew on the grass and, while the sun hesitantly took its place in the sky, Indra noticed Rishi Gautama's daughter, Ahalya.

While none of them had been formally introduced to her, everyone knew her as the sage's daughter. Indra had never seen anybody as stunning as the girl. She was the most beautiful creature in that ashram and she seemed to blend in with the atmosphere of the ashram. Seeing her only added to the charm of the day.

Indra had heard that Ahalya was the daughter of the Creator of the world and she had been created from all the beautiful aspects of every conceivable beauty of nature. He had never seen any girl like her. The soft demeanour, the smile, the face, the eyes, the long hair...she was indeed different. She didn't seem earthly—she was surreally beautiful. Later, Vishnu, who always seemed to know everything about everyone, told him about her and how she had been handed over to the sage to be brought up.

Ahalya had become a significant reason for Indra liking the ashram and soon, a cause to discuss numerous issues with the sage after their learning hours! While Indra was quite discreet about his desire and made sure no one had any inkling about it, he couldn't get over the first time he had seen Ahalya. She had been watering the plants in her grove and he was completely smitten by her looks. That image had stuck with Indra and he found himself thinking about her often. He was wondering what this was and why she never looked at any of them. Did she even speak? Did she even know who he was? He wondered why it seemed as if she was not too concerned with anything and simply moved around oblivious to everything and everybody around her.

The movement of everyone else waking up brought him back to earth, only to realize that Ahalya wasn't there. Yet another day without getting to learn more about her!

As usual, everyone got busy with the day's work—ablutions, scriptures, chores...

The days were getting longer and warmer. Soon, working without a dip in the river was getting impossible. After a tiring day, Indra decided to take a dip in the river at sundown. He had begun to like it after the first time he had done it. It was quiet and serene at that time. Indra walked up to the high rock perched at one end of the stream and dove into the deep water. He found the swim exhilarating, as that was the only time his body got all the exercise he needed, besides cutting trees and chopping wood. After some time, when he felt that his muscles were crying for some rest, he went and stood at the shallow end of the river. He took a dip and emerged from the waters, pulling his long tresses back and letting every drop of water caress his impressive frame. The water droplets swam down his body, clinging to him as if they didn't want to let go of any inch of his magnificent body. The broad shoulders leading down to the strong torso were nothing short of divine, but the water droplets were destined to just slip down and merge with the waters of the river and lose that single moment of glory they had just received—caressing the divine frame of Indra!

Indra opened his eyes to notice Ahalya sitting on a rock in the distance. Yes, it was indeed her! Had she seen him? Well, who else was around? The splash of his dive must have made her notice him. Well, he had never heard her speak, but it's not possible that she hadn't heard him! And even if she doesn't hear, well, she surely must be able to see!

Suddenly, Indra was conscious...he took another dip and pulled his hair back, except that this time, he consciously made a splash and noise, just in case she hadn't noticed. She still didn't move and there was nobody around. Indra decided to speak to her. He swam towards the rock, splashing more water than usual. His heart was pounding.

As he looked up from the water while swimming towards the rock, he stared at Ahalya's face. She definitely possessed a divine beauty, which was beyond imagination. The simplicity itself was meticulous and inconceivable. She, too, was looking at him. Both of them kept staring at each other, speechless for a long time. The river had stopped making ripples around Indra. One could hear a leaf fall in the distance and the breeze rustle the dry leaves around. A lock of Ahalya's hair stirred in the wind and brushed against her eyes. This sort of jolted her back to the moment. Indra, too, was brought back to the moment by her sudden movement. He was about to say something when she smiled and got up to leave.

Indra tried to stop her but suddenly, the words were stuck within him. He couldn't even find his voice, as if...as if, he had just turned dumb. Ahalya was leaving and he hadn't even told her his name! She gave him one last look from the distance and left smiling as if she understood his nervousness. Indra hit the water in anger and frustration, splashing it all around. It only angered him more when he realized that even the water seemed to be laughing at him.

Indra stayed there for long, soaking in every moment of what had happened. He was wondering what had made him so tongue-tied? Was it her looks or was this…just how it was meant to be?

The sun was smiling over the horizon, as it, too, seemed to have noticed Indra's nervousness. He decided to ignore it—why bother about the setting sun anyway? Indra stepped out of the water and lay down on the rock. The slight breeze cooled his wet body and his dripping loincloth—this was his usual practice; he didn't believe in carrying an extra pair of dry clothing for after the swim. He found that this was the best way to enjoy the moments after a swim. His long hair was spread on the rock, dripping water. Once again, the struggle of the droplets began but, this time, they were absorbed by the heat of the rock and the wind.

It was beginning to get dark and, soon, it would be time for the evening scriptures and rituals. Indra didn't want to miss them. Not that he felt that they would ever be of any help to him, but he didn't want to be a cause of annoyance to anybody. Besides, Ahalya also joined everybody in these sessions.

Indra found his footsteps move faster than usual. Soon, he was in his cottage, changing for the evening rituals.

Rishi Gautama was always on time and students arriving after him was unacceptable behaviour. Indra, however, was earlier than usual because that was when Ahalya used to set up everything for the sage—his asana, his water, etc. By the time Indra reached, all that had been done, but Ahalya was not there. He waited and took his position right in the front corner. This was a good place, not in the direct line of vision of the sage but literally opposite where Ahalya used to sit!

Soon, the others started coming in, followed by the sage. The chanting of the scriptures began but no Ahalya. This had never happened before. Indra was disturbed—why was she missing? The entire session, she did not turn up. This was something that had never happened before. He began to wonder if her absence had something to do with what had happened at the river that day.

The rituals soon came to an end without Indra even realizing it. The night was long and the wait for the next evening was even longer. Suddenly, it seemed that the sun was in no hurry to rise and once it had risen, it was in no hurry in its journey to the west!

'My Name Is Indra'

Ahalya was sitting on the rock, like she had done the previous day. Indra had been soaking in the waters for long. He finally swam towards the rock noiselessly.

He quietly rose from the waters, looked straight at Ahalya and said, 'Didn't see you for the chanting yesterday evening...' He noticed that she was smiling.

'Why? Were you waiting for me?' asked Ahalya.

'Well, no, I mean, yes... Actually, I was just wondering...' Indra struggled.

'What?' asked Ahalya, staring straight at Indra.

'No, I mean, I was wondering if you were unwell...' he enquired hesitantly.

There was a deafening silence for some time. Indra was worried that she might leave all of a sudden, like the previous day.

'I am Indra.'

Ahalya smiled and said, 'I know. Father speaks often about you.'

This surprised Indra, 'Oh, really? Good things, I hope…'

The sudden pauses and silent responses upset Indra.

'He thinks highly about you,' Ahalya suddenly broke the silence.

'Really? And you?'

'What about me?'

'What do you think about me?'

'Do you want me to think about you?'

There was something about the way she spoke and looked at

him, which was beginning to unsettle Indra. Why was he feeling like this? He had never quite felt like this...

'You didn't answer me,' Ahalya persisted.

Indra kept staring at her face. He had lost his words. That face was just not mortal. She was divine...ethereal. Her long hair flirted with the wind. Her white saree, tied loosely, could barely hide her shapely hips and legs. Her delicate shoulders and slim arms were the work of a master sculptor, but it was her penetrating doe-eyes that made Indra very uneasy. They were fearless, had pride of conviction and a self-awareness, bearing no shade of arrogance. How could some eyes *say* so much?

Indra suddenly saw her leaving. Without realizing it, he jumped out of the water and stood in front of Ahalya. Water caressed Indra's massive frame, his hair dripped water and his loose dhoti clung to his body, hiding less and revealing a manly frame. Ahalya was shocked and stood motionless. She had never seen a man in such youthful bloom. She let her eyes roll over his body, unabashed, unashamed and unmindful of her actions. Indra could feel her eyes all over him and an odd sense of joy rushed through his veins. He didn't want this moment to pass.

Indra extended his hand towards Ahalya's but she moved a few steps back. She could see Indra even better now. The setting sun, now hidden behind his head, did its trick. The golden halo formed by the sun gave him a celestial look, while the clothes clinging to his wet body made him look divinely sensuous. Ahalya wanted to keep staring at him. Time stood still.

A strong breeze shook both of them out of their reveries. The sun played a trick on the two; it had set without either of them realizing it. Ahalya ran from there and Indra kept staring after her. He, too, wanted to run after her, hold her in his arms and crush her with his passion, but his feet were stuck to the ground;

he just couldn't move. By the time he could, she was nowhere to be seen. He kept staring at the direction in which Ahalya had run, till the breeze made him shiver. Indra didn't want to go. He wanted to stay there forever and wait for her. She would come the next evening again. Suddenly, everything else had lost meaning for Indra. He seemed to exist only for Ahalya.

Ahalya did come the next evening and the next and every evening thereafter, and so did Indra. Ahalya looked forward to the evenings and for Indra, nothing else mattered in the whole day. Suddenly, that was the most sacred hour for both, when they would be alone, together, when nothing and nobody else mattered.

The Call

Life has a strange way of taking unexpected turns. Mitra had come to see Indra the previous day…rather, to take him back 'for the time being', is what Mitra had said.

There was trouble back home and Mitra felt that Indra was needed there. While it was a great feeling to be wanted, Indra wasn't sure of his feelings about leaving the ashram, which he had so reluctantly joined and only lately started to like. So much so that somewhere in his mind, he thought, he belonged here. However, he understood that although he liked being here, this wasn't his home. This wasn't the place that would lead to the objective of his life. His place and his sphere of action were not a serene ashram; it was the world stage, which was calling him, calling him to act, act upon the very rationale of his existence.

Mitra had mentioned something to him, which had kept him awake the whole night. His people back home were facing some trouble from the demons.

'Demons? You mean the people who trouble sages?' Ahalya asked.

The innocent question brought a smile to Indra's face. 'Well, they don't just trouble the sages! There is a world outside the world of sages, and these people trouble others too.'

An embarrassed Ahalya smiled. She was trying to understand the urgency of the meeting, which Indra had communicated to her after asking her to meet him in a hurry. The missive had brought her here, at the grove, to find a pensive Indra. She knew the moment she saw him that something was amiss.

'So, what will you do?' continued Ahalya.

'My people are planning to wage a battle against some demons and they want me there.'

Ahalya wasn't sure if there was joy in the voice or sadness or reluctance.

'And you don't want to go...'

'No, no! Of course, I want to go...'

Ahalya's face fell, which Indra noticed and added, 'That is what is bothering me. One part of me wants to go and the other wants to stay. My mind says this is the moment I have been waiting for—my people have felt that we need Indra for this. But...'

'But what?' asked Ahalya staring at Indra, who was looking up at the sky.

Indra looked at Ahalya, placing his hands on hers. 'But my heart wants to stay here, with you.'

Ahalya smiled and asked, 'Has Father agreed to allow you to leave?'

'Yes, Mitra has spoken to him and he has allowed it,' Indra answered to Ahalya's disappointment.

'And...' Ahalya prompted.

'I am leaving now. Mitra is waiting for me.'

He took her hand in his. 'But promise me you will wait for me. I will be back. For you.'

Ahalya held back her tears and said, 'I will, but it would have been better if you had spoken to Father once about us. Lately, he seems to be preoccupied with something, I don't know what. He seems disturbed. Often, I have found him staring at me oddly. I can't fathom that expression.'

'Maybe he is concerned about your coming of age and is looking for a husband for you?' Indra suggested with a smile.

'I would sense that, but I don't think that's what he is thinking. There is something... I don't know what it is... Leave it. All I can say is do come back soon. I have lived here without you earlier, but now, I can't live without—'.

The distant shadow of a person interrupted Ahalya. She distanced herself from him by a few steps.

It was Vishnu. He was heading towards the grove when he stopped. He was surprised to see Ahalya and Indra together. Indra looked in Vishnu's direction and said, 'I think I have to leave... but I will come back. Wait for me...' These were Indra's last words before he headed towards Vishnu.

Ahalya noticed a disturbed look on Vishnu's face. Indra pulled him along, the two had some conversation and, soon, they were gone. Ahalya suddenly felt very lonely, as if this calling away of Indra was heralding something ominous. As if this was going to be a life-changing event...but for whom? Him or her?

Part 2

The Rise

The Enemy

'Just who are these people?' asked Indra.

'That indeed is a tough question and a sad reality,' Mitra responded. The expression on his face displayed the same emotions as his words. Indra was confused. What could that mean? 'Well, they are...' Mitra hazarded, 'They are the Asuras, Rakshasas and Danavas.'

Noticing that the answer did not seem to mean anything much to Indra, Mitra explained, 'The Rakshasas and the Danavas are a different kind of people. Their lifestyles and mannerisms are different. They are often wild and loud in their behaviour. Their dressing and food habits are different. They even look different...'

'Look different? How?' wondered Indra.

Mitra smiled, 'Well, not quite different, except for their complexions—they are not as fair as us. Some are quite dark-skinned. They eye our women all the time and often try to capture them. Once captured, one never hears about them. Among the Rakshasas, there are some really bad ones like the Yatudhanas, who are rumoured to even eat humans.'

'Are you serious?' Indra asked, repulsed.

'Well, one can never be sure of such things. Once we had captured a few of the Rakshasas, and we heard them say this. As I said, till you don't see them, you can never be sure. But then why wait for them to commit such acts? Our sages have been quite disturbed by some of them and so we need to act.'

'And how do they disturb our sages?'

'They disturb the yajnas and other rituals of our sages,'

Mitra responded. 'When our sages are performing their rituals, they disturb them by sending animals or by blowing wind and dust...'

'Blowing wind? You mean they can do that?' asked a surprised Indra.

'Well, some of them know tricks. Tricks like creating illusions. Some are even known to change shapes and take the form of animals, like bulls and dogs. They dirty the sacred groves of our sages and even the *yajna-sthalas*, the yajna spaces. They dirty the water of sacred rivers and ponds, from where we drink water. Often, they just harass our people. There is no reason, except to attack and overpower. Some of them seem to only thrive on evil—evil intentions and evil designs to rule and destroy. Many times, we have been attacked for no reason.'

Indra found that quite strange. Is this some sort of war for fun? He had never quite heard about it before. 'Why now?' he wondered aloud.

'Well, it's not sudden. We have been ignoring some of their misdemeanours and often avoiding them completely until they did not bother us directly. But lately, these skirmishes have increased. I think they are trying to subdue our rising presence in this area...'

'And us?' asked Indra, looking straight at Mitra.

Mitra smiled. 'Us too. Yes, we are also expanding our sphere of control. Space is might and the more space we have under our control, both directly and indirectly, the greater power that gives us.'

'Indirectly?' Indra didn't quite understand the term.

'Indirectly...through alliances, including the friendship and support extended to some tribes and groups in fighting their enemies,' explained Mitra.

Indra nodded. 'Have there been any major battles or just skirmishes?'

Mitra smiled. 'Well not many of the encounters have been planned. They have happened as and when something goes wrong.'

'And who has been waging these battles from our end?'

'Well, all of us, ably supported by your friends, the Maruts. Varuna has been in charge, but his sense of law and righteousness often comes in the way of defeating the enemies, which needs a combination of valour and guile! You know what I mean, right? While we are on the side of fair play, they are not. How long can battles be won on just fair play if the same is not reciprocated from the other end? So, it boils down to might is right and I feel we should fight our enemies in the same way they do. Fair if they are and not-so-fair if they aren't. Once, when...' Mitra's voice trailed off.

'When what? Tell me!' urged Indra.

Mitra smiled. 'Once, two of them seemed simply invincible. Sanda and Marka were just not defeatable and we were having a tough time bringing them under control. They destroyed for the sake of destroying. While many of their ilk are known to do so, these two excelled at it and had become quite a nuisance. There were quite a few battles in which we were losing our men and time.'

'Then?'

'We sent some spies from our side to understand their weakness.' Mitra smiled at Indra. 'Often it is our women. But not for these two—they could be tempted with something much simpler: your favourite drink, soma!'

Indra looked down in embarrassment. 'Relax,' smiled Mitra, 'I know about your penchant for the root, just as it is a favourite with nearly all of us. So, we offered them the drink and they soon changed sides! Battle over!'

'Really? As simple as that?'

'Well, in this case, yes, it was. But not all of them are that simple. There have been battles, some quite long-drawn and bloody. Loss of life has been enormous on both the sides, besides the loss of animals. We have lost lots of our cows and bulls, who we need for many reasons. They have been bothering our subjects too. That's one of the ways of harassing us, of course.'

'Often, we have been helped by providence, like in the case of Makha. He, too, was unmanageable and a lot of lives had been lost in trying to subdue him. While we were reaching a stage of frustration, he was just not willing to give up. He thrived on blood and battle. We had tried everything but nothing seemed to be working.'

'Then?' curiosity was getting the better of Indra.

'As I said, luck was favouring us,' Mitra responded with a smile and continued, 'This happened entirely in front of people. On the battlefield, while he was standing with his bow, which was as large as he had been, the string of the bow snapped against his head and his head rolled over on the ground! None of us could believe what we had seen. It happened so suddenly that it took us a while to understand that he had died on his own.'

'That's it? I mean such a person dies by himself? That's kind of unbelievable!'

Indra found Mitra smiling. 'Are you sure, there was no unfairness there?'

Mitra smiled. 'Not that I know of! Maybe a wind blew some ants to the end of the bow, which weakened its string, which "unfortunately" snapped!'

'Vayu?' asked Indra, wide-eyed.

'Well, that's what the rumours said; I am not in the know. I don't know anything about it beyond this,' said Mitra looking elsewhere.

'Oh really!' said Indra smiling. 'And what about Varuna? You mean to say, he, too, thinks this is "providence"?'

'Well, since there was no way anything else could be proven, he too let it pass. But I guess he has some doubt about this. He is supposed to have blessed the ants with the ability to seek out water. Wherever they dig, they find water,' Mitra informed Indra.

'And his guilt was taken care of!' said Indra sarcastically. 'By the way,' asked Indra, 'aren't some of us Asuras too? So, how are they enemies?'

Mitra smiled, 'Yes, you are right...but these Asuras are different.'

Indra gave Mitra a questioning look.

Mitra seemed more pensive as he continued, 'They have been a wayward bunch. They don't care much for order and lawfulness. They thrive on breaking rules and going against what seems to be the order of the day. They cannot accept rules; they prefer to live a life of unruliness. There is a difference in mentality here. They seem to be becoming our chief adversaries. It becomes tougher to defeat them, as they are one of us! They use the same means of warfare against us as ours, the same yajnas and even worship the same gods.'

'As if this is not enough, their evil ways have made them create new hymns and prayers with evil intentions. Some of them, unknown to us and their preceptors have given rise to new scriptures, if I may call them that. They are literally "*Asuri*", something we wouldn't want to follow, and something that's clearly evil, with devious intentions.

'Indra, we have to understand that while we want to win

battles for the larger cause of goodness, we can't be one of them. This distinction must be maintained to bring a semblance of equilibrium on earth. We must make sure that our way of living and thinking thrives since the civilization that we leave behind has much to gain from us and nothing from them. They are everything that we are not. This message must be brought home and, soon, before the earth is ruled by them.'

Indra had never seen Mitra so serious. Somehow, every word he said seemed to make so much sense to Indra.

After a pause, which seemed like an eternity, Indra asked, 'And where do I come in?'

Mitra was brought back to the moment, 'You...ah you! Some of us think that you need to take charge of the battles now. You are young and the Maruts are good friends of yours and listen to you. Along with them, create an army and wage wars against our enemies. Let us get rid of them.'

'Why me?' Indra was still not clear about what Mitra had to say.

'You are young. These enemies are new and tackling them needs new ways of thinking based on the changing circumstances. We have done our bit and think that, in this changing scenario, we need new blood and new ways of thinking. You could just do well, better than us, I feel.' Mitra was looking straight at Indra.

While Indra felt good, he was still sceptical, 'And Varuna has agreed to this? Won't this go against his sense of "fairness"?' the sarcasm was not lost on Mitra, but he decided to ignore it.

'We have discussed it with him and Mother too. While he is not quite amenable to the idea, let's face it, he, too, is tired. Battles aren't his forte any more. We have seen him waging wars, but those were different times and enemies. These are changing times, changing realities and he accepts it, even if he doesn't say so. His feeble resistance was a dead giveaway.'

'So, there was resistance!' Indra didn't sound too pleased.

'Now come on,' Mitra came closer to Indra. 'That's really not fair. What do you expect? That he should change the way he thinks? Would you do it? And before you answer that, let me tell you, it's all very easy to answer theoretical questions, so don't bother. It's time you take charge of this realm, save the system and establish a rule of law. For this, if some new laws must be implemented, go ahead. But remember to maintain the right equilibrium of the society that we have established.'

Indra saw this as an opportunity and knew that this was going to change the way everybody looked at him. This was his chance to prove that he was different and was the one to reckon with.

'I am sure, we haven't made any mistake,' Mitra was looking straight at Indra.

Indra got up from his place, kept staring at Mitra and then simply hugged him. Both said nothing for some time. Mitra knew that his machinations would not fail and Indra knew that he was obliged to Mitra and would never fail him, and the world would remember him till it existed!

Vala

'It is difficult to understand these enemies, especially when some of them had lived among us... Rather, they were one of us,' said Raudriya, one of the Maruts. Indra was listening.

'But enemies are enemies.' Indra heard himself say, putting the shoot of soma—which he had taken an intense liking to—down, its juice trickling down his lips. 'Why is this discussion so important and how does it matter who they are—from within us or without?'

'It does, Sakra, it does,' said Bhadrajaneya, the one with a beautiful wife. Indra was often addressed as 'Sakra' now, which meant powerful. The shoot often made Bhadra, as he was called, emotional. Although he was ruthless in the field, he displayed an affectionate side once a few drops of soma went in him!

'It does...' he repeated. 'It does.' After a brief pause, as if he had forgotten what he was saying, he added, 'Eliminating outsiders is easy, but killing one of us isn't. There is no major guilt when one is killing those who harm us and deserve to be eliminated. It's part of our responsibility towards our kind. If it is a matter of who exists—them or us—then the battle becomes very easy—it's us! But when this decision has to be taken between *us* and *ours*, it is not easy.'

Now, this was probably one of those rare nuggets of wisdom from Bhadra, but it sure was succinct enough to be considered. Everybody looked at him, but he was oblivious to everyone's glare, as the shoot of soma was working on him. 'This, Sakra, is what is making things difficult now,' was Bhadra's concluding remark.

Indra found everybody quietly acknowledging the rare display of wisdom by Bhadra—he sure did make sense. Such a dilemma—if one can call it that—had not quite arisen earlier. This could precisely have been the reason why Indra had been made responsible for it. While Indra still felt an enemy was an enemy, he couldn't disagree with Bhadra completely because he hadn't quite fought a full-fledged battle, however insignificant it may be. Participating in battles and taking charge were two different things. Earlier, he had been part of some minor skirmishes, but things were different now. Besides, this was an important opportunity—he felt that he was being observed this time. By whom? By everybody—Mother, Varuna, Mitra and Varuna's close associates.

If Indra failed, it would be an embarrassment to both him and Mitra, who seemed to have put his reputation at stake by suggesting Indra for this battle. This was the moment that could catapult him to a position, which had been weakened under Varuna, who was losing popularity among his own people. It was time to rise and shine and not just sit and allow this moment to pass.

'I tend to agree with you that we need to act,' Indra found himself saying. Once again, the heads were nodding—not helping much in strategizing, though. This was both a blessing as well as an impediment. If no idea was forthcoming, he was free to do what he thought was the need of the hour, except that there was no way to be sure that what he was going to do was correct. While he sure wanted to usher in some sort of a revolution in warfare, he wasn't going to miss out on the tried-and-tested methods.

'Vishwaroop,' called out Indra, 'I want you to start the sacred yajna, which should ensure that our offerings benefit our folks.'

Vishwaroop was the son of a sage and had taken over the

mantle of performing sacrifices and yajnas from his illustrious father, who had never missed the mark. Vishwaroop acknowledged Indra's instruction and promised to begin first thing the next morning.

'Good,' nodded Indra, 'now that that's done—and yes, Vishwaroop, you can take whoever you want to help you...'

'No, I don't need anybody,' replied Vishwaroop, 'I can do this myself. I would rather have everybody help where might is needed. I think you will need all of them and more.'

There was no denying that, thought Indra. While he had the entire army at his beck and call, one would often find that they could do with more when they were in the midst of a battle.

'So, who can tell me more about this fellow called Vala?' asked Indra, looking around.

'Vala is a dangerous creature,' Vidyut responded, quick as lightning. 'Vala is dangerous because he cannot be trusted and he is considered to be the bravest of them all.'

'Why? I mean how?' wondered Indra looking at Vidyut, who was known to be sharp and fast with his information. One never had to question his abilities on gathering information.

Vidyut continued, 'Besides all the bravery, he is often assisted by the Panis—'

'Panis?' enquired Indra.

'Yes, Panis. The tribe of people that steal cattle. They thrive on stealing cattle and Vala hoardes them in his cave.'

'And does what?'

'Well, we don't know what he does but one thing is certain, he hoardes them in his cave, depriving people of the benefits of the cattle. Cattle are wealth and people who lose them are suddenly left poor,' explained Vidyut. 'He is very powerful,' continued Vidyut, 'he has been troubling us and the common folk and is quite a nuisance to the majority. This quality of making others' life miserable, unopposed, has made him both arrogant and brave—a terrible mix to have in one's enemy!'

Indra was listening intently. That was the quality of Vidyut's information. He never hid anything that could be disturbing. He said it all.

'But this time, he has gone a bit too far...' Indra looked at him, shocked, just as everybody out there, who had been listening to Vidyut intently, was. 'This time it is not scores of cattle...He has also imprisoned Ushas in the cave. Ushas, as you know...'

Indra got up from his seat...the name was not unheard of, remembered Vidyut. Ushas was an important entity in the community and besides that, this was an old story for Indra.

There was a palpable silence around, as everybody had Indra's skirmish with Ushas etched in their minds.

Ushas commanded a lot of respect. There was no doubting her significance in the community and the fact that she had been a force to reckon with, for that matter, she still was.

One day, Ushas had been returning in her chariot, pulled by about a hundred horses. She had just run through the sky, declaring the arrival of the day and left for her abode, as tomorrow was yet another day. Indra had often seen her rushing at great speed as if she was flying in the air. Her control over her steeds and her garments flying all around, with her golden hair, cascading behind her, were simply mesmerizing. Indra had often tried to stop and speak to her, but she didn't seem to be bothered about anybody, especially Indra.

Ushas's nonchalance had seemed to be arrogant to Indra and a personal affront. Besides, all Indra had wanted was to speak to her, which wasn't asking for the Sun, who she seemed to be in love with. Her love for the illuminating brilliance of the Sun was known to all. Had Indra been jealous? Well, no! But that day, something within him had moved him to do what no one had ever done before.

Indra had stood in the way of Ushas. Her hundred-steed chariot needed to be given way and Indra, atop his huge black bull, had been in no mood to move, as he had reached there before her. Indra's bull had been moving very slowly and Ushas had to halt, seeing Indra's pace. She had yelled from behind for the interloper to move—did he not know that the roads were to be kept clear for her?

Just what did Indra hate about this woman? The fact that she was in love with Surya, or the fact that she ignored Indra as if he did not exist or was it her free-wheeling attitude that irked him or that he had never seen a woman who was this fiercely independent? None of these aspects would have bothered him if only she had acknowledged his existence. *Reason* sure had been a casualty that day, as too much of soma had put Indra's reason to sleep. Seeing Ushas from a distance had been enough for Indra to take a stand, which he knew would lead to a confrontation.

'Are you deaf?' Ushas had demanded from behind Indra, which had jolted him back to the moment. 'Or are you drunk on youth and ignorance?' she had asked angrily, as she had been forced to slow down.

A few more moments later, she had repeated, 'Will you move, you arrogant man, or do you want to find yourself under the hoofs of my steeds?'

A needlessly enraged Indra had been waiting for the ultimate provocation. It was time to put this arrogant woman in her place, let her know that he was no ordinary youth—he was going to be someone to reckon with and that had better happen right then. 'Later' was never an option for him.

Indra had moved ahead and steered his bull to face Ushas. When he had turned around, Ushas's glow had fallen on his face and she had noticed Indra. This was the same youth who was known to be with the sons of Rudra. His mane had been flying all over and there sure was something about him. While she had heard about his methods and his confrontations within his family, none of that interested her. She had simply needed to pass and not be held up.

'Are you moving or do you want me to charge and trample you down to dust? I am not used to being delayed,' Ushas had shouted, reining her steeds, which also seemed to be uncomfortable being stationary. But Indra had been in no mood for negotiations because, for him, words in such situations were a waste of time. Indra had felt no need to explain himself and, from a distance, he had charged without warning.

Indra, atop his bull, had hurtled towards Ushas, who barely understood the act or the reason behind it. The bull had seen red and had been unstoppable. Seeing the two, Ushas had tried to steer her chariot aside, but she had never done this before. She was not used to 'giving way' and this silly youth had challenged her to do exactly what she had never done!

A hundred steeds were not easy to manoeuvre and, just like their mistress, the steeds too weren't used to turning or moving. Indra's bull had hurtled towards the chariot and Ushas had just managed to turn eastwards, as the bull and its rider had charged into her chariot. The enormous force of the impact had thrown Ushas to the ground and the reins of the horses had fallen from her hand. The horses had fallen all around. Ushas had been thrown to the ground with a force that she had never experienced. She had rolled down the banks of the river, Vipas, which was flowing nearby.

With the clash, Indra had got down from his bull and walked towards the river, where a drenched and injured Ushas had been trying to understand what had just happened. The dishevelled and ragged Ushas's face had given away her fear. Indra had loved that expression. Ushas had been scared when she had seen the bloodshot eyes and menacing structure of Indra. She had tried to wrap herself with the shreds of what had been her clothes until a few moments ago and had run for her life. Behind her, all she could hear was Indra's loud laughter—the laughter of victory, the laughter of having tamed an arrogant woman, the laughter of killing the free spirit of an independent woman. The fleeing Ushas had known that she would never be the same again; her life would never be the same again.

This incident was still fresh in Indra's mind and in that of everyone present. However, Indra seemed to be infuriated by the fact that Ushas was in the custody of Vala.

Indra realized that all eyes were on him. He understood that they were all wondering if he would undertake this at all since they knew about his enmity with her. 'Before you tell me anything,' Indra said, looking at nobody in particular, 'let me make one thing very clear. My differences with Ushas are personal and it has nothing to do with the responsibility entrusted upon me. If at all, this difference can never go beyond our community—I don't want a rank outsider, an enemy at that, to take advantage of such situations and, least of all, get away with taking someone of such importance hostage.'

There was a sigh of relief among many, as they all revered her, irrespective of her difference with Indra. They were glad that Indra was not letting his personal issue come in the way of rescuing her, not that he had ever done such a thing before.

'We will have to get her back and everything else that has

been held hostage, and soon,' Indra said, pacing restlessly. He grabbed a few more soma shoots and chewed on them frantically. He was known do this whenever he was agitated or excited.

There was no time to waste. They had to act and act immediately. 'Vishwaroop,' Indra reiterated—his voice heard by all, 'I want you to begin the yajnas first thing tomorrow morning, without fail.'

'I will, Sakra!' replied Vishwaroop, looking at the direction in which Indra had left, followed by the others. Vishwaroop then saw something move in the nearby shrubs but decided to ignore it.

The Slaying

The battle lines were drawn. Indra was armed with bows and arrows, maces and all that could be of help. The Maruts and others were also ready and raring to go. Indra and his boys had drunk some soma to ensure that they had the energy to last the day and fight without any emotional pricks of conscience coming in the way!

Vala, on the other hand, was missing, though his army was in position. Indra was upset to see that his adversary had not come for the battle, clearly demonstrating that Indra was not worth his while. For Indra and the unruly boys of Rudra, Vala's army was enough.

This angered Indra all the more because besides being a personal affront, the demon was also questioning the decision of the elders of his community.

The battle began at the sound of a huge gong. The Maruts stormed towards Vala's army, which had heavy weapons with sharp edges, spikes and huge spears. Some were on steeds but most of them were on foot. They seemed to be hungry for war and excited by the sight of blood. They were unruly and laughed with an evil sense of joy. Indra found them quite unorganized and often rudderless. While this could be an advantage, Indra needed to understand whether this was a deliberate ploy to mislead him or whether it was the reality.

Indra could see that his boys were beginning to get tired and so were the opponents. Soon, he saw some of them retreating but Indra's boys were not charging at them. The gong announced the end of the day and Indra noticed that everyone had been waiting for this moment. The ground was littered with the bodies of Vala's soldiers, though there were hardly any casualties from Indra's army. Needless to say, all of them were tired. Indra decided to do something about it.

They were camping close to the field, near the river bed. Soon, everyone retired to their camps and there was an uneasy calm.

Indra was jolted out of his thoughts by the arrival of Ahibhanava, the one with the brilliance of serpents. Ahibhanava was a spy from Indra's camp, unknown to anybody. He reported that there had been significant losses of life in Vala's camp, but that had hardly been a deterrent. They had lots of people to fight for them, so they could last for days. Also, the entrance of the cave was well-guarded by a special force, which seemed to be equipped with some unknown strength or power. This was disturbing, as Indra was in a hurry to prove to the elders that they had not made the wrong decision by trusting him with the task of killing Vala.

Ahibhanava had left without anybody even noticing his entrance and exit, leaving Indra in a pensive moment. If the first day was inconclusive, the days that followed weren't any different either. Indra was worried—just what was making them so formidable? Ahibhanava, too, felt that there was something more to them than just physical strength. The injured were fit to fight the next day, which seemed odd to both Ahibhanava and Indra. They wondered if they were missing something.

Indra learnt that back in the tribe, people were questioning the sanity of handing the battle to Indra. Some were questioning it openly and all fingers were being pointed at Mitra. Indra was upset about this. He couldn't believe that this was happening.

He had already quaffed a glass too many of soma for the day, when he saw Ahibhanava walk into his tent one night. He looked distinctly worried. While he was known to bring worrying news every day, that day seemed different.

'Go ahead, spread the gloom, my dear,' said Indra.

Ahibhanava was silent. He knew he hadn't been of much help but was also aware that the information he had brought today was significant. He went closer to Indra and whispered something in his ear.

Indra's expressions changed and before Ahibhanava could complete, he stood up. Anger flashed across his face. He poured another goblet of soma, drank it in one gulp, grabbed his sword and stormed out of the tent. Ahibhanava followed him.

When some of the guards saw them and tried to follow, Ahibhanava indicated that they were to be left alone. Nobody was required. The two walked through the tents, the occupants of which were oblivious to what was happening. Indra slowed down when they reached close to the farthest tent. Behind the tent was the *yajna-kshetra*, where Vishwaroop had been performing yajnas since the day the war had begun. Indra stood aside and noticed Vishwaroop perform some rites quietly. He had just finished the day's work and was preparing to share the offerings with the Maruts. The offerings were organized in a huge golden plate, which was sent to everyone in the army.

Just when Indra was about to charge, he noticed a shadow at a distance. Ahibhanava pulled Indra back in the dark. Surprised at the intrusion of his steps, Indra looked at Ahibhanava, who had put his finger on his lips, indicating Indra to be quiet. Ahibhanava then gestured Indra to look at the shadow. Indra was shocked to see one of Vala's generals!

Vishwaroop then took the plate of the offerings and put

half of them in a silver container and gave it to the general. The general, smiling and bowing to Vishwaroop, walked away into the darkness of the night. Indra was about to charge when, once again, Ahibhanava restrained him, whispering, 'He is not our enemy, ours is this one,' he said, pointing to Vishwaroop.

Just as Vishwaroop was spreading the offerings in the empty portion of the plate to make it look full, he noticed Indra standing in front of him. Vishwaroop was flustered and instinctively looked in the direction where the general had just left.

'Who was he?' demanded Indra.

Vishwaroop kept quiet. He wasn't sure what he was supposed to say.

'I asked—who was he?' Indra thundered.

Vishwaroop knew that he had earned the wrath of Indra and it would be better to own up than lie. He responded, 'He is a general of Vala.'

Indra could barely believe what he just heard.

'And what was he doing with the offering?' bellowed Indra.

'I give them a share of it every day,' Vishwaroop said, barely audible.

'You are helping our enemy? Why?'

An uneasy pause was broken by the thundering voice of Indra, 'WHY?'

Vishwaroop said, 'They are related to me.'

'How? How are they related to you?'

'My mother...'

'Go on, you traitor, I am listening,' demanded an impatient Indra.

'My mother belongs to their tribe and my grandfather is their guru. I couldn't betray them in their moment of crisis,' Vishwaroop responded with the reason for his betrayal.

'But you could betray me? Me? Here I am trying to understand the reason we keep losing, despite having such brave warriors; meanwhile, you are busy working for them. You have stabbed me in the back,' Indra accused, losing his composure.

'I can explain... I was equipping our men too,' reasoned Vishwaroop.

'But that wasn't your task. You were supposed to equip only our folks, not yours! And if you had a problem with that, you should have said it. But you chose to remain silent and dig my grave!' yelled Indra for the world to hear.

'Helping one's people is not a crime,' Vishwaroop responded defiantly, which surprised Indra and Ahibhanava, who had maintained a distance.

'You will give me lessons on crime? A traitor is teaching me what crime is?' No sooner had Indra said this, his hands reached the sword at his waist. Even before Vishwaroop could realize it, Indra pulled out the sword and beheaded him.

Ahibhanava stood there shocked! He had not expected this. He did not know how to react.

Indra looked at the dead body and then at the head that had failed him. The eyes stared at him defiantly, even in death. Indra kicked the head towards the flames of the yajna, which had not died yet. Indra would not need the offerings any more. He retraced his steps back to his tent. He knew he had no reason to doubt the effectiveness of his boys. It was the sage's son who was to be blamed for the delay in releasing the hostages.

Indra was not going to allow anybody to come in the way of him and his victory. Ahibhanava, still in a state of shock, followed Indra.

Tomorrow the war would be over.

The Battle

The war ought to have been over long back. With an army of Maruts and the ferociousness of Indra, it sure was a surprise for many back home that the war was not over. Besides, no one had thought that Vala would be able to stand his ground in the war for so long. Besides having underestimated Vala, many were beginning to doubt the decision of entrusting Indra with leading the army. But Indra was not willing to accept this.

With the traitor, Vishwaroop, gone, Indra had hoped that one element of the divine intervention would be taken away from Vala. But someone like him, who had resisted for so long, would definitely come back with a vengeance, probably better prepared. Indra understood that this had to be discussed with his army before they took the wrong message. If there was one thing he knew about war, it was that rumours could spoil the morale of the people who were fighting for you.

The next day was overcast, as if the skies were reacting to Vishwaroop's death. There were some murmurs in the army about the incident but nothing was being said aloud. Indra was not going to wait till he heard something. He sent word that he would address everyone about something very important and, till then, nobody should listen to any unsolicited rumours.

At the appointed hour, the small but brave army assembled outside Indra's tent. He gulped down a goblet of soma and stepped out to face those who deserved to know the truth. He looked at all of them and saw mixed emotions on all their faces. In the corner, he noticed Ahibhanava but decided to ignore him, as no one in the group knew that he was spying for the army. Indra believed that no one should ever know who, among them, was a spy, even if it was for the enemy.

'I have been thinking for the last few days,' began Indra, 'about why we were not able to end this war, which ought to have ended several days back. I never doubted your abilities even once,' he asserted while looking around, 'but we cannot deny that the war has been on an equal footing.'

Some nodded in agreement.

'While they were more, you boys have been more than a match for them. But even then, we seemed to be defending more than routing them until a few days back, if not earlier. I knew that the problem lay elsewhere.'

Some glanced at each other, wondering what was coming.

'I didn't have to look too far. The problem was not with any of you or your capabilities to take on this evil tribe, that has held hostage our cows and, above all, Ushas. Our offerings to the gods were being shared with the gods of our enemy.' The army of Maruts looked at each other. 'Yes, you heard me right. Our very own Vishwaroop was helping them.'

A look of disbelief was visible on every face. 'If it is unbelievable to you, it was even more difficult for me to believe, until I saw it with my own eyes.' Indra narrated everything that had taken place the previous night.

'I hate traitors and there is no place for them in my army!' bellowed Indra. 'I have got rid of him. We will now fight without any divine help. You will now fight on the merit of your strengths. We won't need yajnas and sacrifices conducted by traitors!'

Indra looked around. While some faces looked content, some still looked worried. He knew he had to address them and not let them pass. A small doubt can grow into a larger issue faster than a small plant manages to stand with its roots. If he needed his boys to fight for him, he had to answer their doubts.

'Some of you seem worried,' he said looking at one of them. 'Feel free to clear your doubts right now. Don't hesitate.'

'But... But wasn't he a son of the sage?' came a feeble voice from the back. Some nodded and others looked back at him.

'Yes, he was,' replied Indra.

'Are you not the son of Rudra? Does that make you any less of a person? If one of us was going against us and working for our enemy, what would you have done? Pardoned him? Would he not be more cautious the next time? This is war, my friend, and every delay costs lives... Lives of our friends and those we love and care for. You can't let war be perpetuated by the acts of a traitor.

'There is no sin greater than letting your own people down, deceiving them and fighting for the enemy.' Indra noticed that some of them were already nodding in agreement.

'I will not allow that,' Indra continued, without looking at anybody. 'If there is any sin, let it be mine and mine only. I know I have committed no sin, as I am here for a task—a task that I have been trusted with by the elders for our community. I am not going to disappoint anybody and nor will I let anybody raise a single finger against you all, who have been battling the enemy with all your might and spirit. I can't let a traitor malign any of you.'

The army was visibly moved. Raudriya walked up to Indra and said, 'We understand you, O mighty Indra, and we respect your decision. Though, I must admit, until a few moments ago, we weren't sure if we agreed with your decision but, right now, there is no doubt in our minds... Or at least in my mind, that what you did was right.' He looked around and saw all of them nodding.

'There, Indra,' said a smiling Raudriya, 'We all agree on this. You have led us from the front, like no one had earlier. We will charge with equal vigour and will not let you down.'

Indra was moved. He looked at Raudriya and hugged him. There was visible cheer among all of them and Indra knew that the war would be over soon.

The next couple of days were crucial but the advancement of Indra's army was visible. Each passing day was taking them closer to the cave where Vala was supposed to have held the hostages captive. His generals were retreating and losing morale, which was not being adequately restored by Vala, much to Indra's surprise.

The Release

It wasn't too long before Indra realized that not many of Vala's generals were left in the battlefield. Some had deserted their own army, while others were dead. There were even feelers being sent out by some that they were willing to surrender, as they were not able to hold up. Besides, the morale of the army seemed to be missing because Vala himself was missing from all the action. With the leader gone, the army was rudderless and simply giving up.

Soon, the war was over, earlier than anticipated. Though the war seemed to have been won, Vala was nowhere in sight. Despite being closer to the cave, Indra's army still had to enter it.

It was close to noon when Vala's army was routed, with some of their generals surrendering. Indra and his army then reached the opening of the cave. With great difficulty, the huge boulder at the opening of the cave was moved just enough for people to get in.

Indra sent Vala's general inside the cave before his generals and finally, he entered. Vala's men were petrified and had to be pushed by the points of the spears held against their backs. For Vala's men, death was imminent either way so they had no choice but to advance. What lay ahead was unknown to them.

A deafening silence greeted them, with darkness all around. Indra and his generals were prepared for any incident. All of them were aware of the fact that Vala was a sorcerer and Indra only wanted to ensure that none of his men bore the brunt of Vala's evil means, which were unknown to everybody, including his own generals. To make matters worse, now that Vishwaroop, who might have been of some help to them against Vala's sorcery, was not with them. But Indra was not letting this come in the way. He had held a couple of Vala's men outside, as a back-up. Some of them might be aware of Vala's magic and could help, if those ahead of him were unable to.

The cave was getting darker and darker because the light from outside was very feeble and didn't penetrate the cave once they turned right, which was the only way. Vidyut suddenly came from behind with a blazing torch, which would show them the way ahead. This was some respite to everybody. At a distance, they could see the shape of a person meditating. The generals of Vala, being pushed by the spear-points whispered 'Vala'. Soon, they had surrounded Vala, who seemed oblivious to the presence of the enemies around him. No one trusted him and his next move, which could be anything.

Indra was getting restless. While they were all staring at Vala, Indra's eyes were seeking the hostages. Suddenly, he noticed something shining and glittering in the distance. Even before he could go closer, there was some movement in an extreme corner and he saw Ushas, chained to a pillar. He was shocked and surprised to find her so helpless and sad. His anger knew no bounds, as he felt that the demons had no right to defile his folks, irrespective of the fact that he, too, had differences with her. But that's between them and no outsider had any right to even touch her.

Ushas looked up at the sudden movement in the cave and she noticed Indra. There were tears in her eyes, which moved Indra. He simply broke the wall that the generals had created ahead of him and, with a loud shriek, he beheaded Vala! Everyone standing around him was shocked, as no one had expected that.

But Indra was not going to give so much thought to a demon that had harmed his people for long enough.

Seeing their leader dead in front of them, Vala's generals fell to their knees and begged for forgiveness. They did not want to die and pleaded for their lives. Indra was not interested in them and headed towards Ushas straightaway. With violent blows, he broke the chains tying Ushas down and helped her stand up. Her usual brightness and vivaciousness were missing. She was tired and dishevelled and devoid of any energy. Indra gestured towards one of his generals and instructed him to take her away immediately in his chariot.

Ushas was taken away outside the cave. Before turning towards the entrance of the cave, she turned around to see Indra, not sure of what to think of him. She smiled feebly—it was a smile of gratitude and Indra responded with a smile. He knew that his earlier misdemeanour with her had been forgotten—not that he had ever considered it one.

Indra asked Vala's other generals to be taken away and asked Vidyut to stay back with his torch, along with some of the other Maruts. Indra had a hunch that the cave needed to be explored, as there was more to it. Vidyut did warn Indra of the fact that Vala could have some evil spirits locked around and it could be dangerous. Such words only egged Indra on to go further. Besides, the cows were still to be found.

The cave seemed to be larger than what they had imagined. The deeper they went, the bigger it seemed to get. It could just as well have been a small village in itself. Soon, they could smell the cows. There was a small opening from where some light and breeze were filtering in, which had allowed the cows to survive. There were scores of them and, needless to say, Vala had taken good care of them. They had fodder and water, except that they were all chained. Indra gestured the others to release them and take them out. Soon, all of them were being guided out of the cave.

Suddenly, something caught Indra's attention. The light from the small opening in the cave made a side of the floor of the cave glitter, much like stars in the night sky. Indra inched closer to the place, only to be dazzled. There was a pile of stones, all of different shapes and sizes. He picked a handful of them, amazed at the range of colours. Vidyut picked up a few as well and Indra could see their glitter reflected in his eyes, and he smiled.

These were precious stones that Vala had unearthed and kept for himself—rubies, emeralds, diamonds and sapphires of different shapes and sizes. They were mesmerising to say the least. There were chests upon chests full of these. Indra knew that this treasure had to be carried out and taken with them, as it couldn't be left behind. He asked the others to take as many as they could and instructed them to send more soldiers from outside the cave to make sure that not one of the stones was left behind.

Soon, all the cattle and the stones were out. Indra's chariot had already left with Ushas and they were returning with the booty. Indra was happy at the outcome. While crossing the river, he looked at the chest close to him and for no apparent reason, just picked up a handful of stones and dropped them in the flowing river. 'Go, waves! Take these to the people of the world! It's theirs and I give it back to them.' Saying so, he picked up fistfuls and one by one, threw them all in the water, not before throwing them up in the sky. The setting sun threw its light on the gems before they fell in the stream while some rolled onto the earth nearby.

The army smiled at the beautiful sight of the stones rolling down the earth or settling down at the bottom of the shallow streams. There was joy and happiness all around.

Indra came home victorious, with the cattle and the gems from the cave. Ushas, too, was back to safety. There were joy and celebrations all around. All the pain and hardship were forgotten. Mother was happy and so was Mitra. Surya bowed at the rising fortunes of Indra, as he, too, was pleased with Ushas's return. Sometimes gestures were better than words.

It was time for celebrations for all, except...

The Father

It was time for celebrations for all, except Vishwaroop's father—Sage Twashta. He was not a part of the celebrations, as he felt that his son had only been doing his duty and he hadn't failed his people. He had been working for the tribe and the community. Twashta was not going to let this pass so easily. His son's death—nay, murder—had to be avenged.

Twashta felt that the matter needed deliberation. Thus, he had raised it with Varuna. Varuna had brought up the matter a couple of times with Mitra, Vayu and others, but nothing had come out of it. No one seemed interested in discussing it, as, suddenly, the end seemed more important than the means. Varuna was surprised at the mindset, which was alien to him. He felt that Vishwaroop should have been tried later by the people and Indra had no right to take such action, which seemed impulsive.

Varuna was surprised that even Mitra seemed to ignore the issue and so did the others. Just what had happened to the rules of the community? Varuna was starting to feel more and more neglected. He noticed that his methods were becoming more of a shackle to the people around him and were suffocating them. He felt that they were becoming increasingly reckless and beginning to like living in the moment, much like Indra. Varuna's approach, which was following the norm, was more of an impediment to them.

Soon, much like the others, Varuna, too, did not want to pursue the matter and that disturbed him. Was he becoming old and weak? Did he also not believe in the rules he had laid down and followed diligently all this while? Was he, too, changing, like the people around him? Varuna was shrouded in these thoughts of self-doubt and soon realized that no one had noticed how he had turned reclusive. Everyone was busy with the new star on the horizon and the discussions everywhere were of how Indra had freed the cattle, Ushas and, of course, the priceless gems that had brought great wealth for all. It's not that Varuna was not proud of these achievements but somewhere, according to him, Vishwaroop's death was hovering over them like an ominous cloud, which would burst one day.

Twashta was not a part of the many celebrations. The community had found a new hero and he was the toast of the town now. The sage retired to a cave, where he was often seen meditating. He wanted to be left alone. Besides, no one wanted anything to do with him after the news spread that his son was a traitor.

Apala

'Who's that?' asked Indra when he noticed a woman, all huddled and covered from head-to-toe walking towards the forest.

Pavaka, the pure, and Indra were lazing around under a tree after having gone up and down a hill a couple of times, a daily activity to keep themselves active and energetic.

'That?' replied Pavaka, 'That's Apala, Sage Atri's daughter.'

'Wasn't she supposed to be married away to someone in another village?'

'Yes, but unfortunately, she has had to come back.'

'Come back? What do you mean by come back?'

'Well, I don't know exactly, but from what I have heard, there was some problem with her and so her husband...' Pavaka trailed off.

'Her husband what? Tell me!' Indra insisted.

'From what I know, she has been driven out of his house. Poor girl,' Pavaka shared, feeling sorry for the girl.

Indra was surprised. He wasn't sure what to say and do. He kept lying in the grove along with Pavaka.

While, lately, the celebrations were getting a bit overboard, Indra sure did like and appreciate the sudden adulation. Better still, Varuna seemed miffed about something, which added to Indra's joy. Despite this, there had been too much celebration of late and Indra was already beginning to get tired of it all. So, occasionally, he would escape to this part of the grove, which not many knew of. It allowed him some anonymity, as no one ever came by there, except Pavaka or a couple of them.

Soon, Pavaka excused himself to attend to something urgent. Indra decided to stay back and enjoy some moments of solitude. He suddenly found himself thinking of Apala. Indra remembered her as a quiet but immensely beautiful girl. She was the daughter of Sage Atri and was usually known to keep to herself. A couple of times, she had seen him when he had been to Sage Atri's house with Mother, but not much otherwise. He remembered being told about her marriage, but to be 'driven out' of her husband's house was unheard of. Also, he had seldom seen anybody covering herself the way she had. It sure was intriguing.

Something within him stirred. With the thought of Apala came the sudden desire for the shoots of soma. While Mother had mentioned a few days back that he seemed to be getting too fond of the shoot, Indra wondered what made him want it then. He looked around to see if he could get hold of a few of them, but no, there weren't any there.

No sooner had he realized that there was no soma there than his urge to bite into the crunchy fresh shoot intensified. Why is it that when we know something is not available that our desire for it increases? A sudden restlessness gripped him and he felt that he needed to have soma right then. While Indra found this sudden feeling odd, he recognized that the need to bite into the shoot was real. Right then, he could give anything to lay his hands on it.

Suddenly, he noticed Apala at a distance coming back, holding onto a bunch of soma shoots and biting into them. From a distance, he could hear her take crunchy bites of the shoots. He couldn't help himself and suddenly went and stood in her way. She was shocked and looked at him. There was an awkward silence for some moments.

'Sakra?' Indra heard the soft voice, laced with surprise.

Indra noticed some juice trickling down from the sides of her mouth. He kept staring at the slight stream of the soma juice.

'Is that you, Sakra?' wondered Apala aloud, 'Just look at you!' She was definitely awed by the masculine frame of the man in front of her. The long tresses, which were not used to be bound, just like the man, were pulled back. The penetrating eyes, which missed nothing and the slender neck on the two bare and broad shoulders, were nothing short of desirable.

'Won't you sit for a while?' Indra asked.

Apala looked at him and said, 'Yes, of course, why not?'

Indra directed her to his grove and soon, they were talking as if they had known each other for ages. Indra was surprised to find Apala so forthcoming and frank. He soon learnt that her husband had driven her away because she had developed a skin disease, which needed immediate attention. While Apala was speaking about all this, she was constantly biting into the shoots carelessly and Indra didn't lose sight of the juice trickling down the side of her lips. Indra could no longer resist. His fingers moved towards her lips, as if to wipe them. To Indra's surprise, Apala closed her eyes and before long, Indra found his lips closer to hers. Soon, Indra was licking the trickle of soma juice off of the side of Apala's lips and found her enjoying every moment of it. Gradually, his lips moved to her lips and both of them enjoyed the tender moment like they had never done before.

The sudden closeness and physicality surprised them both. Not once did Apala make an effort to pull away and not once did Indra feel the need for restraint. It was as natural as the buzzing bee sitting on a flower. The bee never sought permission from the flower, just as the flower never felt the need to object. For Indra and Apala, the moment and their actions needed no explanations.

Time had stopped for the two. Apala had mentioned how her husband hated her for her skin disease and how her father had been unable to cure her. Indra realized that she had barely moved her clothing—she seemed uncomfortable.

Indra asked tenderly, 'Do you trust me?'

Apala looked up and said, 'I am here, with you...now. Would I be with you...like this...if I didn't?'

'Then come with me,' said Indra, getting up from there suddenly.

'Where?' asked Apala.

Indra kept his finger on her moist lips, 'Just come with me. You won't regret it.'

Indra led Apala deep inside the forest to a place Apala had never known existed in so many years. Soon, they came across a small pond with white lilies in it. Apala had never seen the pond before. Indra stood there, staring at the pond.

Indra stepped into the pond. He looked back and held his hand out to her. Apala, unmindful of what was going to happen, gave him her hand and just followed him. There was something in those eyes, which was making her not think about anything, anything at all.

Soon, the lilies made way for both of them. Apala's loose clothing was drenched and revealed a shapely build underneath. Indra left her in the middle of the pond and walked to the other end. Apala couldn't help stare at the man and his frame—the bare torso and the lower half of his body, which the water more than revealed...Apala closed her eyes.

Indra picked up some mud from the side of the pond and walked back to her. Suddenly, Apala felt Indra slide off her clothing and apply the mud on her skin with his hands. Apala wanted the moment to never end. She had never felt like this before. She had never felt a man's hand moving so sensuously, massaging her body. This␣a bliss she had craved for. After what seemed to be eternity of rubbing his hands all over her, Indra went back for some more of the mud. By the time he was back, the mud had been washed off of Apala's bare body. Indra repeated what he had just done and Apala simply didn't want him to stop. She could hear herself moaning softly, as his hands massaged her all over.

Indra was smiling and he, too, had a strange feeling within himself. He had never ever felt a woman before. His hands slid down her body, carefully and caressingly. While the mud was rough, some parts of her skin were unusually rough too. Indra was mindful of the mud rubbing over those parts but he didn't miss the fact that she would close her eyes and make soft moaning sounds when he touched her there, as if she wanted him to go on and on and never stop.

Indra went through the whole exercise three times. Not once did Apala say anything and neither did Indra. The sun shone down on the two. Indra noticed Apala's skin glowing like never before. Her wet hair fell all over her face and the face had the beauty of all the flowers in the forest.

Indra found himself going very close to her. He led her out of the water, under a tree and embraced her. Apala didn't object and simply gave in to him, as if she had always wanted this. The two bare bodies on the mud were a sight to behold. Neither of them knew how long they were there but soon, the two were lying on the earth, unmindful of their state. There was no inhibition and the fact that the two had not uttered a word just didn't matter, since the bodies had spoken...the unspeakable.

Indra led Apala once again to the pond and this time, he meticulously peeled off the mud from her body. Apala had once again closed her eyes. After what seemed to be eternity in the pond, Indra led Apala out of the water. Only the sun was witness to Apala's lustrous skin. The rough skin from her body was gone! She was the most beautiful woman ever! Apala's joy was visible on her face and in her eyes.

Apala gathered her clothes, which were drenched, and wrapped them around her. She looked at Indra once before leaving. There was joy and gratitude in the eyes. She needed no words to thank Indra for what he had done to her—her tear-glazed eyes were enough. She was now the woman she always wanted to be.

Indra saw Apala leave. He went back to the pond and dipped himself neck deep, as if he, too, wanted to soak in the experience that he had just had. It was the first time that Indra felt like a man—a male who had...who had...Indra took a dip in the pond and walked out of it after what seemed like ages.

The lilies had seen it all. Each of them had acquired a pink shade suddenly. They were blushing from what they had seen. All of them were jostling to catch the last glimpse of the man leaving their waters—his huge silhouette against the setting sun was majestic, royal and erotic.

The secret of the magical powers of the pond were known to no one, just as what they had seen would be known to none, except their Sakra and the lilies, of course, who were still blushing and had developed beads of dew on their petals, much like the ones that had gathered on Sakra's forehead!

Namuchi

After the victory over Vala, Indra was included in the group of elders and was made to sit between Varuna and Mitra. While this was a great moment for Indra, he was surprised to find that Varuna wasn't upset about this. Varuna had taken this elevation of a reckless boy to sitting with them as the natural course of Indra maturing. While it sure was a surprise for Indra, there was no time to mull over such matters.

There seemed to be a growing buzz about some things that were not quite explainable. Some people had brought the news that the river waters were beginning to lower lately. Just how was this possible? While there were no immediate answers and no sure way of corroborating the matter, one had heard that this had happened more than once by now. Some even complained that a few of the cows were missing again, which had also not been corroborated as yet. Although no one could prove it, everyone at the gathering of elders realized that some of these complaints were becoming quite frequent.

While the initial complaints had been ruled out, when they became more frequent, Varuna had sent some of his men to get to the bottom of the matter and report back in a few weeks. Indra found these happenings odd but left it to the wisdom of the elders to decide the course of action.

All the conversation and discussion was making Indra weary, which was indeed odd. Indra suddenly felt as if he needed to breathe. He realized that he was feeling dizzy and needed some fresh air. He was fidgety and feeling increasingly uneasy. Before it was visible, he rose and started to walk out of the small enclosure. Everyone noticed him leaving, but no one noticed his discomfort.

As soon as Indra stepped out, he realized he was unwell. Something was wrong; he had never felt like this. He found himself standing under the shade of a massive tree besides the river. The cool breeze would do him good was what he had thought. But even before he realized what was happening, he fell to the ground with a huge thud. The last thing he knew was that he was holding onto the trunk of a tree.

Someone was observing him from afar. It was Namuchi, who was happy that the job was done. He walked away feeling satisfied that he had just disarmed the most cunning person of them all. Indra needed to be cut to size before Namuchi unleashed his reign of terror. He had waited long enough, especially after he had learnt about Vishwaroop's death. He knew that Sage Twashta would be of no help since he had gone missing after his son had been beheaded by Indra. Thus, these people had no access to the magical help that they so needed but they didn't recognize it. It was indeed the right time to wrench power from these people. Namuchi's tribe of the Dasas would rule now! All his moves so far had been effective.

Namuchi had started with winning Indra's confidence—who was the new sun on the horizon for these silly people after the victory over Vala. His most recent step, just the previous day, had been getting a promise out of Indra in a drunken stupor!

After Indra had killed Vala, Namuchi had realized that Indra's methods were now being accepted. Subsequently, Namuchi had hatched his plan and worked towards this day! He came close to Indra, with the help of the herb, of course. Namuchi had recognized Indra's weakness for soma and had seen him taking off quite often to chew on the stems or drink goblets of its juice at a time. Soon, Namuchi had become Indra's partner in such sojourns, often just the two of them.

During many such drinking sessions, Namuchi would say things to get close to Indra and, soon enough, they were close. Lately, after being inducted in the core group of senior administrators, Indra had been growing increasingly bored of the proceedings and Namuchi had used this boredom to his benefit. They say, the higher you go, the fewer friends you have and Namuchi took advantage of this. Indra suddenly found a confidante in Namuchi. He was always there when Indra needed a non-judgemental companion.

The previous day, however, had been a master stroke. While both of them had quaffed many goblets of soma, their drinks had not been the same. Namuchi had added an extra herb in Indra's goblet without his knowledge. This herb had made Indra very tired and his throat had been parched. He had repeatedly asked for more of the drink, which had led to a state of uneasiness. Indra had ended up drinking more and more without realizing that the dry throat had actually been the result of the extra herb that Namuchi had been adding to his drink.

When Indra had held his throat and asked for yet another goblet of soma, Namuchi had offered a goblet full of it. Just when Indra had extended his hand to take it, Namuchi had withdrawn the goblet and flashed an evil smile. Indra had found this odd and wondered what sort of a joke this was. Namuchi had made his move then, 'Sometimes, you scare me, Sakra, you, who are so powerful.' Namuchi had learnt that Indra often liked being addressed as Sakra.

'What do you mean?' Indra had wondered aloud.

'What if you kill me one day?'

'What kind of a joke is that, Namuchi? Why would I want

to kill you?' Indra had asked, trying to get a hold of the goblet.

'Well, you killed Vishwaroop and Vala. I belong to the same tribe, you see,' the shrewd Namuchi had responded, extending the goblet just a little.

'They had betrayed and stolen from my people. I did not kill them because they were not from my tribe. What sort of a conclusion is that, my friend?'

Namuchi had handed Indra the goblet, which he had gulped down even before Namuchi could see him do so. Namuchi had been glad that the herb had worked. Indra had been sweating and adequately agitated—just what Namuchi had wanted. 'Give me more,' Indra had yelled, throwing the goblet on the ground.

Namuchi had indicated to his attendant to go in and get more soma. The attendant had gone in to do as he had been instructed.

'What were you saying, my friend, about me killing you?' Indra had asked, laughing.

'Well, I only said what I am hearing these days,' Namuchi had responded, hanging his head in despair, not losing sight of Indra for a moment. He had seen that Indra's face was flushed and his eyes were drooping. He sure had had enough soma and now was the time.

'What are you hearing? Don't weave unnecessary yarns, my friend, come to the point. Where is your man? How long does it take him to get my drink? My throat is parched. I wonder what is wrong with the weather today,' Indra had said.

'People are saying that your people are after us. You people will eliminate us Dasas and Daityas very soon, the way you killed Vishwaroop and Vala,' Namuchi had responded softly.

Hearing this, Indra had erupted, 'Just what is this *your people* and *our people*? Where did you get this from? We are all one. I have only killed those who have wronged. If this was done by any of my brothers, I would have done the same. I think something is wrong with you. Besides, you are brave and strong and I am your friend! Why are you worried about anybody killing you? Stop this nonsense and can you yell at that man of yours who has gone in for what seems like hours?!'

'Well, you might be saying all this under the influence of soma now. But when your people insist, you might kill me too,' Namuchi had insisted sadly, with a long face.

'I don't know what to say to you. I think you have been drinking a few too many goblets of soma. By the way, too much of soma can make you feel sad and insecure! So, my suggestion is stop drinking it. Leave it for me. I suddenly seem to have an appetite for it!'

Just then, the attendant had brought in freshly prepared drinks in two large goblets. Indra had taken both of them and had been about to gulp one down when Namuchi had held his hand. 'Promise me something, before you drink that one.'

Indra had looked at Namuchi, bewildered, 'What?'

'Promise me,' Namuchi had said, still holding his hand, 'that you will never kill me when it's day or night. You won't hurt me with either an arrow made of any prevalent metal or by hand or using any other weapon that is wet or dry.'

'What nonsense is this, Namuchi? You are my friend,' Indra had responded, trying to pull his hand away. But Namuchi had gripped it firmly; Indra could barely move his hand.

'Yes, I am your friend...today. Tomorrow is another day and I am scared of you,' Namuchi had feigned.

Indra had been both surprised and amused. He had laughed and responded, 'Done, my friend, I give you my word. I will not kill you in the day or night or with anything that is dry or moist or with my arrows made of any prevalent metal or by hand.' Indra had looked at his big palm and realized that there indeed was someone who had been scared of it! 'Anything else? Could you please let me drink this now? I feel like I am dying!'

Namuchi had let go of the hand. Seeing Indra gulp down both their goblets of soma, he had smiled. He had just ensured that he could not be killed, not even by the mighty Indra.

Now, there was nobody between him and the throne of Indra's tribe. One thing was sure; Indra would never go back on his word!

'You won't forget your word, will you?' Namuchi had asked.

'This is the word of Sakra, your friend… Have faith in me. You are my friend…'

Namuchi had smiled at Indra, who had fallen off to one side. His long hair had been all drenched in sweat and his body had been sweating profusely. His arm bands had been about to break open, as they were unable to hold onto his bulging muscles for long. Namuchi had gestured to his attendant, who had taken Indra inside and made him lie down comfortably.

The poison had not worked before the next day. Namuchi had nothing to worry, as nobody would ever know about him and the poisonous herb he had used on Indra.

The Ashwins

Saraswati was sitting beside the river. It was her usual spot and she loved to sit there alone, serene and contemplating. Many had often said that she was similar to the river. Her long, flowing hair was like the silent waves of the river and her white robe was as clear and clean as its waters. Her face was always smiling and radiating the calmness of the river.

Saraswati was very close to Ushas and had lately been worried about her. While Ushas was grateful to the young man who had saved her life, somehow, she was unable to reconcile her conflict with that man and then the same man saving her from imminent danger. Saraswati had tried to explain to her that while Indra was rash and hot-headed, he meant no harm. Saraswati remembered someone saying that the moment he had learnt that Ushas was in captivity, he had been disturbed. If he truly despised her, as Ushas thought he did, then why had he been disturbed? While Ushas did not have an answer, she sure was disturbed, as she had been in captivity for too long. Had that young man not come in the nick of time, Saraswati wondered what would have happened to Ushas?

With this thought, Saraswati smiled and offered a silent gratitude to the young man, whom they called Indra. While he was often brash, there was something about him. The breeze was blowing through her hair and fluttering her loose white robe. She loved to sit there and soak in all that she could. She let the waters of the river caress her feet.

A loud thud brought Saraswati back from her thoughts. She

noticed a young man fall in the distance near a tree. She rushed towards the tree to find Indra sprawled on the floor, unconscious and sweating profusely. She looked all around, but no one was there. She was worried and wondered what she could do. She rushed to the river and brought some water in her palms to sprinkle on his face. The cool sprinkle made Indra open his eyes. He was trying to say something and all Saraswati could understand was 'Ashwin...'

She called some people from a nearby grove and with their help, she managed to take the near-unconscious Indra to the Ashwins—the twin physicians. One of them made him lie down on the floor and requested all of them to leave the cottage. He looked at Saraswati and she, too, left the cottage, leaving the two brothers with him.

The twin physicians were the most handsome of them all. They loosened Indra's garments and tried to understand what could have happened to him. Indra's eyes were red and his body seemed to have swollen up. His lips were thick and eyelids were drooping. The slight foam around his lips convinced them that he had been poisoned.

The two brothers immediately made Indra sit up. While one of them patted his cheeks to wake him up, the other started crushing some herbs and salts in a pestle. He made a small concoction and helped Indra gulp it down. No sooner had he done that than Indra started to cough and soon, he started vomiting in a tub, which was kept ready for him to do so. The throwing up was very painful for Indra and soon, he lost consciousness again. The physicians cleaned him and made him lie down. They sensed some commotion outside the cottage.

One of them went out to find Mitra and other members of the council standing, wanting to know what had happened. One of the Ashwins informed them that Indra had been poisoned but was safe now. The word poison made everybody wonder who could have been behind this. Mitra was visibly angry and Varuna looked pensive. The Ashwins asked all of them to leave, as it would be a few hours before Indra regained his senses. Once he was well, they would drop him home. Besides, there was nothing to worry about now, as they had got all the poison out of him. Also, the poison had not been seriously harmful, though too much of it could have been fatal and not getting him to them early would have been dangerous. The assembled folks tried to thank the Ashwins, but they said that if there was anybody who ought to be thanked, it was Saraswati, who had brought Indra there in time. They all looked at her, standing aside. Varuna walked up to her and expressed his gratitude. She just smiled.

Soon, everyone had left, leaving the two brothers to tend to Indra. Saraswati, however, waited outside, as she thought that she might be of some help.

For the rest of the day, Indra was woken up to take some concoction and fell asleep again. The Ashwins took turns to care for him. By late night, the swelling on his body had reduced. While his eyes continued to seem reddish, there was no denying that he had lost a considerable part of his stamina. The herb sure had been deadly.

It was not before late night that Indra regained consciousness. He was weak so the Ashwins let him lie down. They apprised him of his condition and gave him some gruel to drink, as his stomach had suffered immensely. While he was still very weak, he had not lost his aggression. Indra was angry at Namuchi for betraying him and his trust. He would not leave this betrayal unanswered. The Ashwins smiled at him and told him that he would need to listen to them if he wanted to get on his feet soon. Indra wanted to know if the poison was out of his body. The physicians assured him that it was, except that the intake and the forced expulsion had made him weak. Fortunately, the herb, did not affect his system much.

Indra woke up feeling much better the next day. Saraswati had come to see him and he thanked her profusely for getting him to the physicians in time. She simply smiled and sat calmly, much like the river flowing by. Indra was aware that she did not speak much and often just smiled. Indra was also aware that she was very close to Ushas but did not want to rake up the matter. Besides, it didn't make any sense to talk about her.

Later, the physicians helped him go home but got him to assure them that he would come over, if he was feeling better, as they would need to make some formulation and give it to him without any delay. However, if he was not able to come, he should send word of his inability to come. Indra assured them that he would do as they said and that he was already beginning to feel better. He was sure he would make it back to them in the evening.

After resting for the day, when many people, including Mitra, Varuna and some of the Maruts, came to see him, Indra decided to go and see the physicians. When he reached there, he was surprised to find Saraswati waiting along with them. He smiled at her and sat down in a corner. Seeing him, one of the Ashwins got down to prepare the concoction while the other sat with him to ask him some very basic questions.

Soon, the mix was ready and Indra gulped it down with water. It tasted very bad and seeing Indra's expressions, all of them were amused. Indra was embarrassed, but he regained his composure soon enough. After some uncomfortable moments of silence, Indra asked, 'Do you know what was mixed in my drink?

I mean what was the poison?'

The Ashwins looked at each other and one of them picked up a small root from the corner and said, 'This.'

Indra looked at it with disgust but did not take it in his hand. 'But I must say that this was not used to kill you.'

A surprised Indra looked at both of them one by one, and asked, 'What do you mean by that?'

One of the Ashwins said, 'Anyone who understands that this root is poisonous also understands that it cannot kill. Besides, someone who understands roots would also know which ones would be lethal.'

Indra was perplexed by this information.

'The question, then, is,' said Saraswati, speaking for the first time, 'why was it given to you at all?'

While the question was valid, there was no answer. Saraswati and the physicians were staring at Indra. He was wondering, what to say.

'Could it be to intimidate you?' asked one of the physicians, 'Or...'

'Or what?' asked Indra.

'I don't know what,' said the physician.

'Or to get some assurance or a promise or something like that out of you, maybe?' Saraswati suggested, staring straight at Indra.

Indra now remembered his conversation with Namuchi and the assurance he had given when he direly needed the drink. While in that moment, it seemed insignificant and meaningless, things were now falling in place. Indra told them about the conversation and the assurance. The three of them looked at each other. They knew that they had a task on hand and would have to find a way to circumvent the assurance.

After a long time, Saraswati broke the silence, 'Can you tell us what your promise had been?'

Indra thought hard and said, 'I had said that I would not kill him at night or during the day and with a weapon which was neither wet nor dry.'

The Ashwins looked at each other. 'What kind of assurance is that?' one of them asked.

But Saraswati was thinking hard. She asked, 'Are you sure that's all?'

Indra remembered, 'Oh yes, one more thing: I would not use arrows made of any prevalent metal or my hand. I wonder what that was for.'

Saraswati was staring hard at Indra. 'Anything else?' she enquired persistently.

Indra found himself thinking, but ended up saying, 'No, that's all...Yes, I am sure.'

It was late and they knew that no amount of thinking was going to help. So, they decided to part. Saraswati never spoke after that. Saraswati and the Ashwins were in deep thought. Indra was worried that he had created a dilemma for himself with his assurance. How was he going to teach Namuchi a lesson?

On his way back, Indra met Raudriya. Indra learnt that Namuchi had been up to mischief during the day. He had uprooted many of the trees from the sacred groves and hurled them towards the sages' huts. Many of them had fled from there. Also, some of Namuchi's people had poured water on the sacred fires lit by the sages, who had been performing some rituals.

Indra was visibly angry but, this time, more at himself than at Namuchi. He knew that he was responsible for this. If only he had not gotten so close to him and had not given him such an odd assurance, then Indra would have killed him right now. Indra was in a rage, but he felt restricted. He knew he had to do something before Namuchi became too dangerous. The council was anyway battling with many other problems, such as the declining water of the river and the sudden disappearance of cows. They shouldn't be bothered with this new menace of Namuchi.

Raudriya suggested that they storm his bastion and kill him, but Indra held him back, saying that he needed a couple of days to recoup and get back on his feet. Raudriya dropped him home and left. Indra spent a sleepless night, blaming himself for what had happened. Somewhere in the back of his mind, he knew that the physicians and Saraswati would help him. He didn't know why, but he felt that they wanted to help him.

Saraswati's sudden interest in him bewildered him. Why was she so caring, when earlier, she had never even interacted with him? He had only seen her a couple of times when she had come to meet Varuna and Mitra, and once or twice when she had come to speak to Mother at the sacred grove. Besides, she was so close to Ushas that it sure was surprising that she would want to help him. Indra slept with these thoughts on his mind.

The next day was cloudy and dull. Indra was feeling uneasy. He had heard that Namuchi was planning to attack with a small army and Varuna wanted him to lead the charge. Indra was in a dilemma. If he led the attack and stuck to his word, wouldn't he be obliged to let Namuchi go and not kill him? With nobody else equipped to kill him, Namuchi was nearly invincible. What had he done?

Saraswati

Indra rushed to meet the Ashwins. He found them busy making some concoction. They asked him to wait.

They were soon joined by Saraswati, who had something in her hand, which was wrapped in leaves. They sat in a corner close to the window of the hut. Looking at Indra, she said, 'I am sure you have heard about the violence unleashed by Namuchi. This is exactly why he made you give him that assurance. This is mainly because he knows that there is none other than you who can match him in the battlefield.'

Indra looked down. He knew he was to blame. Saraswati was not done, 'Next time, be careful when you befriend someone. It's not for nothing that we often say: stay with your own.'

While Indra didn't quite agree with this, he knew that this was definitely not the time to debate on the subject. He was keen to know just how the three of them were going to help him, as he was sure that they had discussed this matter or that they had some plan.

Indra was getting visibly impatient. Saraswati noticed this and remarked, 'Learn to calm down. This restlessness doesn't allow one to think clearly.'

One of the Ashwins raised his hand and patted Indra's back. He then handed Indra a goblet with a concoction, 'Try this...it's better than soma!' The joke was not lost on Indra, except that he was in no mood to smile, though the rest of them were.

Indra took a look at the amber-coloured liquid and took a sip of it. It was thick and sweet. It tasted nice. 'What is it?' he asked, looking at the liquid. The physicians smiled at each other, till one of them said, 'It's called madhu. This is going to be the next soma, except that it will be more healing and will have curative powers. It is made by the bees and will be available in its purest form.'

Indra was intrigued to know that the bees would be making it for them. While it tasted nice, Indra wasn't sure if it could be compared with soma. But, once again, he decided against voicing his opinion. He suddenly noticed Saraswati staring at him and the physicians.

The Ashwins offered a ladle of it to Saraswati, who just dipped a finger in it to taste. She smiled and said, 'It indeed is nice.' The Ashwins smiled at each other feeling good. After all, they had been working on this for some time and they knew that they had created a great offering for everybody.

'Anyway, let us get back to this,' Saraswati said. 'Just to be sure, Indra, can you just tell me once again what promise has been extracted out of you?'

Indra didn't like the words, 'extracted out of you' but knew well enough to keep quiet, lest he be reminded of his error by the matronly Saraswati, who had made it amply clear that she was here with a purpose.

Indra cleared his throat and reiterated, 'That I will not kill him when it's day or night, with arrows made of any prevalent metal or my hand or with any weapon that is wet or dry. I guess that's what I have promised him.' Indra hated every word he repeated and, somewhere, he felt that Saraswati knew it. She only wanted him to repeat it to make him realize the gravity of it all.

'Right,' began Saraswati, 'before we begin, do you want to honour your words?' Indra was surprised by the question, especially when this had not even crossed his mind. Saraswati continued, 'Especially when this promise was extracted out of evil intentions and not honouring one's words for the larger cause of saving your community should be pardonable.'

Indra did not like the idea of going back on his word. He kept quiet for some time and looked at Saraswati as he responded, 'While I do agree that the promise was extracted out of me by evil design, I still think I should honour it. It's my word and not that of some Dasa like him.'

Saraswati smiled and said, 'I am glad you said that. You are not a Dasa like him nor are you a Daitya.'

'So, let us understand what you have assured,' said Saraswati. 'You will not use your hand to hit him or kill him. So, that has been ruled out. You will not use your arrows made of prevalent metals, which is iron, so, arrows are ruled out. The other metals that we use are also ruled out; so are the other weapons that you might use, like an axe, a dagger or any heavy object made of iron. That leaves us with no weapons, as such, right?' As Saraswati proceeded meticulously, Indra found the implications of his assurance weighing on him.

Saraswati took out something from the leaves. It was dark in colour and quite unattractive. 'This is sisa. It has not been used yet, besides it hasn't even been tried or tested. I believe Vishwakarma is working on this supposed metal. He doesn't know much about it, except that it is hard and can be shaped, provided we give him directions on how to make it usable.'

Indra took the dark piece in his hands. It was cold and hard. He wondered how this could be shaped into a weapon, but that was a query for later. 'But it is dry...' Indra trailed off.

Saraswati looked at it once again. 'That's another issue. But before that, can you make an unknown weapon out of this; I mean can you suggest something?'

Indra was still toying with it and suddenly, he said, 'If the edges can be sharpened enough to cut, it might work. Also, a round shape would help me swing it.'

The others saw him gesturing how he would use it. Indra noticed them looking at him; he put it down. 'Fair enough, you work on giving it a shape,' said Saraswati, 'But the dry and wet is still a problem.'

'So is the time,' added one of the Ashwins.

Indra said, 'That can be taken care of. I can attack him before dawn, which is neither day nor night.'

It suddenly seemed so simple and all of them smiled at the ease with which Indra had said it. Indra, too, was surprised that it had suddenly seemed so simple.

The Ashwins looked at each other and then one of them said, 'I think we can take care of the wet and dry weapon. Foam! The foam on water is neither wet nor dry...it's just bubbles. If we can cover the weapon with foam, then it is neither wet nor dry. We are done!'

Saraswati was happy. They had solved the problem. 'Now, you do one thing,' she said, giving the dark object to Indra, 'Go to Vishwakarma and explain to him how you want this shaped. I have already spoken to him about you and he will be expecting you. He will do this on priority.'

Indra was staring at Saraswati, 'Can I ask something? Why are you helping me?'

Saraswati smiled and asked, 'Shouldn't I?'

Indra hesitated, 'No, that's not what I meant, but, nonetheless, why?'

Saraswati looked at Indra, 'Life is not just strength and aggression. Yes, you need strength to survive, but there is one more thing that one needs—wisdom. You must know when to do what and how. Knowledge of everything is the key. When I see young people like you, I find you all not thinking of what to do and how. I often find you and those naughty boys of yours rushing everywhere without knowing why. I can foresee the pitfalls of a growing society like ours. The council, too, judges only on the basis of strength.'

'So strength is not the only important thing for you?' Indra asked.

'That's for animals! They survive on strength. The likes of you and me, we need to give equal weightage to wisdom and intellect, which only we have. That's the sharpest weapon with us and, much like your arrows and axes, it too needs to be sharpened regularly. Strength is only needed in battlefields but wisdom is needed everywhere.' Indra was more than impressed by what she said.

'But you haven't answered, why me? Why are you trying to help me?' Indra insisted.

'Because you are the next shining star on the horizon!' she said proudly. 'The older folks have survived without using much wisdom, except when it came to them instinctively or impulsively. But your kind will need it at every step. I wanted to impress upon you the importance of thinking, strategizing and using your intelligence before rushing into a battlefield. Times are changing and you will need it more often than before.' Indra was impressed and was at a loss for words. The Ashwins, too, were smiling. 'Besides,' continued Saraswati, 'You will need the help of the twin brothers more and more often.' She then looked at the Ashwins and said, 'They will be able to find new cures and antidotes for the growing number of enemies that you are bound to make along the way...'

Indra was suddenly overwhelmed by their faith in him. They

looked up to him and were willing to strengthen him. They were true supporters of the community and he was thoroughly impressed by the fact that to progress, one needed faculties of all kinds. Just as he would need the strength and the will of the Maruts, he would need the brains of the likes of Saraswati and the magical support of the Ashwins and more. While there sure will be one leader, he will need the support of many.

Saraswati had just performed a very important task, the ramifications of which would never be forgotten by Indra, ever! Indra realized that if he won this battle, it was clearly their win and he would not hesitate to acknowledge their contribution.

'Now go! Rush to Vishwakarma. He is waiting for you,' said Saraswati, smiling. The Ashwins, too, were glad that an important message had been given to Indra, that they had managed to cure him and that he was back on his feet.

Indra got up to leave. He had barely reached the door of the hut when he heard Saraswati call out, 'And go slow on that favourite drink of yours! It's good only when taken in moderate quantities. Too much of anything is harmful...'

Indra smiled and stepped out.

Battle with Namuchi

The following day was important for Indra. This was the first time he was going into a battle where he was not just equipped with the strength and power of his army but also the knowledge of wars and a measure of intellect to destroy his enemy. A battle is half won when one has prepared and strategized.

Indra was also aware that his enemy, Namuchi, was both arrogant and overconfident. That, by itself, was a big flaw.

When Indra met Namuchi on the battlefield, he was beaming from ear to ear. He had that arrogant look about him, like he was far superior. He shouted at Indra, 'So, my dear Sakra, how are you planning to kill me? I have already disabled you—' Suddenly, his facial expressions changed, 'Unless, of course, you are planning to go back on your word?'

Indra looked straight at him, 'I am a man of my word and I don't intend to go back on my assurance to you, though it wouldn't be a sin if I did, as you had gotten that assurance out of me by guile and deception.'

'A word is a word, my dear friend,' laughed Namuchi.

'I don't need to learn that from a Dasa like you,' Indra hurled his words at Namuchi, which were no less than a weapon.

Namuchi was angry at the mention of the word 'Dasa'. His hands flew back to his quiver to pick an arrow, but he stopped short of doing so, and said, 'I guess I should be fair. So, what weapon do you want me to use? That choice I must give you, shouldn't I?' Namuchi asked, smirking at Indra.

Indra smiled and responded, 'I have taken no such assurance from you, so why bother?' Namuchi listened in surprise as Indra continued, 'Strong and brave people don't disarm their opponents. So, go ahead, weakling, you can use whatever you want!'

Namuchi was visibly agitated. He shot an arrow at Indra, who guarded himself with his shield. The arrow just fell to the ground. Soon, Namuchi ran out of arrows and axes, which he kept hurling at Indra. Indra just stood there defending himself with a shield. Eventually, dusk fell and the battle had to stop. Namuchi threatened Indra, 'You won't see the sun rising tomorrow.'

Indra smiled at Namuchi, 'Let the sun decide who will see it!'

Namuchi was known to worship the rising sun every day, which brought him to the banks of the river early in the morning. He would finish his ablutions and wait for the rising sun. Indra was waiting for him the next morning. Namuchi had just finished his ablutions and there was some time for the sun to rise.

Indra sprang in front of Namuchi. He was surprised. 'It's not time for the battle yet. What are you doing here?'

'I have come to see you.'

'This is not the time to negotiate. It's the time for my rituals and I don't discuss anything with anybody,' said Namuchi dismissing Indra.

'But aren't you my friend? Won't you even listen to me?'

'Developed cold feet already?' smiled Namuchi. 'The war has just begun.'

'I have come to end it. I think it's a waste of my time,' said Indra, advancing towards Namuchi.

Namuchi was aware that Indra was not to be trusted; rather his entire community wasn't to be trusted. He inched towards his bow and arrow, which he always carried with him. He was surprised to see Indra heading towards the river. Indra was knee deep in water when he turned around to look at Namuchi, who looked perplexed.

Suddenly, a wave came from nowhere. Indra dipped something in the foam that had formed due to the wave, and hurled it towards Namuchi. The disc-like object was sharp, with saw-like edges. It sliced through Namuchi's neck like a knife through butter. Namuchi's head was severed from his body and it rolled on the ground. It was all over in a fraction of a second, even before Namuchi could realize what was happening. Indra shouted, 'Look, Namuchi, it's neither day nor night, my weapon is not made of iron or any of the prevalent metals and the weapon was neither wet nor dry.'

'Cheat! You cheat! I curse you... You will pay for this...' Namuchi sputtered accusatorially, his voice trailing off.

The battle was won even before it began. The sun was smiling on the horizon. It had just sent its first rays to see if Indra had completed his task.

Indra: The Warrior

It was time to celebrate. The council of elders was very proud of its decision to send for Indra, who was now being referred to as 'Indra: The Warrior' within the community. Everybody was praising his skills and his means, which were both innovative and strategic. His aggression was being talked about and somewhere there was a feeling that he was just a few steps away from being made the chief of the tribe, which had both expanded its boundaries and influence over several years.

The council had inducted him in all its discussions quite seamlessly. Mitra was very happy with the developments and was glad that Indra had not failed him. He felt that Indra's leadership skills were just what they needed in the changing times. Though he still needed to learn to rein in his aggression, it would surely come to him with time. Besides, youth is rash and battles can't be fought without such unbridled aggression, especially when the rules and norms of the tribe were being ignored by the new set of enemies. The Dasas, Daityas and the Danavas had been raising their heads a bit too often. Also, with the tribe growing geographically and in terms of population, diverse people had started coming in. This had led to governance suddenly becoming an issue. A few years back, things had just been about defending the tribe but now, it was about both defending and acquiring land and animals. The society was changing and so were its needs, demands and, of course, standards.

Varuna was beginning to feel worried. While the area of governance had increased, so had many other issues. Some of his established laws were not being accepted by a few of the new tribes under his governance. It was beginning to be felt that the ideas of one were being imposed on the others. While this would lead to an internal rebellion, society couldn't exist with differing rules for people. Expansion had led to new problems, which hadn't been accounted for in the past. Suddenly, Varuna felt that he was losing his grip on matters that had been simple. A society that exists without any norms or flouts them at will—whose foundation changes with time—is dangerous. Varuna could sense trouble ahead.

He also noticed the members of his council often mentioning that they should refer certain matters to Indra. His means were not quite palatable to Varuna, but they sure did bring results, there was no denying that. However, this could not be the reason to disobey the set rules. While Varuna was glad about the changes and progress that Indra had brought about, he could never empathize with Indra's standards. Varuna felt that Indra's aggression would be his undoing. The violence was another issue. Indra never brought anybody to book—he simply killed them. Ever since he had started going to battles, nobody was punished, they were simply killed. Vishwaroop could have been brought to the council for trial, but he had been killed and so had Vala. Vishwaroop was the son of a sage and sages were important for society. Varuna was worried about Twashta's absence and he wondered what that meant.

Varuna was of the opinion that the sages were critical to their society. Their knowledge of the scriptures, ritualistic offerings to the Creator and others, sacrifices and yajnas were of prime importance to their society. A growing segment of the sages had taken umbrage at the killing of Vishwaroop. While there was no denying that what Vishwaroop had done was wrong but did he deserve to die for it? Varuna felt that some of Indra's actions were impulsive, unthoughtful and had no precedence. The sages were of the same opinion.

There was a simmering discontent among the sages about Indra. While none of them had voiced their opinion on this, Varuna was worried that this discontent could snowball someday into something major. However, somewhere, Varuna had also decided not to voice his opinion. People were beginning to think that Varuna was growing insecure with the rise of Indra and that his discomfort was stemming from a sense of his loss of power and influence, which was not the case. However, this was not apparent to many. The general feeling was that whatever Indra's means, he brought results and that's what mattered. While this was a very personal opinion, such matters could not be resolved socially. Varuna was disappointed that no one saw the future the way he did. It had nothing to do with him losing power; he was willing to relinquish it at any moment, but only to a deserving person, not to someone who was rash and impulsive, like Indra. He was too young to understand the gravity of the chiefdom.

While the celebrations of Indra's victory were on, the issue of the dwindling waters in the rivers and the streams was not lost on the council. This was an unprecedented issue and the council couldn't quite understand the reason behind it. The missing cattle, too, were beginning to become a concern. All the caves nearby had been checked and none of the cattle were there. These complaints had an alarming regularity about them. The recent battles had taken up quite a bit of their time. The spies, too, had not reverted to Varuna, which was odd. This had seldom happened. It was possible that they would come back without any information but not returning was both odd and worrisome.

The First Signs of Danger

There had been too many celebrations. Somehow, people were just not tired of celebrating Indra's victory over Namuchi, especially the strategic means of the victory. But the council seemed to be troubled with a new problem, which they weren't able to get under control.

The latest news had gotten everybody worried. One of Varuna's spies had been found dead at a high altitude. Varuna had sent him to find the reason for the dwindling water in the rivers and streams. It had been quite some time since he had not returned, which was unusual. Varuna had sent some people to look for him and they had found his dead body. What was odd was the cause of his death. He had been bitten by a serpent. When the body was sent to the Ashwins to understand the nature of the serpent that had bitten him, they were also at a loss. According to the physicians, they had never come across such a snakebite. This serpent seemed different. The spy had not died just of its bite. There were enough signs to show that he had been both shocked and traumatized before dying. No ordinary snake could have shocked anybody in the community, not even the children, who regularly came across the slithering creatures at every step. This one had to be different and there must have been something unique about it. Besides, the physicians were well aware of all the existing species of snakes based on whether they had an antidote for their venom or not.

This incident brought all the celebrations to a rightful halt. The council was meeting again to understand how to tackle this problem, which wasn't even visible. In this case, the enemy was unknown and tackling something which was not visible was much like trying to 'see' air! The fact that a spy had been killed made one thing very clear; the enemy was smart, extremely intelligent and had recognized the spy, which was a surprise because nobody other than Varuna knew the spy, not even the members of the council. How had the enemy recognized the spy and killed him? What was the information that he had gathered and how could the council manage to get that information, which was becoming extremely critical? Did it have anything to do with the vanishing waters and cattle? Or was this killing not linked to the other problems?

There were too many questions and no answers. Just how were the people to get to the bottom of it all? The death of the spy had added to their fears. There were rumours of all kinds. Some said that a demon had drunk all the waters of the streams, others said that a snake demon had killed one of the Devas. Some even said that the cows were being killed to deprive the children of milk and the Daityas were eating the meat of the cows. The rumours were spreading like wildfire and, soon, everyone seemed to have their own version of this new menace.

The council knew that they had to do something, and soon, before the fear grew in people's minds. Sages were asked to perform yajnas and sacrifices and make offerings to the Creator. Children were not allowed to venture far, lest they be bitten by some snake or be kidnapped. In the midst of all this uncertainty, something unusual happened, which shook everyone to the core.

The sacrificial altar of the tribe was at a high altitude. All the yajnas and other rituals, like sacrifices, were conducted there. In the centre of the space was a small enclosure, known as the *yajna-vedi*, which was reserved for the holy fire to be lit and oblations to be offered. Someone had desecrated the yajna-vedi by throwing the carcass of a dog in it! The entrails of the dog had been pulled out and scattered all over it. The altar, which was carved out of stone, had also been chipped away from the sides, indicating that efforts had been made to break it. There was blood smeared all over the vedi, which bore telltale signs of mischief with an intention to disturb and create chaos.

There was a general feeling that this menace was the doing of someone who wanted to spread fear among the people. It had led to more rumours. There was fear in everybody's hearts and the council was being accused of not doing enough to address the matter. All the battles had been forgotten and soon, there were murmurs that the council was ill-equipped, lazy and scared of this new demonic force. Some were even proposing that a new council be constituted because the present one was too old to adapt itself to the changing face of adversity. People were now saying such things openly. Fear had suddenly made everyone forthright. It seemed as if everybody's survival had been questioned and, thus, they were voicing their concern.

The council had never faced such a situation. More than the enemies from outside, there was a sudden fear of an uprising from within. Until the desecration of the yajna-vedi, people were divided in their opinion. But since then, there was only one view: everyone was in grave danger and the present council wasn't equipped to tackle it. They needed divine intervention. The Creator was disappointed with His people and was probably withholding the waters, killing cattle and had desecrated the yajna-vedi—it was a sign, a divine sign that things were not in order and something ominous was about to take place.

However, what Mitra heard was not told to anybody. He had heard that this was the price they had to pay for killing the son of a sage. The obvious reference was to the killing of Vishwaroop. The sages were the representatives of the Creator and killing one of their sons had been a grave crime and nature had not taken well to it. Due to the mistake of one person, who chose not to give Vishwaroop a fair trial, the entire society would have to endure hardships and imminent destruction. Mitra could sense that some sages were behind these actions but did not bring it to his lips.

While Mitra didn't believe in it, he was worried about the spread of this news. If the people believed this, it would mean the end of Indra, even before he got to begin. Besides, one didn't know how Indra would react to it. This worry was eating into Mitra and he knew that he had to do something about it.

Ahibhanava

Indra knew that extraordinary events needed extraordinary steps. He sought out Ahibhanava and decided to take matters into his own hands. Varuna and the council's means were ancient and he needed to do things his own way.

'I am sure you are aware of the new problem that seems to be growing by the day,' Indra said to Ahibhanava. 'I need your help, Ahi.'

'Go ahead, chief, just tell me what you have in mind,' responded Ahibhanava—or Ahi, as his friends called him. Although, Ahi did not like the short form because it meant serpents and undermined the very meaning of his name, he decided against mentioning it to Indra.

'I am worried about this new problem that we are faced with. I don't know why, but something tells me that the enemy is trying to reach me or is expecting me to react. I think it has something to do with me. I want you to somehow get to the bottom of this. I don't care what you do or how you do it, just get it done.'

Ahibhanava took a sip from the goblet that Indra had offered, not missing a single word uttered by Indra. He, too, had been worried about the sudden events, though he did not know where to begin.

'Do you think you can help?' Indra wondered aloud.

Ahibhanava's expressions changed, 'While I am not sure how, I sure will. Have faith in me, Sakra, I will have something for you.'

'By when, my dear Ahi, by when?' Indra asked desperately.

'Give me a day or two, not more...' said Ahibhanava, still thinking, not knowing why he even said a day or two!

Indra nodded in agreement but added hastily, 'Discretion is key, Ahi. I don't want even your brothers to know about this.'

Ahibhanava smiled, and added, 'Always! You can rest assured about that.' He quaffed the goblet and left.

Indra was feeling uneasy. Somehow, nostalgia was gripping him. While it's odd that he should find himself thinking of anything else, he couldn't bring himself to not think...about her.

Lately, Indra had found himself thinking a lot about Ahalya and his days at the ashram. He wanted to visit her and seek her hand in marriage from Guruji. He hadn't even realized that it had been a long time since he had left the ashram—time had simply flown by. Neither had he heard from the ashram nor had he sent any message or a messenger.

One day, Indra found himself heading towards the spring to be alone. He found the cool breeze and the water very soothing and relaxing. Besides, that was one place where nobody bothered him, as not many knew about it.

Indra stayed there for very long, till the sun indicated that it was time for him to depart.

When he reached his cottage, he was surprised to find Ahibhanava waiting for him. Seeing him, Ahi smiled and said, 'You might want to change into something cleaner before I say anything, my friend!'

Indra knew the smile and went in, saying, 'You better have something important for me.'

Indra came out in a crisp new garment. His hair tied and held back by a dry band. He had two goblets of soma in his hands and handed one of them to Ahibhanava.

'So, what do you have for me?' Indra asked, looking straight at Ahibhanava.

'Sage Twashta is behind all this,' Ahibhanava responded cryptically.

'What do you mean?' Indra asked, looking rather shocked.

'This new enemy of yours is Vritra. He is the son of Sage Twashta and Vishwaroop's brother. All this is happening in retaliation to the death of Vishwaroop,' Ahibhanava explained.

'Are you sure?' asked Indra. Ahibhanava nodded.

'Tell me more,' instructed Indra.

Vritra

'Yes, you heard me right,' Indra was addressing the council. 'Vritra is the son of Sage Twashta and he is creating all these problems for us.'

Everyone present there was shocked. Mitra kept quiet because he had heard similar rumours but had not managed to get them verified.

'How do you know this and how sure are you about it?' asked Varuna.

'I have my sources,' replied Indra, which surprised everyone. While Varuna was not happy with the answer, he could see that Indra sure had learnt from him. Just like him, Indra, too, did not want to expose his spy, but what was even more surprising was that he had his *own* spies. Regardless, this was not the time for all these differences.

'So, what do we know about him?' asked Varuna.

'Vritra has magical powers,' Indra began. 'He can shapeshift—one of his forms is that of a serpent. He can take the shape of an unimaginably large serpent, which can be both fearsome and deadly, as we have seen in the case of your spy,' he concluded, looking at Varuna.

There was a palpable silence in the room. 'Where was he all these days?' asked Mitra.

'From what I know,' Indra replied, 'he was a bit of a recluse and had left his father long back, especially because he was interested in such magical sciences that his father didn't quite approve of. But after Vishwaroop's death, Twashta sought his son out. By then, Vritra had acquired many magical powers and... and has even got a small army, so to say, which he has trained.'

Shock was writ large on every face there and some members of the council were even looking at Indra angrily. Sensing animosity, he said, 'In case any of you are thinking that all of us are facing this threat because of me, let me tell you something. Vritra was planning to attack us sooner or later. He has ambitions and there was no need to acquire such powers if he didn't intend to use them. Where else would he use them if not against us since we are the largest tribe today? Besides, can you imagine how emboldened he would have been if his brother had been alive?' Some faces lost their frowns, but not all. Indra continued, 'Vishwaroop's death has only got us the trouble earlier than when it would inevitably reach us. So, please, get off the delusion that if Vishwaroop had not been killed, we would have been safe. We would not have been. Besides, let me make one thing very clear: killing Vishwaroop was important, not just for winning that battle and rescuing Ushas and the cattle, it was also important to send a strong message to those who are thinking of going against us,' Indra asserted conclusively, radiating a strange authority. They were powerful words and not a single person in the room wanted to stand up to such statements—not one.

'But what has the dwindling water got to do with this... Vritra, right?' asked one of them.

Everybody nodded in agreement at the question and Indra realized that one important thing had been missed out.

'Yes, that is an important development that everyone needs to know. This Vritra and his people have created obstructions.'

'Obstructions?' enquired quite a few voices. 'What are those?'

'They,' Indra began, 'are walls created to withhold the waters and channelize them elsewhere. While building these walls is not easy, especially when the water is flowing, Vritra has definitely done this over a period of time. This was the final part of his plan before attacking us, as the dwindling of the waters was sure to take us to him. He knew that. While right now, he is not channelling the waters anywhere, he sure can do so. If those channels are opened, then reversing them back to us could be difficult.'

Indra's thorough information on the problems was not missed by anybody, and while some were still upset with him, there was not one person who did not marvel at his ability to present the situation and be on top of the information. Varuna was impressed and it was visible on his face. Mitra couldn't help but smile all throughout, which looked rather odd, considering the predicament that they were in!

'We need to act fast,' said Indra, 'before it's too late. Also, early action will enable us to learn about his skills and capabilities, which could be beyond what we have just learnt. Let's face it: he is no ordinary Dasa or Daitya. There is more to him and his magical capabilities. It's not going to be just strength but also a lot of intelligence.' Indra couldn't help but realize that he was speaking Saraswati's language.

This new enemy had created a fear psychosis all around. The council was worried that it would spread and have adverse repercussions on the growing might and respect of the community both within and among the other tribes. A society that is constantly fighting cannot evolve culturally and materially—this was something to reckon with. Also, the council felt that they were in a stage of change. The new enemies were engaging them in new methods of fear and war was an eventuality they had to accept. Also, the council needed to change with the times. Old laws were either not relevant or not tenable, as the rules of engagement were constantly being challenged. The old order called for a change and the new leader was visible to all.

Varuna could see that he and his methods were being seriously challenged. He was coming to the conclusion that he would soon need to anoint someone who was more in charge than him and who that someone was was no secret. Though he wasn't sure if this was the right time to anoint Indra as the next chief and if he was up for the responsibility, he knew that there was never a right time for such a thing. Indra sure seemed to be on top of his game. This, however, was war. One had never seen his administrative abilities, but the council was there to guide him through those. The question was: would he listen to the council?

'So, have you thought of anything?' Mitra's question to Indra brought Varuna back to the problem at hand.

Indra got up from his seat and, looking straight at Mitra, said, 'I thought all of us were going to discuss that.' Before Mitra could say anything, he continued, 'I have thought of something, but we need to put all our heads together to be sure that we succeed. Also, this is not going to be a singular job, like the earlier ones. We will need the might of all, as we are up against quite a formidable force—someone who has powers beyond ours.'

Varuna found himself saying, 'Do let us know your ideas and let us discuss those. With all your skills and knowledge on this new enemy, go ahead, tell us what you have planned.'

Indra was surprised by Varuna's calm demeanour, which radiated a sense of trust in him. There was a sudden respect for him. He smiled and said, 'While I am not sure how we will engage with him, one thing is that we need to know about his full potential. Also, we have not seen him as yet. So, I think...' Indra trailed off hesitantly.

'Go ahead, Sakra, go ahead...' Mitra egged him on.

'I think the best way to know him and his capabilities is to engage him in a small battle to begin with. Let's face it: it could be fatal to us but we will know what he is capable of. Also, we need to arrest his father, if we can, as we can charge him with treason. At the moment, he is dwelling in a cave, where I have already put two people in disguise who will keep us informed about his movements. This way, we will be able to pull Vritra out as and when we need to. It will also allow us to make sure that we have something to make him vulnerable,' Indra concluded, taking a deep breath.

Everybody was hanging onto every word he uttered. 'As I said, we will have to equip our army for any consequence. This time, we will need all of you to back us up,' Indra added, looking at Varuna and Mitra. 'We will need you all to be ready, once we understand his powers.'

'What about the initial engagement?' asked Varuna. 'Who do you have in mind for that?'

'I will go along with a select group of the Maruts,' Indra replied looking at Vayu, who smiled and nodded in agreement. 'This engagement will be more of a fact-finding mission to gauge Vritra's capabilities and to get to see him. However, there is a possibility that we might still have underestimated him. We don't know, but an engagement will reveal him and that is necessary,' Indra elaborated.

There seemed to be no opposition to his plan so far. 'Another important thing,' Indra continued, 'We might need some weapons suddenly. Everybody must be on standby. While I don't know what kind of weapons, we will need to react quickly once we do know. Also, the sages will need to perform yajnas and sacrifices just to counter any evil powers that he might try to exercise.' Indra added as an afterthought, 'I don't want them to side with

Vritra's father at this stage. Not now.'

Varuna frowned, 'Why would they do so?'

'I can just never trust them; I am sorry to say so. I feel that someone needs to ensure that they don't go against us from within while we are fighting the enemy without. One battle at a time,' Indra asserted.

'Leave them to me. I will speak to them,' assured Mitra.

'So, what next?' asked Vayu.

'It's wartime!' cried Indra.

Vishnu

The sudden arrival of Vishnu in the midst of all this chaos surprised Indra, but Indra sure was glad to see him. Vishnu had continued at the gurukul when Indra left. Vishnu brought back the memories of the gurukul, which suddenly seemed like a distant memory. Indra had been so busy lately that he hadn't realized how long it had been. *I haven't had the time to go back to the gurukul...as I had promised Ahal—*

Vishnu entered the cottage, interrupting Indra's thoughts, 'How have you been, Indra?'

Indra got up and embraced him, 'I have been busy but have missed you all. I am so glad you have come. Seeing you takes me back to the good old days. Come, sit...sit next to me, my friend.' Vishnu smiled and sat next to him on a couch. Noticing Vishnu looking all around, he asked, 'You look a bit tense, is everything alright?'

'Oh no, nothing...' mumbled Vishnu.

Vishnu had just been surprised to find Indra in a small cottage full of weapons and vats. Indra was following his gaze and noticed him looking at the vats.

'That is something you must try... Is anybody there?' he said while clapping his hands. Immediately, an attendant ran in. 'Pour a goblet of soma for my friend,' Indra instructed.

'You are quite a king here,' remarked Vishnu.

'King? What's that? No, my friend, we are ruled by a council. Varuna is the head of the council. No king here,' Indra explained.

The attendant re-entered and handed a goblet to Vishnu.

'Take this and tell me how you like the drink.'

Vishnu took a sip of the drink offered to him and said, smiling, 'It is good!'

'Tell me about the gurukul. Is everybody good out there? How is Guruji and—' Indra had barely finished the statement when Vayu walked in.

'We need to go for the discussion about... Oh, I am sorry,' Vayu stopped mid-sentence on seeing a stranger sitting with Indra.

'Oh, don't worry about him,' said Indra. 'He is my friend from the gurukul—Vishnu, a king of his kingdom!'

Vishnu felt embarrassed by this introduction. He folded his hands and bowed in acknowledgement of Vayu. 'I am just a head of a very small piece of land, rather a small island, if I may add.'

Vayu smiled and responded, 'Oh, so you have come to join us in the battle? That's nice!'

'No, no, he has come to just meet me,' Indra started explaining but stopped halfway and addressed Vishnu, 'My friend, if you want, you can join us. We are up against a formidable enemy this time and I am sure you can be of great help.'

'I would love to, provided you are leading,' said Vishnu. 'That way, I will get to learn from you. I have heard much about your warfare skills.'

Indra was flattered and patted his back, 'You can't be serious, but I would be honoured and much flattered if you do. However, I don't want to force it on you.'

'No, not at all. Please count me in.'

'You are in!' Indra exclaimed, visibly happy.

Vayu smiled at the good news before saying, 'Indra we need to go. Everybody is waiting for you at the council hall. We are meeting to plan for the attack.'

Indra, realizing that the meeting had skipped his mind, said, 'Oh yes, come, let's go. Let's not delay any further. Vishnu, you can join us. However, if you are feeling too tired, you can stay back here. This is your cottage! Just ask for anything you need from the attendant outside and he will send it.'

'I guess I will stay back,' said Vishnu. 'You can brief me when you are back.'

'Sure,' Indra responded as he left for the council meeting with Vayu.

Vishnu kept staring at the door from which Indra had just left. He had heard about Indra and his popularity and was glad to see him in charge. However, while he was in charge here, he sure had lost out at the gurukul. His lady-love was... Vishnu decided not to think about it. But he had to tell him... Someone had to... But would this be the right time? When he is so busy with something that seemed very important, it would not be appropriate for him to break the news. He could wait...wait till the end of the war maybe. Also, knowing Indra, he might behave very unpredictably, which could be disastrous. Besides, what difference could he make now anyway? Vishnu thought, taking another swig of the interesting drink that had been offered to him.

At Vritra's Lair

Vritra's lair was dark, wet and dingy. An unfathomably huge serpent lay coiled in the corner, hissing. In his serpentine form, Vritra was larger than any serpent one had ever seen. He was unearthly, dangerous and fearless—all three of which made him quite invincible. No one had seen him, except some close associates, who did what they were told and no one dared to object to his whims and desires because it could have dangerous and unknown consequences. In his serpentine form, Vritra could burn someone to death, dissolve them in his poison or simply stun them to death with his eyes. No one was there to tell the tales of his dissatisfaction. None lived to even report his slightest disappointment, as there wasn't anything like that. One either did what he was told or one didn't live to see the next moment.

Vritra was waiting for his messenger to get news. He had worked hard enough after his father had given him all the powers that he had needed. His father had retired to the mountains but not before ensuring that Vritra had all that he would need to avenge the death of his brother. Vritra had only one desire and that was to control these creatures who called themselves the Devas. They made the rules for everyone else to follow and those who didn't became lawbreakers and these Devas took it upon them to rule over everybody. Who gave them these powers? Who made them the rulers? These creatures were gaining ground and were now claiming more land and water. Water was the lifeline of these pastoral people and that is why he wanted to stop its flow. The source of water had been stopped without them realizing it because they were too busy making rules for the land.

While his father was upset with the death of his brother, Vritra took the opportunity to ask his father to equip him with all that he would need to face these creatures. He wanted to rule over all land and water, bringing in new laws. He had already stopped the rivers and would soon change their course. The Devas would perish without the river water, in parched lands. Nothing would grow on their land and they would be brought to their knees. He had already stolen thousands of their cows, another source of their livelihood, without them realizing it. Foolish set of people, these Devas!

Suddenly, he heard someone breathing. Vritra raised his hood to see Pani waiting to speak.

'Yes, my cattle-thief, how many have you gotten today?' hissed Vritra, staring at Pani.

Pani was sweating, as he found visiting Vritra quite a task. The atmosphere in this lair was noxious. Pani could never fathom what it was: Vritra's presence or his gaze or the air. But for Pani and his people, Vritra was an ally. They were secure with Vritra on their side, or rather, with them on the side of this formidable force against these Devas, who felt so smug about themselves and their rules of law. For time immemorial, the law of the land had been might is right. Suddenly, these Devas brought in something called the *law*! Silly people who restricted themselves and their people with these things invented just to harm their own selves. But they, the Panis, weren't obliged to follow these laws. They did not believe in all these silly things. They stole cattle because they felt like it and there was no stopping them, at least not since Vritra seemed to have had similar ideas.

Pani suddenly felt numb and he knew that he was being stared at. 'Did you come just to stare at me or do you want to tell me something?' hissed Vritra. Pani realized that Vritra, in his weird serpentine form, was coiling his tail around Pani, which he hated because it choked him. However, Vritra did this to everyone when he wanted to disarm them and make them say all that they knew. Pani immediately rattled off, 'I have some news. I believe the Devas are planning to attack.'

'Planning to what?' yelled Vritra. 'What did you say? Attack who? Me?'

Pani knew that this wasn't the best of news to take to Vritra, but if he heard it later, that could just be the last day of his life. He fearfully informed Vritra, 'Yes, I have just heard it. They are upset with their loss of water and...'

Vritra's huge eyes were close to Pani. He was feeling numb again—the eyes were very unsettling. Even if there was anything that he wanted to withhold, this moment made it impossible, '...and the cattle, which we have been hoarding.'

With one flick of his tail, Vritra let Pani go. He could now breathe. Vritra seemed to be smiling; there was joy in that face, which didn't seem to know the meaning of joy. Until today, at least Pani had never seen it. 'Tell me more, my friend,' Vritra prodded.

'From what I know, they are planning to attack and release the water and the cattle. The leader of their army is...is...' Pani stuttered fearfully.

Vritra turned to look at Pani and he was about to come closer, when he heard Pani say, 'Indra! Indra is in charge of the army.'

Just the name Vritra wanted to hear. Vritra burst out laughing. The walls of the lair shook with his laughter and a few rocks fell. The ground shivered and moved. The sound of his laughter was reverberating all around.

Pani was scared. He had never seen this side of Vritra. He was roaring. Pani didn't know what to do, but his cattle, too, were at stake and he gathered courage to stay put till he was dismissed. While he was aware that Indra had killed Vritra's brother, he still was not expecting this reaction. Did he know enough about Indra?

'Who is Indra?' was Vritra's surprising question.

'Who is Indra? Are you asking me who Indra is?' Pani was too surprised to hear the question.

'Yes, yes,' Vritra responded irritably, 'I know he killed my brother, but then tell me more about this fellow. Don't behave like my father, who reacts like this at the very mention of Indra. Don't make stories; just tell me who he is.'

'Well,' tried Pani, 'he seems to be the new general of the Devas. He doesn't follow many rules and battles with his own instinct. He doesn't care much for what the repercussions will be of a certain action, he just does them. However, he seems to be quite popular with his people, especially after defeating Vala and Namuchi: two supposedly dangerous Danavas.'

'That's all? I know who he has killed but what more?' demanded Vritra.

'Well, he is supposed to have also killed Sambara, a Danava, just because he had stolen his favourite drink—something called soma,' Pani added, thinking really hard.

'What is soma?'

'It is some kind of a magical drink that these people just relish and I am told Indra more than relishes it. He rather seems to have a weakness for it,' said Pani, who was acutely aware of Vritra's piercing gaze, which implied that he wanted to know more about Indra. 'There are some rumours about him.'

'Like what?' hissed Vritra.

'Well, as I said, this sounds unbelievable, but they say that it was he who was responsible for the mountains being steady—as in stuck to the ground,' said Pani, unsure if he should even be saying these things.

'What do you mean steady?' Vritra demanded, irritated at the piecemeal answers.

Pani knew that Vritra's irritation could be dangerous for him, so he hurriedly explained, 'Well they say that the mountains used to have wings and they flew at their will. This supposedly created problems for their sages, who spent all their time in yajnas—some sort of a ritual to satisfy their Creator and other aspects of well-being. So, Indra apparently cut their wings and since then the mountains don't fly and, thus, the sages aren't disturbed.'

Pani heard a thunderous laugh, like he had never heard before. He simply wanted to leave. 'This fellow is interesting. A true match!' exclaimed Vritra.

Pani could see Vritra slithering in joy, something seldom seen in this creature. His eyes were gleaming and his nostrils were breathing fire. Never had Pani seen anything like this before. He wondered what made Vritra so happy about a piece of information that was so unbelievable.

'And yes, one more thing,' Pani remembered. 'He loves cattle and goes out of his way to release them if they are taken into custody. This singular act has made him a favourite among his people.'

'If there is anything else, then tell me or else leave. I hate silly bits like "favourite among his people".'

Pani was relieved, 'I am told that they might attack any time.'

Vritra didn't find that too important and Pani left, hoping that all the laughter and joy of Vritra would ensure that he and his folks get to retain the cattle they had stolen over so many days.

Vritra knew that his time to rule over the land had come.

The waters had been stopped and the cattle were safe in caves. What else did he need to unsettle these silly people? It was time to rule and make these people follow new rules laid down by the mighty Vritra!

The War

The preparations were done; Indra felt that they should attack, just to gauge the strength and the capabilities of Vritra. While a lot had been said and heard about Vritra, there was nothing like a first-hand understanding of the enemy. It would help him strategize his next steps.

The sages were all on their side. Sage Brihaspati was leading the lot and had ensured that besides the offerings to the Creator through yajnas, whatever aid they needed would be made available to them. They would not be found wanting and there would be no one who would work against the warrior lot. While Indra was glad to hear this, he was cautious nonetheless. Somehow, he just couldn't trust these sages.

Clear instructions were given to a very select group of warriors, who had been hand-picked by Indra. The idea was to make more noise than act, so that Vritra unleashed his might. Since this enemy was an expert in magical arts, which they had not encountered till date, it might be worthwhile to explore and understand, rather than unleash all of their force and find it wanting or unprepared.

No one objected to Indra's methods. Everybody knew that they were up against an unknown foe and it made more sense to allow Indra to decide. It wasn't that Indra was not seeking advice, but there weren't too many members forthcoming on that front either. While the army in general was kept on standby waiting for instructions, everybody who had any experience in warfare was ready to join. This was nothing short of a clash of cultures and the Devas were not willing to lose or even give an inch. Besides, it was also a matter of survival. With the waters completely halted by Vritra's obstructions, and the cattle lost, they were in trouble. The war was no longer a matter of choice; it was a matter of survival. It was about fighting to live.

Battles usually were heralded in the morning, after sunrise. Indra sent his feelers to the opposite side, which was indicating that they would attack in the morning, as usual. The sun had risen. Indra and his small band of people, mainly the Maruts and a few foot soldiers, were ready for combat. Indra waited eagerly for the opponent to make a move. Moments turned into hours, but there was no sign of anything. Indra glugged down goblets of soma, without which he was never ready for war. Besides, it gave him the much-needed nourishment for battles, which were known to extract a lot from you, both physically and mentally and often, for some, emotionally.

Each was waiting for the other to begin. There was a strange stillness and quiet in the air. It was close to afternoon and there had been no indication from the top, as the army of Indra had to rise up to the higher plains. Suddenly, darkness started enveloping them, which was surprising since it was just afternoon and dusk was many hours away. Indra saw this as a sign of Vritra's reaction.

The small army stepped stealthily upwards. While the darkness was unusual, it definitely revealed Vritra's impatience, something Indra was trying to gauge. Vritra had also unleashed his magic as a weapon. The darkness was growing and visibility was falling fast. Indra was prepared and ordered everyone to light torches. Wooden bars were lit and handed over to a select few of them. While it would have revealed their presence, that risk would have to be taken. However, Indra asked for only a few torches to be lit to ensure that the strength of the group was not revealed, which was quite small anyway.

As they proceeded, a storm started brewing in their path. Another one of Vritra's magical moves! Indra was amused; it seemed Vritra was using all his powers on the same day! Indra ensured that they were moving very slowly, just to take time because there was no plan to wage a war immediately. Indra just needed to unleash his close friend, Vata, who alone was enough to create a massive storm, but he was in no hurry. Vata was eager to rout the enemy but was awaiting instructions from the chief and would do nothing till he had been instructed to. Indra knew that an important aspect of any army was its trust in the chief.

At the other end, Vritra was getting restless. He was wondering why they were so slow and if they were scared of his magical powers. His messengers had told him so much about Indra that Vritra was now wondering if he should trust his messengers at all, as this Indra was definitely very slow and what was even more surprising was that he had come with such a small team. One gale from his end was enough to blow them away. Or was he underestimating Indra? Intriguing enough to look forward to meeting him, thought Vritra.

The Panis, who were ready to battle alongside Vritra, were also surprised by Indra's restraint. Was he scared or was he measuring and gauging the enemy? This was quite unlike all that they had gathered about Indra and an even bigger worry was that Vritra was beginning to doubt their information gathering. Would it be pertinent to go down to gather some more information, but risk getting caught or simply wait it out? Waiting since the morning had been both weird and unexpected, but it seemed that they had little choice in the matter. Vritra was also getting irritated that none of his magical moves had been effective.

A few more hours and Indra's army had hardly made any significant progress, which was very surprising. Vritra wondered if he had placed too much trust in the Panis, who could have just cooked up all these stories about this Indra, just to ensure that their cattle were taken care of. This was possible, as they might not be equipped to face Indra and were just ensuring that they were safe under Vritra's protection. Did Father exaggerate about Indra just to ensure that Vritra avenged his brother's death? Vritra smiled, each seemed to have their own selfish reasons to prop up the enemy, when Indra was hardly someone he should have been worried about. Irrespective of the individual biases, Vritra was beginning to think that he needn't fret over this 'threat' and should learn to relax. These Devas were overrated and Indra was a match for just their sort, not him. However, it was good to be cautious nonetheless.

Soon, Vritra received news that Indra's small band of people was retreating. He felt sorry for them. He realized that his weapons were an overkill for these Devas! However, he was also disappointed that there had to be another day of conflict—what a waste, he thought.

The War Plan

While Vritra noticed the retreat, what he failed to take stock of was the elaborate planning in the evening. In a heavily guarded tent, Indra, Mitra, Varuna, some of the Maruts—like Vayu, Raudriya, Vata—and, of course, Vishnu and many of the others, were huddled, discussing the attack for the next day. Sage Brihaspati also joined in later to understand the progress as well as the expectation for the next day. While Indra was not quite comfortable with a sage joining a discussion on wars, he decided to overlook it for the moment because he understood that Varuna and Mitra used to do so, so it seemed normal to everyone. Besides, this was not the time to dwell on such things—there were more pressing matters at hand.

'So, as we can see,' continued Indra, 'Vritra doesn't quite have an army of his own but has Panis to stand by him and support him. While the Panis have no loyalty towards Vritra, they are here for their selfish reasons—they want to keep their loot, our cattle.'

'Does that mean that they may desert Vritra, if need be?' wondered Vishnu. All eyes turned towards him, making Vishnu feel odd.

'Well, probably,' mused Indra. 'One can never say anything on that, as motivations and reasons to stay on can change. From what we know as of now, they don't seem to have any major reasons to support Vritra, besides, I wonder if Vritra needs their help, except for the information that they might be supplying to him.'

'Did any of you get to see Vritra?' asked Varuna.

Indra looked around, 'I don't think so. He was running his tricks from behind that hill.' Indra pointed high up to indicate a hill, which appeared formidable under the moonlight. This comment about Vritra's seemingly cowardly ways brought smiles to the faces of the members of the council.

'So, what are we planning to do tomorrow?' asked Varuna.

'I think we should play this waiting game for another day to make him feel that we are ill-equipped and just when he thinks that we are just a bunch of people, we charge,' Indra suggested. 'The idea is to catch him unawares, as we are still not sure of his bag of tricks.'

Vayu was not quite happy with this slow pace. 'I think we should attack tomorrow.' All eyes turned to him. Indra had just touched the goblet of soma to his lips and at Vayu's utterance, he just looked at Vayu from over the corner of the goblet. Indra noticed some acknowledgement on certain faces. Mitra was looking at him.

'Any particular reason for the hurry?' asked Indra, keeping the goblet down and wiping off a few drops of soma from his beard.

'The water has dried up and all we have out there are calves and bullocks. Let's just get them—there is chaos back home, and—'

'And all of us are just playing the waiting game here up in the cool environs of the foothills, right?' interjected Indra.

Vayu did not respond. Varuna was quiet. While he did feel that the pace was slow, he somehow had begun to trust Indra's instincts in this matter.

'While I, too, am not comfortable with this pace,' Indra said, remarkably calm despite the opposition to his plans, 'what is still not known is the state of our enemy. He is not the usual Vala or a Namuchi. This fellow has many tricks up his sleeve. He is not the regular Danava, with limited thinking! He is fortified. Oh, that reminds me...one of my spies has come back with new information. According to him, high up there,' Indra said pointing to the hill, 'are some ninety-nine forts. Finding him will not be an easy task, let alone eliminate him.'

There was surprise written on all the faces. Indra continued, 'Exercising restrain is not something even I prefer, but the issue is that we still don't know what we don't know! The way he unleashed darkness—do we have a solution to it? Yes, I know we can counter his storm but the way he is displaying his tricks—we don't need to till we decide to. Besides, we are not even aware of the weapons in his armoury. If Vritra didn't do much, doesn't it mean that he, too, is watching us?'

Everyone nodded in agreement, including Vayu, though he was slightly restless, befitting his personality! Sage Brihaspati, who had not spoken at all until then, said, 'While I don't know what kind of weapons you would need to destroy this Vritra, but we can build special weapons for you. I can speak to Tvastr, who can make such things, provided we know what you need.'

Indra found this surprising. A sage speaking about weapons? But he decided not to make any statement that could be counterproductive; who knows who could be of help at what point of time? 'Besides,' continued the sage, 'we also have special weapons with us, I mean they are with Sage Dadhichi. We can get them as and when we feel the need to use them.'

'What are these special weapons?' wondered Vishnu aloud. Once again, all eyes were on him, which made him wonder if the question had been inappropriate. While a few people there were uncomfortable with Vishnu's presence as an outsider, no one said anything, as they were aware that he was a close friend of Indra's.

Indra looked at Vishnu and said, 'These are some very old and blessed weapons. It is believed that the Creator gave these to us at some point of time. These weapons have divine blessings and we take them out if we need them. However, it is inappropriate to use them unless there is a dire need for them. We haven't used them for long now and I sincerely hope we don't need them yet.'

Vishnu was surprised to find such awareness of war and weapons in Indra, especially since none of these things had ever come up during their stay at the gurukul, though he knew that Indra belonged to a warrior community, unlike his.

'I hope that clears your doubts, Vishnu,' Indra enquired. Vishnu nodded and decided that he was not going to ask any more questions that might make him look silly.

'By the way, Rishivar,' Mitra interjected, 'the weapons have not been used for long. I hope they haven't lost their potency.'

'I would think not,' Brihaspati replied. 'Sage Dadhichi knew the nature of the weapons. They could not be kept inside a hut, as their brilliance radiated all around. Keeping them buried underground would only make the soil and the area around it luminescent, thereby drawing attention. So, I remember him mentioning that he has kept them in the wedge of a particular tree. Let me know if you need them. We will need to purify them for about a day before you can use them.'

Indra nodded and hoped that he would not need them.

An Unusual Attack

A few days had passed and there hadn't been much progress, except that Indra had managed to destroy many of Vritra's forts, although he had not been in any of them. Needless to say, destroying them hadn't been easy—each of them was made of impenetrable rocks. Had it not been for Indra's special arrows, no one would have been able to break in.

While breaking the forts had been some motivation for Indra's army and for those who felt that the pace was too slow, Indra knew that he was up against a formidable force and simply attacking would not help. Vritra had many aces up his sleeve and every day, he managed to pose a new and a different threat. While Indra had managed to defend his army well against all of them, one thing he had realized was that he was still just defending. He wasn't attacking as such. He felt that destroying the forts was an achievement, but it still was an uphill task and he had not yet had a face-to-face encounter with Vritra.

There was mixed information about Vritra. Besides the fact that he could take the form of a huge, slithering, fire-breathing serpent, some said that he looked massive, much like all of them, except that he was dark, big and burly. He had long black hair, a huge curly moustache and wore headgear made of metal with horns on it. While the description seemed very odd, Indra understood that this sure was a very different kind of an adversary, who he had to destroy, no matter what.

While all this was going on in Indra's mind, he still hadn't made up his mind to seek help from anybody else. But what had happened that day had been the tipping point. Indra's army had faced the unexpected that day.

Just when they had been feeling good about having destroyed yet another fort of Vritra, they had been attacked by a rain of serpents! Suddenly, serpents had been all over them from everywhere. Indra's small army had been taken aback. The serpents had been flying all around and it had been impossible to escape them. Some soldiers had been bitten badly while others had been singed by the fire that many of them were breathing. Indra had decided to make a hasty retreat and provide immediate antidotes to those who had been bitten by the snakes.

The Ashwins had a tough time treating the snakebites, as each had been equally deadly and different from the other. Those who had been singed had been treated immediately, but the burns had been very different from the ones caused by fire. It had taken the Ashwins some time to understand what these burns were. Something in their fire had released some sort of a liquid that penetrated deep through the skin and just went on burning it deep down. Strange burns they were!

Indra sure did suffer losses due to this attack. Many members of his army were recuperating some were badly in need of rest. While there was no dearth of zeal in any of them and each was raring to go despite the severe injuries, Indra felt that they needed to recover fully before they were in any position to attack. It was at that moment that Indra had felt that he might as well invoke the help of Sage Dadhichi and the blessed weapons. Sage Brihaspati had been sent for and Indra had explained the situation to him. It had been decided that they would need to get the blessed weapons.

Sage Brihaspati had left immediately to get the weapons from Sage Dadhichi.

Sage Dadhichi

Sage Brihaspati walked into the cottage where everyone was waiting for him. They were all expecting to see the celestial weapons that many, like Varuna, Mitra and Vayu, had not seen for a very long time. Seeing Sage Brihaspati walk in empty-handed, disappointment writ large on his face, got them all worried. There was apprehension and fear of the unknown on every face.

Sage Brihaspati looked at all of them wondering what to say or rather how to say all that he had to. He was given a place to sit. There was complete silence in the cottage, with everyone wondering if they should say anything. Sage Brihaspati looked at all of them one by one and then announced, 'I have some bad news.'

Everyone looked at him quizzically.

'Unfortunately,' began Sage Brihaspati, 'the weapons are of no use any more. They have lost their powers.'

'How is that possible?' asked Indra, hiding the agitation in his voice.

'Let me explain,' began the sage. 'Sage Dadhichi had taken the weapons against the wishes of his wife, who felt that sages should have nothing to do with wars and weapons. She felt that these were material possessions and that sages, like him, should rise above them. While Dadhichi did agree with her, he had no choice but to take care of them, as he had given his word to the Devas. As mentioned earlier, he had hidden them in the wedge of a tree in his ashram.

'After several years of the weapons remaining unclaimed,

he took them out, wondering if they were in good condition. When he took them out, he felt that the weapons were lacking their characteristic lustre. He brought a pitcher of holy water and put them in it to clean them. Unfortunately, the power of the weapons got dissolved in this water and they were rendered useless,' Brihaspati explained and paused to breathe.

Seeing the many questions on every face, he immediately continued, 'Lest the power be wasted, Dadhichi drank the water himself and, thus, all the power of the celestial weapons has now been transferred to him.'

Everybody was confused. 'So?' Indra managed to ask.

'So...so, the weapons are useless—they are of no use to us,' Sage Brihaspati said with finality.

There was disappointment and apprehension in the faces of everyone around, but Indra was visibly angry. His distrust towards the sages was only fortified because of this incident and he wondered why they had ever trusted such people. But better sense prevailed and he decided to keep quiet and not say anything that might hurt sentiments at a time when a lot was going wrong anyway.

There was silence in the cottage, as many felt that the last chance that they had to defeat Vritra was lost. There were mixed emotions and everyone was lost in thought. As the only sage in the room, Brihaspati felt like the odd one out. He had been so sure that he would be able to salvage the situation with the help of the weapons and had even assured everyone that he and his folks would help as and when needed. But here was Sage Dadhichi, who had let them down so badly.

The long, contemplative silence was suddenly broken by the arrival of someone in the cottage. At the entrance stood none other than Sage Dadhichi himself.

Seeing him, no one got up as they had for Sage Brihaspati. Seeing this, Sage Brihaspati understood the mood of the gathering. He got up to invite Sage Dadhichi in, but just then Mitra rose from his seat and welcomed him. Soon, one by one, all of them raised themselves from their seats, though the reluctance was more than visible. Needless to say, this was not missed by Sage Dadhichi.

Sage Dadhichi was offered a seat and everyone looked at him, wondering what he was there for. He looked healthy and strong—quite different from the way sages usually looked. He was smiling, as he could sense the anger in each one of them. He hadn't forgotten how Sage Brihaspati himself had been so disappointed and had raged at him for 'letting him down' and how he had 'lost face'. Similar sentiments were visible on every face right then.

Sage Dadhichi looked at Varuna, Indra and Mitra, and said, 'I know all of you are disappointed by what I have done, but I want you to understand that I did what seemed right to me then.' Varuna was about to say something, but Sage Dadhichi raised his hand and asked him to wait, 'Let me explain. The weapons had been lying in the wedge of one of the trees for a very long time when I took them out. Like all weapons, they, too, would have lost their sharpness or edge due to non-usage. That is why I wanted to check them. When I noticed that they had lost their lustre, I dipped them in a pitcher. However, their brilliance immediately transferred to the water; I didn't know such a thing would happen.'

Everyone was listening to Sage Dadhichi wondering what exactly he was here for—to offer an apology?

'But all is not lost, there is still hope,' Sage Dadhichi continued.

Indra moved to the edge of his seat and asked, 'How, Rishivar, how? Please tell us.'

Sage Dadhichi smiled at his youth and curiosity.

'All the brilliance and the power of the weapons has been transferred to my bones after I drank the water!' said the sage, smiling.

'So?' asked Indra, echoing the doubt in the minds of every other person sitting there, including Sage Brihaspati.

'So,' offered Sage Dadhichi calmly, 'you can use my bones!'

'Use your bones?' wondered Varuna aloud. 'How?'

'You can use my bones to make a weapon, which can never go wrong,' Sage Dadhichi responded matter-of-factly.

Mitra got up from his seat and went close to Dadhichi and spoke to him with folded hands, 'Rishivar, we appreciate your sentiments, but we still haven't understood what you mean. We will need to attack the enemy, *now*. We need a weapon *now*.' Mitra's frustration was not lost on anybody, including Dadhichi.

'My son,' the sage smiled at Mitra, 'I am well versed with the situation, as Sage Brihaspati has told me everything. I am aware that you need everything now. That is exactly why I am here and did not send word. Let me explain.' He made Mitra sit down and continued, 'Once my body is no more, you can collect my bones and make a weapon out of it. For you to be able to do so, I am willing to lay down my life—*now*.'

There was shock and awe in every face in the cottage. Indra got up from his seat. Dadhichi was smiling as he continued, seemingly unaffected by the shock, 'You heard me right. I will lay down my life now and here. Then, my bones can be used to make a weapon, which Tvastr will make for you.'

Dadhichi sat down and looking at the ground, said, 'I have lived my life and have attained all I wanted to or could. Once the objective of life has been attained, the body is of no use. I don't need to continue living, as there isn't anything else or more that I may achieve. Besides, if my death is going to serve a bigger purpose, then what more could one ask for? Rather, I see my life continuing in the weapon that Tvastr will make for you,' the sage said, looking at Indra, 'How many here can attain that?'

There were tears in some eyes and disbelief in others. Indra walked a few paces, came close to Dadhichi and bowed down, saying, 'Pardon me, Rishivar, for not understanding you before. What you have just said, I don't think I could have ever brought myself to say, even if it was for the sake of saying. Everyone here is honoured to witness what you just said. This must be recorded in history as the ultimate sacrifice a person can make for his community.'

Sage Dadhichi raised Indra and looked straight at him, 'My son, you are the future of this tribe and in you I trust the weapon made from my body. Go ahead, no one can stop you from having this weapon. It will be your weapon, it will define you and be associated with you. Call it the Vajra! Let it fall on your enemy like thunder!'

Everyone present bowed to Sage Dadhichi and every eye had tears of respect. No one had expected this and no one could have offered this, if they had been in his place. Sage Brihaspati, too, bowed with reverence and escorted Dadhichi out of the cottage to prepare for the ritual. Not a single person spoke thereafter.

Vajra

Sage Dadhichi was escorted to a secluded spot in his cottage, where he sat in deep meditation. Sages of his calibre could enter into meditative states for days without interruption and survive simply on air. While Dadhichi understood that he did not have the luxury of time, he instructed Sage Brihaspati to check back in the morning.

Sage Brihaspati left the cottage with a heavy heart and didn't sleep the entire night, unable to take his mind off the eventful day. He had not known any other act of such selflessness. His moist eyes had lost sleep for the night.

At the crack of dawn, he went to Sage Dadhichi's cottage to find his lifeless body. Tears welled up in his eyes. Sage Dadhichi had picked one of the many cows present to complete the task. Sage Brihaspati brought the cow to the cottage, where the lifeless body lay and it seemed like the cow needed no instructions. It came near Dadhichi's body and started licking it clean. As instructed by Sage Dadhichi, nobody was allowed in the cottage. Sage Brihaspati had never seen anything like this before. Within a few hours, Dadhichi was reduced to bones. Without spilling a drop of blood, the sage had been reduced to just a skeleton.

With the help of some of the awestruck warriors, Sage Brihaspati took some of the bones for the last rites. The rest of the bones, especially those from the ribs, were handed over to Tvastr. He carried the bones with great reverence to forge the ultimate weapon, imagined and seen by none before.

After two full days of working, Tvastr smiled at himself for creating something no one could have imagined. He walked into the cottage where everyone had gathered to witness the new weapon made out of the bones of Sage Dadhichi. Tvastr placed the weapon on a huge plate and concealed it with a large piece of cloth. He placed it in the centre of the cottage, where every curious eye was waiting for it to be unveiled.

Tvastr waited for impact before pulling the cloth off the weapon. Everyone gasped in awe. Indra got up from his seat. Nobody had ever seen anything like this before. The weapon had been forged from Sage Dadhichi's thigh bones and ribs—the strongest of the bones that had absorbed the power of the celestial weapons. It had six prongs, which opened on the outside like the petals of a flower, strong and impenetrable, with the lustre of divinity. It looked big and definitely needed strong arms and hands to even lift it.

Indra folded his hands with reverence before touching it. He knew that this wasn't any ordinary weapon. He was literally holding the bones of Sage Dadhichi, who had given up his life for him. Indra could hear the last words of the sage ring in his ears: *In you I trust the weapon made from my body.* He knew that the sage had trusted him with a responsibility and duty and he had to live up to Dadhichi's sacrifice. Indra felt both pride and responsibility in that moment. He lifted the weapon, Vajra, in his hand and tried to wield it but was stopped by Tvastr. Indra looked surprised. Tvastr smiled and said, 'Let us all go out before you wield it.' The curious gathering stepped out of the cottage and stood on one side of the open space. Tvastr then looked at Indra and said, 'You can wield it now but make sure that you exert the pressure *away* from you.'

Indra raised the Vajra and hurled it ahead of him. Suddenly, there was a loud clap of thunder and a blinding light emanated from the weapon. The tree in front of him was blown to smithereens besides creating strong waves in the river flowing behind the tree. It was both scary and dangerous. Indra was impressed and so was everybody else. Indra bowed with reverence for the weapon, as he knew that this was no ordinary weapon—it was the Vajra, which would remind him and the times to come, what sacrifice is. It was the result of the ultimate sacrifice made by anybody in eons to come.

Indra knew that this was a weapon that would be his forever and it would be used for the benefit of his people. Vritra was sure to be killed by this and that would end the suffering of his people. The reports of suffering that they had been receiving lately had been getting worse. The water had stopped completely, affecting the lives of the people, crops and animals. The calves were dying due to lack of nourishment from the cows, as all the cows had gone missing too. The bulls were getting agitated and were attacking each other and everybody around. If Vritra was not eliminated immediately, there would be anarchy and an uprising among the people. Indra knew that he had to take charge and get on top of all this...soon.

Vritra Awakens

Vritra was listening to all that the Panis were saying. He was amused to find the Panis panicking at the information that they had brought about some secret weapon that the Devas had acquired. Vritra was wondering what weapon could harm him and whether the Devas were naive enough to think that they had come up with something to destroy him!

While Vritra was aware that the Panis were more worried about their cattle and didn't care much for anything else, it suited him to patronize them as their saviour, which added to the Devas' trouble. The way to stifle the Devas was to stop their water and deprive them of their cattle. The cattle were a major means of wealth and without them, the Devas were severely affected. If at this stage he actually joined the battle then this slow destruction would lead to the sheer decimation of the Devas. It was futile to prolong the inevitable, thought Vritra.

He uncoiled himself and took a deep breath, which uprooted a few trees nearby, and breathed fire out, which further burned trees and caused a small pond to dry up. The Panis were happy to see this sign of Vritra's invincibility because in it was their sustenance. While they had full faith in Vritra's destructive powers, which they had witnessed to some extent, they could not trust the Devas. Lately, they had been too quiet and impassive in the battle, which didn't make sense to them. They were definitely up to something. But then, they were glad to see Vritra now joining the battle directly unlike the way it had been so far. While Vritra had no army and needed no one, the Panis were ready to fight support Vritra, but also desert him, if need be! The Panis fought only for their benefit, they didn't have any major allegiance to Vritra or animosity towards the Devas—their allegiance was to their loot, the cattle.

The Battle Royale

The beginning of the day heralded its outcome. It was dry and dull. The sky was clear, but the air was suffocating. There was not even a slight breeze to move the feeblest of the leaves. The stench of animals that had died due to thirst was in the air. Calves were dead and many bulls had been reduced to walking skeletons. People all over were dying of thirst and hunger caused by the poor yield from the land.

Indra had started the day at dawn since he and his army were planning to strike early. After his ablutions, he sat down to have his share of soma, as he needed all the energy and exhilaration that he could get that day. The makers of the juice were surprised by the rate at which Indra consumed it. They whispered among themselves, 'His appetite is surprising...by now, he must have consumed seas of soma!'

But soma was in demand that day. Everyone had had their fill of soma. The Devas were determined to ensure that they strike and strike hard that day. A bit of complacency had set in among the enemies and striking that day would be decisive. They were running out of time and any further delay would have been counterproductive and even dangerous.

Everyone awaited the sound of the conch shell. Indra and his army were moving upwards and were waiting to strike. The Panis were advancing slowly, as they were more interested in defending than attacking. They were guarding their loot and for that, defence was more appropriate a strategy.

At the sound of the conch shell, Indra charged. He pulled the reins of the horses pulling his chariot, which was shining in the sun. The horses neighed and shot ahead, hurtling over the dry, stony path. With the soma in Indra and his army, there seemed to be no stopping this band of youthful warriors. Within no time, Indra had dashed into Vritra's forts, looking for him. He wanted to ensure that he met Vritra that day, no matter what.

When Indra reached the ninety-ninth fort, he knew that he was close to his adversary. He wanted Vritra to be out today but had been warned about the encounter by Sage Brihaspati. Despite all the information they had gathered about Vritra in the time they had taken to reach him, there may still be some things to be known about him. Indra was aware that he could still have some surprises in store. As if to indicate his plan, he stopped before the final fort and looked back. His army understood the look and nodded in unison.

Indra's army hurled huge boulders at the fort and Indra rained his heavy arrows on it. The fort gave in quicker than they had expected. No sooner had the fort's walls given way than Vritra's deadly poison rained down on them. But the army was ready with large shields that prevented the poison from touching their skins. He then rained fire from inside but the shields saved them yet again. Indra's horses suffered minor burns but that only made them more aggressive and at the slightest of the tug by Indra, they neighed and were raring to go, unwilling to wait, much like their master.

Indra charged, followed by his army. There were chants of *'Vritra-han!'*, 'Slay Vritra!', in the air. The air was getting hot with excitement and charged with bloodlust for the enemy. Soma was coursing through their veins. Indra's senses were at their peak in that moment, expecting the unexpected. He was prepared and just as he was looking around, his horses stopped with a sudden jolt. He barely managed to halt and not topple his chariot. Vritra stood in front of him.

The slithering giant serpent was uncoiling himself, ready to face Indra. Indra had never seen a serpent of such size and proportion. His ugly but glistening skin was an eyesore for sure. His huge face was visible once in a while, when he raised his head menacingly to breathe fire and straighten up; the penetrating and mesmerizing eyes did not leave Indra even once. Sage Brihaspati had warned Indra against making direct eye contact, as the serpent had magical powers, and was known to exercise his magic through his eyes. Indra shifted his gaze without diverting his attention from this monstrous serpent.

There was silence, except for the slimy, slithering movements of Vritra. Indra could hear Vishnu from a distance, asking him to strike and kill Vritra right then, but Indra wanted to be face to face with Vritra before he struck. He wanted to see the full potential of his adversary. He wanted to know what he was going to kill. He wanted to give even Vritra a fair chance to fight, even though Vritra had resorted to magic, guile and robbery. Vishnu was scared of Indra's foolhardiness in that moment but decided to stay away.

In his full form, Vritra was definitely formidable—a mountain of a serpent, whose slightest movement shook the ground. The earth quaked in pain and seemed to be crying out under his weight. The clouds in the sky had dried up due to his breath and it was hot all around. Indra could see the menacing tongue leaping out of Vritra's open mouth towards Indra. He shielded himself but knew that the shield would not hold the attack back for long. The venom being spewed from the tongue was corroding the shield and burning it. Indra bent down a little to pick up the axe on the floor of his chariot, invisible to Vritra, and at the very next moment, as Vritra moved his tongue towards the axe, Indra slashed it off with his axe with unexpected precision.

Indra could hear the gasps from behind him. The serpent roared in pain. His eyes were bloodshot and the ground shook, crashing some of the walls of his broken fort, which had managed to withstand Indra's attack. Indra could see the final moments approaching and he was not going to let this moment go. However, before Indra could think, the serpent's tail came hurtling towards his chariot. Indra tried to hack it with his axe but missed, losing the top of his chariot to the tail. The horses neighed and leapt in the air, but Indra managed to control them in time.

Suddenly, as if on cue, a group of Panis attacked. Indra looked at Vata, the gale, the violent Marut, who charged with his group. Vata had been waiting for action and was itching to get back at the petty thieves who had stolen the cows and had been hiding behind Vritra. Vata and his army were not going to let them see another day. Soon, some of them were seen fleeing from the onslaught of Vata and his army.

Vritra, in the meanwhile, had recovered from Indra's attack. Groaning and writhing in pain, he decided to attack Indra, who he had underestimated as a mere young Deva, nothing but an upstart, an irritant at best. But Vritra was now angry at having lost a part of its menacing tongue and he was not letting this go unpunished. Vritra also knew that the others were waiting at a distance and if he charged, some of them were sure to run for their lives.

Vritra flipped his tail and hurled boulders with its breath. Vritra noticed that some of the Devas were retreating—they were abandoning the army. His aggression was fuelled by this and he could also see that Indra was only able to defend. Vritra hissed loudly, blowing away a few trees. The earth had cracked open at a number of places, creating the fear of it caving in, but then, the battle had just begun.

In the distance, Vishnu was wondering why Indra was not using the Vajra—was it ineffective or did Indra not trust its efficacy? What could be the reason for enduring all this destruction when the Vajra could be hurled straightway to end the battle? For a moment, he thought he should remind Indra of that, but then he decided against it because he wasn't sure of doing so. Besides, nobody else seemed to be worried about it or was thinking the same probably. Vishnu was not sure he wanted to get too close to this war. He had come here for something else and that was bothering him anyway. He had gotten involved in this war just to understand the war techniques of Indra and his tribesmen.

Vishnu was not the only one thinking about the Vajra. Varuna, too, was wondering what was keeping Indra from using the weapon. However, he decided against suggesting anything to Indra because, by now, he had realized that Indra had very different war techniques and it was his element of surprise that he sprung on his enemies that made him win each time. So, it was better not to say anything.

Indra was sweating due to all the action. He knew that Vritra would turn violent now and the time to end him was near. Vritra seemed to be coiling himself at a distance, as if to pull himself back, like an arrow against a bow. Vritra felt that this did not deserve to be prolonged any longer and he needed to strike the final blow. He was convinced that there was no secret weapon with Indra, as he was using the same arrows even after being attacked. The Panis had clearly been misinformed and there was no use wasting any more time on this battle.

Vritra coiled himself and with all the pressure of his weight, flew towards Indra. Indra saw Vritra hurtling towards him, which, from a distance, looked like a huge dark cloud. Just when Vritra was halfway through, Indra pulled out the Vajra from the chariot hidden from sight until now, and hurled it towards Vritra. The sudden thunder and lightning blinded Vritra and before he could react, the Vajra hit him.

Indra's throw had been decisive and had hit the target while he was mid-air. When the Vajra made contact with him, Vritra, completely unprepared, fell to the ground with a huge thud. The fall was literally earth-shattering and Vritra did not even realize what had happened to him. The impact of his fall on the ground was so severe that he was half-buried inside the earth, with parts of his body singed and smoking. The air was thick with the smell of his burning flesh. The last thing Vritra saw was the triumphant smile on the face of his adversary!

The Aftermath

Shock and surprise were coupled with a sense of joy all around. The Panis, who were nearly routed, could not believe what they had seen. It was as if a signal had been given to them. No sooner did they notice Vritra fall than they started abandoning the battle lines and ran away. A few were caught but many of them managed to escape. It suddenly seemed that more than the loot, life had become important to them.

Everybody was in a state of joy. There was an air of victory and Indra was proud of what he had done. He was glad that he had not used the Vajra earlier, as it had been important to make Vritra overconfident to let himself out in the open. Indra knew that no matter what deceptive skills he used, at some point, he would exhaust them and come out in the open, thinking that his adversary would be defeated just by the amount of time that had lapsed. Indra knew that all he had to do was remain calm and tenacious until Vritra made the wrong move. He knew that the biggest mistake a side in the army can make is underestimate its adversary; that's when the side makes the most decisive victory—his strategy had paid off!

Everyone had gathered around the burning body of Vritra. Its eyes were half closed and the body was badly bruised. It was a messy sight to witness. Indra gave Vritra one last look and asked some of them to take him away. He knew that the serpent, though evil, was the child of a sage. Vritra's body ought to be handed over to his father, who had lost another son to Indra.

Everybody was now waiting for the ultimate win—the return of their water and cows.

Indra asked Raudriya, along with a few more of them, to go and look for the cows, with one of the Panis to guide them and take them inside. While they were hidden in the caves, like the Panis usually did, Indra didn't want much time to be wasted in searching for them. However, he cautioned Raudriya not to trust them entirely.

Varuna walked up to Indra, smiled at him and patted his back. His face showed pride and Indra was humbled by the gesture. Suddenly, he saw everybody raise their weapons in the air and chant 'Vritrahan! Vritrahan! The Slayer of Vritra'. Mitra walked up to him, embraced him for the great victory and took his hand, raising it up in the air as the chants reverberated all around. The very skies seemed to be celebrating the victory.

Soon, they could all hear the sound of the cows' hoofs on the dry earth. Hundreds and hundreds of them were being brought down by Raudriya and the others. There was an unending stream of them, all being directed towards the plains. They left a cloud of dust on everybody there, but nobody was disturbed by it. The cows left behind a cloud of dust as they ran out. They seemed to be blessing their saviour for reuniting them with their calves.

Hours after the cows' return, it was time to break the walls that had been trapping the water. The dry river beds and the earth needed to be given their rightful water. Indra and a few others went behind the ruins of the forts to find a huge embankment made with rocks and boulders to arrest the waters. While it did seem like a formidable task, they knew that the battle had been won. Those who had tasks assigned to them stayed back and the others left for the plains. The breaking of the embankments began and soon, the water went roaring down its course. There were shouts of joy and a smile on every face. The victory was complete.

Everybody looked at Indra with pride. They had just found their new hero!

The Homecoming

Indra had left for the battle in a chariot but he returned home on the shoulders of his people. He was given a rousing welcome, befitting a hero. There were sounds of drums and cymbals to greet the army. Every face had a smile on it and every old person was blessing them all. One could even see the cows and calves smiling at them all! The earth, too, was soft as if it was shedding tears of joy after reuniting with its life—the water.

Indra was thirsty. The enormity of his act was sinking in. He felt as if a heavy weight had been lifted off of him. Amid all the jubilation, he noticed a sad-looking woman in white standing outside a hut. It was Rishipatni Swarcha—the wife of Sage Dadhichi. Indra raised his hands and asked to be let down. He walked towards Swarcha and saw the pain in her eyes. He bent low, realizing that she was carrying the child of the dead sage, and placed the Vajra at her feet.

The Rishipatni burst out in tears and could barely manage to stand. The women around her held her and took her inside. Indra didn't miss the tinge of hatred in her eyes before she was taken inside the cottage. It saddened Indra and he felt guilty, but he knew that many a thing had to be done for the greater good of the community, however unfortunate and unpalatable they may be to individuals. Besides, it hadn't been his idea or anybody else's, but that of Sage Dadhichi himself. In that moment, that and only that had seemed to be the solution. Indra knew that this might be the ultimate sacrifice anybody could make, but he also understood the state of mind of the woman who was carrying the dead sage's child. Indra's changed expression was not missed by anybody and so was his gesture towards Swarcha, which only won more hearts.

The slight aberration dampened the celebrations a trifle, but only a trifle. The brief episode was soon forgotten and preparations for the celebrations began. Indra went to soak in the wooden vats of warm water. He had had his vat made especially large to fit him and for him to spread his legs, which helped him relax. He reached his cottage to find his bath ready, with warm water and aromatic oils. Indra smiled and just dropped off his clothes to soak in the water. After some time, he looked around to find a few goblets and a jar of soma placed close to the vat.

Indra poured himself a couple of goblets of his favourite drink, quaffed them and rested his head against the edge of the vat. His body was tired and he could do with liquid both outside and inside him. He looked at yet another goblet of soma and instead of sipping it, he poured it down and looked at the liquid flowing rhythmically in front of him, not in him... He kept staring at the slow flow and thought:

> *O soma, the child from the mountains of Saryanavrat.*
> *You flow for me, only me.*
> *You exist for me, only me.*
> *I can be strong like the wind and light like the breeze,*
> *I have drunk soma!*
> *I can carry the world on me, with me,*
> *I have drunk soma!*
> *I can place the earth here, the sun there and*
> *the moon elsewhere,*
> *I have drunk soma!*
> *I can fly like the clouds, flow like the rivers,*
> *I have drunk soma!*

Indra took another goblet and started to pour it on himself, watching it trickle down without even blinking.

> *With you, I have stopped the moving mountains.*
> *With you, I have changed the course of rivers.*
> *With you, I have swayed the clouds.*
> *With you, I will do what none can do.*
> *I have drunk soma and will drink soma.*
> *Soma, flow for me, always for me.*
> *Forever and ever...soma, flow for me.*

Holding the goblet close to his lips, he let the soma flow down the sides of his lips, over his neck and onto his broad chest. It excited Indra to fill another goblet and another and another... till the vat was full to the brim with soma.

The air in the cottage was heady with the aroma of soma. The block of wood burning on the side had stopped throwing long shadows. Its flames were exhausted and reduced to dying embers. They saw Indra in the vat, washing away the joy and exhilaration of the day with soma. They didn't want to disturb him and quietly retreated into the night, not wanting to know anything beyond what they had witnessed and never telling anybody the story of that night—the night that Indra spent with soma!

A New Era Begins

The morning after the battle royale began lazily. The celebrations, which were as much for the tribe as for nature, had lasted the whole night. The calves had reunited with their mothers, who had been starved of motherhood for too long. The water which gushed down from behind the broken embankments had softened the earth. There was happiness everywhere and praise for Indra on every lip.

The morning after, the council met to discuss the past few days and the aftermath of the battle. Word was sent to all the members with the appointed hour. Everyone assembled at the cottage for a discussion. Varuna, dressed in all white, was at his designated place and so were the rest, including Indra. However, it was not lost on anybody, including Indra, that all eyes were on him that day. It was a moment of pride for him.

Varuna rose from his seat, welcomed everyone and said, 'This is a momentous day for all of us here and those who are outside. I welcome you all to this day, which is going to go down in the annals of history as a great day, not because we won a great battle but because this day will change the course of our existence and herald a new era for us.'

There was a look of surprise on quite a few faces, wondering what the change was. Mitra was smiling and his face glowed with happiness and joy. Indra looked curious, just as many others were. Varuna could sense anticipation in every face there, 'To avoid dragging this to a state of intrigue, let me tell you all what I have decided.'

Varuna took a deep pause and then continued, 'I have headed this council for too long, starting from a time when our tribe was establishing itself in the region. If I am asked to assess my days, I would say, I have done my best. But my best need not be the need of the hour any more, as times are changing and so are the expectations from a leader.' Everyone was wondering what would come next.

'Keeping with the changes and the need of the hour, I have decided to relinquish my position and step down,' Varuna announced. Many members looked surprised and some even looked sad. Indra was about to stand up but decided to wait and hear him out.

Varuna could see and hear people fidgeting and discussing under their breaths. He raised his hand to hush everybody and continued, 'Step down to a brighter future and younger leadership.' Varuna looked at a surprised Indra. All gazes shifted to Indra. Varuna continued, 'I step down to make way for Indra!'

There was visible cheer everywhere. Indra was both shocked and surprised. Varuna continued, 'What Indra has done is unbelievable. His sharpness and decisive victory have made him worthy of being our new leader. In this changing world, we need new blood, new thoughts and new means, and I feel that Indra has them all. Besides, the council of elders will always be there to guide him, if needed.'

Indra was moved. He got up and saw Varuna walking towards him. Varuna embraced Indra and could sense many unspoken words and invisible emotions in the tight embrace, something Indra had never felt before. Varuna held his hand and took him towards the seat that had been Varuna's, and made him sit there. Indra sensed pride in Varuna's eyes. He naturally and instinctively touched Varuna's feet.

Seeing this, everybody stood up. Some had tears of joy in their eyes, foremost among them, was Mitra. He had known from a very early stage that Indra would occupy Varuna's place one day and was glad that Indra had earned it. Indra was visibly at a loss for words.

Varuna was not done. He continued, 'I request everyone here to cooperate with Indra and guide him, aid him and stay with him in his journey of leading our tribe from here onwards. With great pride and joy, I would now like to leave the council, as I think I am leaving it all in abler hands and on stronger shoulders.'

Indra got up and said, 'No, you can't do that. The council needs you and I need you to guide us and help us achieve our objectives. Nobody has ever left the council and we could do a lot more if you are with us.'

Varuna was reluctant. He felt that he had had his moment and would like to rest now. The council, however, was not willing to let him go and after a lot of deliberation, it was decided that he would oversee activities related to the seas and oceans. Varuna agreed, as he realized that this would take him away from the hubbub of the plains, which he imagined was going to be a very hectic place henceforth. Varuna could foresee a change that he might not quite agree with, even though it could just be the best for his tribesmen. Under such circumstances, it would be good to be away from it all.

Mitra hugged Indra and was proud that he had seen in Indra what many could not. He could proudly say that even Indra had not seen it in himself. From the hot-headed rebel, Indra had matured well and was much more level-headed now than what he had been. He was beaming with brotherly pride and joy. So was everybody else in the council, who felt that Indra deserved to be the leader of the tribe now. While some were sad to see

Varuna go, everyone was glad that a practice had been initiated of relinquishing the post for an abler and more deserving person, which many had not witnessed earlier. A healthy precedent had been set without any acrimony.

After everyone had settled down, Indra was asked to say a few words. He got up and looked around. He realized that everyone sitting there was elder to him and had been on the council since the very beginning. He was the new one there and it felt very different. While he was proud to occupy Varuna's seat, deservedly, now that he was there, he had mixed feelings about it. He had different ideas of how to run the council and was glad that he could do so now. He could sense all the eyes on him. Indra smiled and said, 'I am unsure if I deserve to be here, but I can assure all of you that I will not disappoint any of you for having faith in me. I thank the elders and take this responsibility with great awareness that I have to follow the path laid down by the elders and those who came before me with just as much sincerity and gravity.' Indra looked at Varuna and said, 'I can assure you that you will never regret your decision.'

Varuna nodded in agreement and so did the others.

As soon as the council meeting got over, word spread about Indra's appointment as the new chief and there was joy everywhere. The Maruts, who were the closest to Indra, started dancing and celebrating. Everyone was walking up to Indra to wish him and congratulate him. No one in the tribe was disappointed with the decision. It seemed like this was everybody's decision, despite the fact that such a change had never taken place before.

After a point, Indra wanted nothing more than to just get away from all the hubbub of the day. He walked towards his cottage to sit alone and contemplate.

On entering the cottage, he found Vishnu waiting for him.

He was glad to find someone who could take him away from the dealings of the day. He was happy to see Vishnu and said, 'Vishnu, my friend, I am so happy to see you here! You are just the person I needed to meet now!'

Vishnu got up from his seat and hugged Indra. Vishnu could feel the warmth of friendship in the tight embrace.

'I heard the good news,' said Vishnu. 'I am so happy for you.'

Indra smiled, made Vishnu sit and said, 'Well, before all that, I must thank you for your contribution during the war. You sure were a great help.'

Vishnu smiled, knowing that he had done nothing significant; rather he had been more of an observer during the battle. 'Well, that was hardly...' Vishnu left the statement unfinished.

'No, no, don't say a word,' Indra stopped him.

After a few moments of silence, Vishnu said, 'My friend, I have come to take your leave. I have been here for quite some time now...'

Indra looked surprised. 'Well, to me, it seems like yesterday that you arrived. I have barely spoken to you at length. I have been so preoccupied with this battle, I feel like I have hardly spent any time with you,' Indra said, feeling sorry.

Vishnu smiled and responded, 'You can't be blamed for that, Indra. This was a crisis and your crisis has been a great learning for me. I am not complaining!'

'I can understand that you need to go, but let me request you to stay back for just a few more days. Let me spend some time with you; that way, I will feel better. Just a few more days, don't say no, please,' Indra insisted.

Vishnu knew that he had come here with a purpose, which had not been achieved as yet, and Indra needed to know. While Indra definitely was busy, he still needed to know what Vishnu did and if not him, who would tell Indra? With all this in mind, Vishnu agreed to stay for a few more days. Indra was visibly happy about the decision and assured him that he would make up for all the days when he had not attended to Vishnu, who had come from far just to meet him.

Who Is Vishnu?

'This friend of yours...What's his name?' asked Mitra, who had come to discuss something important with Indra.

'Who? Vishnu?' asked Indra.

'Yes, I think that's the name—who is he?'

'He is a friend from the gurukul. Why?'

'No, I was just asking. He has been here for quite some time now.'

'Oh yes, he had come to see me since I had left the gurukul in a hurry.'

'And stayed back?'

'Well, he stayed back to help me in the battle,' Indra explained, wondering why they were even discussing this.

'Stayed back for the battle?' Mitra looked puzzled. 'He doesn't look like someone who has fought battles. I mean one look at him and you would know he has never fought a battle.'

Indra looked sharply at Mitra, 'Just what are you hinting at?'

Mitra smiled and responded, 'I am not hinting at anything. I was just asking, as he seems to be quite curious. He keeps moving around all day and asks a lot of questions to a lot of people. A bit weird, I think.'

'Oh that!' Indra laughed. 'That's Vishnu for you. He is very curious and never settles for an answer. He has to verify every statement as many times as he can! He was the only one in the entire gurukul who had the maximum questions for Guruji.' Indra stopped and then continued, 'Besides, he belongs to a different society. Everything that he sees here is different for him.

His community, I believe, do not fight wars. This was something different and he wanted to see and understand what our wars are like, that's all. I wouldn't read too much into it.'

'And where is he from?'

'He is from some distant island. I believe his land is surrounded by white gushing waters and he and his people live there,' Indra recalled from what he had once heard Vishnu say. Mitra was quiet and didn't say anything. Indra noticed Mitra's silence and said, 'Is something bothering you?'

'Well, not exactly. I mean I am unable to point to the exact issue...but this fellow, I mean this friend of yours makes me uncomfortable. Don't ask me why.'

Indra came close to Mitra, offered him a goblet of soma, and said, 'Here, sip this and stop worrying about him. Anyway, he is planning to leave in a day or so.'

Indra noticed that Mitra was happy about his last statement. Indra was amused at this unusual thought and that too about Vishnu. I mean, what harm can someone like Vishnu cause anybody? wondered Indra.

Indra decided to put this conversation behind him, as he felt that Mitra was being unnecessarily apprehensive. Indra knew Vishnu better than anybody else and he had always been a friend. Well, he was different because he belonged to a different place and people, but he was not someone to be worried about. In that moment, Indra also realized how little he knew about Vishnu, except for the fact that he lived on some remote island. He knew nothing about his family, his background or his people. Indra felt bad for not having taken enough interest in Vishnu, who, on his part, had come all the way to meet him and had helped him during the war. Indra decided to make up for this and that too the very next day.

Vishnu Speaks

Next day, the sun barely managed to show up, as dark clouds gathered in the sky, heralding the beginning of the rains. The parched earth had spoken words of love to her long-lost lover, the sky, who was ready to make love to her. Ancient lore says that once upon a time, or rather before time even existed, the earth and the sky were lovers who were in an eternal embrace. The two would not release each other, till the cruel world decided to separate them for its own selfish reasons. The sun wanted to shine, the winds wanted space to blow over, the waters wanted to wage wars, and the trees and plants wanted to show off their beauty. In the process, the earth and the sky were separated and since then, they have lived a lonely existence. When the sky's longing to unite with his love, the earth, gets unbearable, he sheds tears, which fall on the earth in the form of rains. The earth bathes in the tears of her partner and blooms like never before. The dry, parched earth dresses up in greenery and sprouts life from within herself and both earth and sky are joyful. The two long-lost lovers' union brings fruitfulness and a bounty for the world, the same world that had wanted the two lovers to separate. The irony of life!

Seeing the overcast day, Indra decided to treat Vishnu to the rains that he might not have experienced. Indra sent word to Vishnu that he would be meeting him in a few hours for an experience of a lifetime. Vishnu received the message with surprise but waited for Indra at the appointed hour.

After a few hours, he heard the sound of a chariot approaching his cottage. He stepped out to find an empty chariot drawn by a charioteer, whom he had not seen earlier. The young man kept sitting on the chariot, folded his hands and said, 'My Lord has asked me to take you to a place where he will meet you.'

'Where?' wondered Vishnu.

The charioteer smiled, 'I am not at liberty to tell you, but if you could come with me, you will not regret it.'

Vishnu liked the man, who seemed to be very charming. Vishnu decided not to question him and proceeded to climb into the chariot, only to realize that it was quite high! He wondered how Indra had managed to control the chariot, which was both very high and seemed quite robust, especially with the two huge horses pulling it. When he stood on the chariot and looked around, he realized that the chariot indeed was very high and the earth seemed oddly far! When he was looking around, he could see the charioteer awaiting his orders, but he found something very odd. The charioteer had no feet. It was then that he realized why the charioteer had not alighted from the chariot when he had reached Vishnu's cottage.

'I have not seen you before, what is your name?' Vishnu asked the charioteer.

'Aruna, my name is Aruna and I have been recently appointed as Lord Indra's charioteer,' he replied. While it would belittle Aruna to ask him about his handicap, Vishnu couldn't quite understand why Indra had appointed a charioteer who had no feet. Sensing Vishnu's dilemma, Aruna, said, 'Shall we proceed?'

'Oh yes, please go ahead,' Vishnu replied, unable to hide his hesitation. He decided to keep quiet and not embarrass Aruna.

'Are you wondering about my feet?' Aruna asked candidly.

Vishnu was embarrassed at the direct query. He couldn't believe that he had been so transparent. 'I am sorry, Aruna, if I made that so obvious, please don't mind my behaviour.'

Aruna smiled, 'No, My Lord, you don't have to feel sorry about it. If anyone should be apologetic, it's my destiny, which made me ill-formed. But it's not an embarrassment any more since My Lord Indra gave me this great opportunity to prove that my handicap is not one at all!'

Vishnu was impressed by the positivity of the man and couldn't help appreciate both the charioteer and his master, Indra. 'So were you born like this or did you...' Vishnu wondered aloud.

'It's a long story, My Lord, but then we have a long way to go too,' mused Aruna and continued, 'I am the son of Rishi Kashyapa, a renowned sage of our society. He has two wives, Kadru and Vinata. My father had blessed my mother, Vinata, that she would have only two sons, but they would be the pride of our society. On the contrary, my stepmother, Kadru, had wanted many sons and that was her only requirement. Soon, my stepmother had birthed many sons and my mother had held me inside her for too long. One day, out of frustration and her inability to bear the delay, she forced me out of her. I hadn't formed completely and when I was born, my lower half was ill-formed. Since then, I have been like this. But my father taught me all that I could learn and My Lord Indra decided to make me his charioteer, when no one found me of any use!'

Vishnu was both surprised and impressed. He had never seen someone who wanted to give an opportunity like this one to a person who could barely walk. He had also never seen anyone who would never walk in his life being so positive and happy with himself. The more Vishnu observed these people, the more he was impressed by them. There was something so very grounded about them, so honest and true. They were very direct and straightforward, without any intrigue and deception.

They expressed their joy and sorrow and at the same time, their anger, too, was dangerous.

Soon, Vishnu started enjoying the cool breeze blowing through his long hair and caressing every pore of his body. It had started to drizzle and there was wetness in the air and the aroma of joy that the earth was already beginning to experience. The clouds were getting darker and, soon, Vishnu could barely make out if it was day or dusk.

After what seemed like quite a long but enjoyable ride in Indra's chariot, steered by the most interesting person, Aruna, they came to a grove. It was uninhabited and quiet, awaiting the storm and the rains. Out of nowhere, he found a nubile and delicate-looking beautiful woman waiting for them. Aruna indicated to Vishnu to follow her. Vishnu was rather surprised at the turn of events and simply allowed himself to go with the flow, not knowing what awaited him.

Vishnu followed the woman through a winding path, which suddenly opened to an isolated pond. Vishnu was surprised to even find a pond there, as nobody from outside could have even guessed that. There, at the edge of the pond, he found Indra waiting for him. He looked handsome in his white dhoti and bare torso, with the wind whipping his mane in all directions. There sure was something about him. Indra greeted Vishnu with a warm embrace, as always, and said, 'I want to make up for all the neglect I have heaped on you. I hope you didn't have trouble travelling this far?'

Vishnu smiled, 'I didn't even realize I was far till you mentioned it. Your charioteer is a very interesting person and didn't make me feel like a guest. It seemed as if I was the master of this place and the chariot. He made me feel at home.'

Indra smiled, 'I know what you are saying, that's the skill of

Aruna, a very happy and contented person and very loyal too. I am glad you felt that way.'

'I want to show you something, come with me,' Indra said, grasping Vishnu by his shoulders and directing him to climb a small hillock. Soon, both of them were at the top from where they could see a huge expanse of land and valleys. Vishnu had never seen a sight as divine and celestial as this one. It was breathtaking. 'What do you think?' asked Indra pointing to the valley.

Vishnu was speechless. He looked at Indra and then back at the valley. Indra was smiling at him, 'Exactly, that is exactly how I felt when I saw this place—speechless!' Indra exclaimed, reading Vishnu's mind.

'So, what is this place?' Vishnu found his voice.

'I am going to make this my capital!' announced Indra. 'Amravati. That's what my capital will be called. One of the most beautiful places on earth—the envy of everybody and a place like none other in this world!' Indra was beaming with pride.

Vishnu was surprised. 'A capital? Whoever thought of that?'

'I have!' replied Indra. 'My kingdom will have a capital. It will be the seat of power for my kingdom, the centre of my land and space from where I will rule the earth one day.'

Indra was staring at the vast expanse ahead of him, the end of which was only the horizon. Vishnu was rather surprised at the vision and thought process. He had never come across anybody who could think so far ahead in the future or of anybody who thought of expanding and even building a capital for his people. Vishnu realized that Indra and his people were way ahead of others and Indra was an administrator with a vision. He could see it in Indra's face and his demeanour. Vishnu wasn't sure if he was just impressed or whether, at that moment, he was jealous of Indra, too, for thinking what he couldn't even imagine.

'What do you say, my friend?' asked Indra, patting Vishnu's back.

Vishnu found himself saying, 'If there is any one person who can do this, then it's you, only you, Indra!' Indra smiled at Vishnu and said, 'I knew you would believe in me. You are the first person I am sharing this vision with; I am yet to share this with anybody else. Come, let's go,' Indra turned back.

The drizzle had just turned into a mild rain, the wind was blowing and the trees were shying away from the caress of the naughty winds. Indra and Vishnu were now standing near the pond, which had lilies in them. 'This is my secret abode,' said Indra pointing at the spot, where he had spent many a memorable moments of his life, unknown to the world outside. 'No one is aware of this place, except a few very close people, and now, you,' Indra shared and Vishnu was visibly impressed.

Indra pulled off his lower garment and jumped inside the pond, much to Vishnu's surprise. He was neck deep and called Vishnu. Initially, Vishnu didn't know what to do but he, too, disrobed and got inside the water. It was soothing and he had barely immersed himself in the waters, when the sky opened up and it started to rain. The feeling was unimaginable. The sky poured water down like never before. Vishnu just closed his eyes to take in the moment. Soon, he could feel the soft, caressing touch of maidens who swam out from nowhere. Vishnu let himself go with the flow and decided to enjoy and get lost in the moment. Vishnu experienced bliss and an unimaginable happiness, something he had never done before—a pleasure so sensuous and so beautiful that he never wanted to emerge out of it. Vishnu wanted to stay in the water, with the thick curtain of rain enveloping him, in his inexplicable ecstasy. It was a moment that he had never envisaged. Vishnu knew that he would be ever grateful to Indra for this day. Vishnu opened his eyes to find that the rains had stopped and Indra was in the water with him at a distance, sipping goblets of soma and smiling at him. 'What was that?' muttered Vishnu.

Indra laughed out loud, the sound of his laughter echoing in the silent spot. 'Shh...' said Indra putting his finger on his lips, '...just stay quiet and enjoy the feeling.'

Vishnu closed his eyes and sat in the water trying to recollect all that had happened, but all he could remember was the feeling of soft hands all over him, which gave him immense joy and satisfaction, goblets of soma, massages and food, all amid the rains! It was incredible and unimaginable. 'Was it all maya—an illusion?' wondered Vishnu aloud.

Indra's laughter reverberated all around, 'Now, that's you! Maya! You are so preoccupied with this matter! You haven't overcome this since our days at the gurukul!'

Gurukul! Vishnu was suddenly reminded of the prime purpose of his visit—*gurukul*.

Indra noticed the change in Vishnu's expression through the misty curtain of the rains. 'Is everything all right? Are you feeling well?'

'I am fine, I am good,' muttered Vishnu. 'I have never experienced such joy and happiness before, my friend, so I am just...confused...but extremely happy.' He stepped out of the water only to realize that his garment was muddied. Indra pointed to a small enclosure in a distance. 'You will find fresh garments there, my friend.' Vishnu was impressed by the preparedness. He hurried towards the enclosure to put on fresh clothes.

Indra saw the disappearing Vishnu and he, too, got up to change. Indra noticed a change in Vishnu's demeanour but decided against asking him anything, lest it spoil the moment.

However, Indra couldn't dismiss it from his mind and kept on wondering what had suddenly gone amiss.

Soon, Vishnu was out looking fresh and relaxed. His long hair was dripping wet, but his face still had the worrylines, which had flashed across when they were in the water. Indra, too, changed into fresh clothes and, soon, they were ready to head back.

Aruna charged and the chariot was flying in the air. Vishnu closed his eyes to take in the moment and, soon, they were back home. Indra noticed that Vishnu was unusually quiet, but decided to let him be.

At the cottage, Indra said, 'My friend, I have planned a lavish dinner for you tonight. I will have someone inform you when its time—'

'Can it be just you and me at the dinner?' Vishnu interrupted Indra midway.

Indra was rather surprised at the request, as he was planning to call a few of his friends but agreed. 'As you wish, my friend. It will be just you and me.'

Indra saw Vishnu walking towards his cottage, and he left wondering what had gone wrong with Vishnu after such an exhilarating experience. Was it something that he had said? But he could barely remember saying anything annoying! Indra decided against speculating and thought of letting the matter rest until dinner time.

Indra decided to host the dinner at his cottage, instead of hosting it in the grove, under the sky, as he had planned earlier, sensing that Vishnu might want some privacy, especially after he had requested it to be a private matter.

Soon, it was time for the feast. Vishnu was impressed with the spread. The cottage smelt of rare fragrances and vats of soma were laid out for him. He sat at the small, raised structure in front of the large, elevated platform with numerous bowls of Vishnu's favourite foods, fruits and sweets. Vishnu realized that Indra had not forgotten anything from their days of friendship at the gurukul. The more he saw Indra the more he was impressed by his friendship and attention to detail.

Indra got everything laid out in front of them and asked all the attendants to leave them alone. Vishnu was glad that it was just the two of them in the cottage. Indra poured goblets of soma and offered one to Vishnu, who had also started liking the drink. He took it and both of them quaffed it together, with a few more goblets being downed in no time. Earthen lamps had been lit around the cottage for illumination and a few had been placed on the table to show them the spread. The drink and the food were making the atmosphere quite heady and the conversation was going nowhere in particular.

Suddenly, Vishnu said, 'I came here with a purpose, my friend.' Indra gave him a questioning look, to which Vishnu replied, 'I had come to tell you something...but you were so busy with the war...that...' his voice trailed off.

Indra was waiting in quiet anticipation of the news. He saw Vishnu hesitating and realized that this matter must have taken the colour off Vishnu's face in the morning. Indra decided not to push him and allow him to come out with it.

Vishnu resumed trying to complete his statement, while sipping soma, '...that... that...I could not tell you. But I have to tell you...now...or else, I will never be able to tell you... Besides, if there is any one person who ought to know about this, it's you,' Vishnu continued hesitantly.

It was tough to gauge the cause of such hesitation—was it the nature of the news or was it the drink that was acting differently on Vishnu? Indra was beginning to get concerned and was unable to bear the suspense of it all.

Indra egged Vishnu on, 'Just say it...don't hold back.'

Emboldened by Indra, Vishnu said, 'Ahalya...'

'What about Ahalya? What happened to Ahalya?' Indra enquired urgently.

Vishnu put his goblet down, 'Ahalya got married.'

'What?' Indra thundered. 'No! Tell me you are joking, Vishnu, tell me you are joking.'

Vishnu looked straight at Indra and repeated, 'Ahalya got married.'

'To whom?' Indra managed to ask.

'Please don't ask,' Vishnu requested.

'To whom?' Indra demanded, his voice thundering across the cottage. Vishnu could not bring himself to say anything. Indra was staring at him, his eyes welling up with tears of rage, his nostrils flared and his veins throbbing in his temples, 'TO WHOM?' he thundered again.

'To Guruji!' Vishnu responded feebly.

Indra was shell-shocked. His silence was the lull before the storm. Without warning, Indra shouted in pain, held the rug on the platform and pulled it hard. Everything on the platform clattered down onto the ground with a loud noise and he threw his goblet of soma towards the wall of the cottage. Indra was visibly in pain. Vishnu kept sitting opposite him, expecting the worse. One of the lamps fell and its oil spread across the room. Soon, a curtain nearby caught fire.

Vishnu tried to pull Indra away from the cottage but was unable to shake him out of his pain and sorrow. Soon, the attendants who had been waiting outside rushed in and were shocked to see the scene. They, along with Vishnu, managed to take the sad and heartbroken Indra out of the cottage, just as one of its sides caved in due to the fast-spreading fire. Indra sat on a small rock outside his burning cottage, staring at it. With the cottage, he saw everything burning down—his hopes, his wishes and his love.

Vishnu felt guilty for what had happened, but then, it wasn't his fault. Someone had to be the harbinger of such bad news. People had gathered around on seeing the fire. Soon, there was smoke rising from the part of the cottage that had caught fire and people were scuttling out of it. Indra sat alone, staring at the ashes—the ashes of his love and desire. He couldn't bring himself to believe what he had just heard.

How could Guruji marry Ahalya?—this was the only thought that kept echoing in his mind till he could no longer bear it. He entered the remains of his cottage and found a vat of soma in a corner. He lifted the vat and put its edge to his lips, and drank and drank...

The Day After

The next day, Indra woke up with a heavy head. He realized that he had had too much soma and was barely able to walk. The stench of burned rugs and curtains was still heavy in his partially burned cottage. He staggered up and managed to sit against a wall. He realized that he had sprawled on the floor all night. His eyes were heavy and he could feel the dried tears near his eyes. His garments were stained with soma and, soon, the events of the previous night came to him clearly.

He realized the import of Vishnu's news, which reminded him that he had invited Vishnu for dinner but there had been no dining that night. Indra gathered himself reluctantly, cleaned himself and changed into fresh clothes. Then, he sent for Vishnu, as he was keen to know more. He still wasn't aware of how and why Ahalya had to marry her father. The very idea was nauseating for Indra.

The attendant came back with the news that Vishnu was not in his cottage. He seemed to have left. 'When?' demanded Indra.

'Not sure, but someone saw him leave in the morning,' the attendant replied.

'Morning? How early?' wondered Indra, realizing that he had woken up very late—it was well past afternoon.

Indra was angry and frustrated. While he was disappointed that Vishnu had left without meeting him, it was not Vishnu that bothered him, but Ahalya. What could have happened? What could be the reason for her marrying Guruji? Why and how did she consent to such an unimaginable arrangement?

While Indra was aware that Guruji wasn't Ahalya's biological father, the world knew it, but what was a man who brought up a girl since her childhood, if not her father? How could he have married Ahalya? What about her? Did she consent to this or was she forced into it? Questions shot across his mind like stars in the dark sky. It was getting unbearable for him. Indra drank soma straight from the vats. He did not have the patience to pour it into goblets nor did he think that goblets could be of any help.

Indra stepped out of his cottage, feeling frustrated, dejected and heartbroken. He was disturbed and couldn't understand what to make of the whole thing. The joy of the victory over Vritra had been long forgotten. He could battle demons, but he was unable to battle this rejection. *Rejection?* Well, sort of. Indra had hoped that he would soon go back to the gurukul and seek Ahalya's hand in marriage. Now, he had learned that all this while, she had been married to Guruji. If this was not a rejection, what was? But Ahalya? How could she?

Indra had to meet her. He kept walking towards the horizon, staggering on his way, not knowing where he was going. Indra was lost in thought and his personal tragedy. He had to meet her, he had to know why she married a man who was like a father to her.

Indra and Ahalya

It was still dark when Indra reached the gurukul. The sun was fast asleep and would not wake up for quite a few hours. Guruji usually left early for his morning ablutions. Indra stood behind a thick tree, waiting for Guruji to emerge from his cottage. It was dark outside and the world was sleeping. He had to meet Ahalya alone to know what had transpired. He would not confront Guruji without knowing the facts.

Soon, the door of the cottage opened. In the faint light, he could see her, a dark silhouette of a woman handing over his pot and clothes, before the old man headed for the river. The door closed and the light was imprisoned in the cottage, much like the girl he loved.

Indra waited for Guruji to be well past the cottage. This wait was longer than eternity for Indra. Convinced that the old man was gone, Indra tiptoed towards the cottage, his heart pounding away for the world to hear and pushed the door slightly. Ahalya was on the cot, in one corner, and woke up with a start and said, 'Is there something you forgot—'. She stopped mid-sentence when she saw the huge frame in the door. She recognized the shadow. She knew that body, the smell of that body, she knew that heartbeat.

Ahalya ran towards Indra and embraced him, 'Where had you been? Where had you been?' she demanded, tears streaming down her cheeks. She was beating him with her delicate fists and crying uncontrollably. Indra stood there, motionless, letting his silence speak for itself. He felt her heart pound against his chest and the sheer warmth of her body awakened his emotions and passions. Indra closed the door behind him and brought her to the cot.

Ahalya was inconsolable and nothing could stop her tears. Indra cradled her face in his hands and lifted it to look into her eyes. They were sad and telling the tragic story of a girl who had been tied to an old oak tree, a goat sacrificed in the fire of yajnas and oblations to an unknown god. The constant flow of tears stemmed for him. Indra could not help himself; he kissed her eyes as she closed them—not to stop the tears but to feel the warmth of her soft eyes, something she had not known or experienced in her cold, distant marriage. This was the moment she had waited for all her youth, which was now being wasted in serving an old man's quest for knowledge and enlightenment.

Ahalya craved for the human touch and warmth of a man. She wanted her flesh to be worshipped as a temple and not as a ritual. She wanted warm hands to feel her and treat her body as a musical instrument and not as the pages of an old scripture. She wanted to moan and cry out loud in the pain of joy and ecstasy. She no longer wanted to be muffled in a union that was yet another chore, laid down as per the norms in the pages of some old scriptures; that was not a celebration of love. Ahalya was a young woman trapped in a cold marriage and Indra's warmth melted the moments of pain away. He took her in his arms and the two were lost—lost to the world, lost to reason and lost to societal norms.

The flickering flame of the lamp saw two bodies melt into one, desperate for love, breaking the silence of the hour with passionate moans, rebelling against the norms of the world, breaking the rules of matrimony, throwing caution to the wind.

The solitary flame in the room chose to extinguish itself, lest it be called to witness the passionate moments. It was unsure of what it saw and heard.

Regardless of their context, the world hates transgressions.

The Curse

Sage Gautama was on his way to the river, the moon shone brightly, as if it was only trying to show him the way.

Suddenly, he stopped to see a snake sitting in his way. He had seldom seen snakes in this area and was rather surprised to find one. Besides, sighting a snake had a deeper meaning. He was wondering if he should see it as a message or simply ignore it. The snake seemed to have felt the approaching footsteps and reluctantly moved away into the bushes. He decided to ignore the sighting and moved along, though the thought could not be banished from his mind.

He had barely taken a few steps ahead, when he saw another snake. This was really unusual and he stopped. The snake was staring at him from a distance, as if it was waiting for him. The sage felt that ignoring the first one had been a mistake, and not taking its message had made it reappear. But what was it trying to convey? What was it trying to hint at, if at all?

While he had ignored the first sighting, the second one, which was an extremely unusual happening, sure did indicate that he was making some mistake and that he should not proceed further. He seemed to be on the wrong path. He was forced to rethink. Just what was he doing wrong in what had been his practice for ages? He has never sighted snakes in such a quick succession before. Besides, sighting a snake indicated a change. What was going to change and how?

He took it as a divine ordain and retraced his steps back home—a decision that was going to be fatal—*fatal for whom*?

Sage Gautama had barely reached his cottage, when he noticed that the door was ajar and in the faint light from the distance, he could see the huge frame of a man emerge. The reluctance of this man confused him and before he could raise an alarm, he noticed Ahalya trying to distance herself from the man. She was unable to pull herself away from him. What was this? Ahalya was seeing someone in his absence and that too at this hour?

The sage rushed towards his cottage and before anybody could realize it, he was right in front of them, catching both of them unaware. Ahalya immediately distanced herself from the man and went inside the cottage. In the faint light of dawn, the sage was shocked to see Ahalya's dishevelled state. Her saree was barely covering her and the smudged bindi on her forehead was telling a story of sin. A sin at the *brahma-muhurta*, 'the hour of gods', the hour of *swadhyay*, of 'self-realization', wasted away on basic instincts of the animal kind and that too with another man. Sage Gautama was both ashamed and shocked to see his wife standing defiantly at a distance, offering no explanation whatsoever, not that he needed anything to be explained.

Indra stood transfixed, making no effort either, though he did seem a trifle worried for Ahalya. The sage found his voice and demanded, looking at Indra, 'What are you doing here, you shameless man?'

'I came to meet Ahalya,' Indra responded calmly.

'At this hour? Don't you have any shame? And was this just a meeting? You could have come during the day when I am around!' he bellowed. He then looked at Ahalya, 'And you! You shameless woman, will you collect yourself and make yourself more presentable or do you want to announce your sinful act to the world?'

Ahalya instinctively gathered her clothes and went inside and emerged in a few moments.

'I am shocked that this is going on behind my back.'

'That is not the case, Guruji... I only came—'

Indra began explaining, but his statement was cut off by the sage, who yelled, 'Shut up! Don't you dare call me Guruji! A man who sleeps with his gurupatni cannot be my student.'

'Gurupatni?' asked Indra aloud.

'Why? Didn't anybody tell you that she is my wife?' asked the sage.

'No, Guruji, I didn't know that the girl who had been your daughter for so long has now become your wife!' Indra responded defiantly.

'Indra!' shouted the sage. 'You dare not comment on matters divine and beyond your understanding. Base men such as you would never understand divine ordains.'

'Divine ordains? Or is it just lust, Guruji? Marrying a girl who was your daughter till the day before your sudden marriage is now a divine ordain? Aren't you even ashamed of yourself? What kind of an example are you setting for your students and society?' Indra demanded.

'Society? What do *you* know about society? People like you don't make society. It's my kind who makes society and makes norms for society. I don't need to take lessons from you and your kind.'

'Go fight wars, Indra, that's your role! Leave society and its norms for sages like us.'

'So that you can do what you like? Make norms to suit you and spoil the lives of innocent girls? Cast away innocent lives to servitude? Continue your lustful ways under the guise of scriptures? Throw young girls' lives away, reduce them to a meaningless existence? Shame on you, Guruji! Shame on you!'

'You dare not speak to me like that in my house…and,' he paused to look at Ahalya, '…that too after doing the unmentionable in *my* house, with *my* wife!' the sage threatened, shivering in anger. 'I will not have you here a moment longer.'

'I don't want to stay here, in this prison where innocent lives are sacrificed in the beds of old men,' Indra scoffed. Looking at Ahalya, he added, 'Come with me, Ahalya. You don't belong here. You deserve better.'

'Ahalya! You dare not move from there. I am not letting this unholy liaison become a norm in society,' the sage commanded, coming in between them, stopping Indra from advancing any further.

Ahalya did not move an inch but stared defiantly at the sage, hurting his feelings.

Indra looked at Ahalya and exclaimed, 'Ahalya! Come with me. I can assure you; he can do nothing. You are mine and I am not going to let you stay in this dungeon with this sick man!'

'Sick man? I curse you, Indra! You will be sick and will suffer from a debilitating disease, which will never allow you to touch another woman in your life!' Sage Gautama raged, sprinkling a few drops of water from his pot on Indra.

A shocked Indra stood there motionless. He knew a curse uttered by Sage Gautama was potent. Ahalya was shocked and pain was writ large on her face. She moved towards Indra, but the sage's voice stopped her.

'Ahalya! I curse you to a stony inertness. You will lead a meaningless existence, standing mute testimony to your sin so the world knows what happens to women who look beyond their husbands. A life without a husband is a life without meaning,' the sage thundered, sprinkling some water from his pot on her.

Ahalya stood motionless, shocked at the words uttered by the sage, her husband, her father. However, somewhere in the recesses of her heart, she was happy. She had experienced love, even if only once. Moreover, she wouldn't have to share her bed with her father any more.

Stony Inertness

Time stopped. It had just witnessed an event that would be recalled time and time again. Life would never be the same for anybody from that moment onwards. Generations would recall this event as an example of the ultimate transgression.

What everyone seemed to miss about this incident, though, was that a woman, who had been wronged earlier, had been wronged yet again. No one saw the pain and unhappiness in her life and her destiny. From being created to break the arrogance of a celestial maid, to being brought up by an old sage, to being married off to the same man who raised her, to displaying impeccable sexual restraint as a partner, to being cursed to stony inertness for attaining sexual fulfilment for the first time in her life, Ahalya had endured it all. And ultimately, she had been framed as the fallen woman to teach the world a lesson.

Some would say that she had made a mistake; others would say that she had done it on purpose and curse her; still others would hail her; but no one will know what she had felt. No one will know her views on her action. No one ever felt the need to ask her. She was simply cursed to be a stone and stones don't speak.

However, if such stones did speak, they would tell a bitter truth—a truth that could change the course of the life of women who were born to serve undeserving men. Such stones would cry in anguish and shed tears of blood for the way women's lives were predetermined without anyone asking them what they desired. Such stones would shout in pain for being the first and only creatures on earth to be ruled by men, making women examples of virtues based on the standards set by men to benefit themselves.

If stones could speak, they would tell many a story of unholy alliances in the bed, shameful lusty liaisons in the name of holy matrimony, thrust upon women under the guise of norms and rules made by men to safeguard their positions in society and, of course, their beds. Some would be eulogized for sacrifices as defined by men and some would be slammed for the smallest of misdemeanours ordained by the same men.

Such stones would also have pointed out how similar misdemeanours by men—their transgressions and sins—had been overlooked. They would help men recall the numerous errors of those who made the norms of this world, and reveal how they would never be made examples of unacceptable behaviour. Their bad behaviour would be considered an exception or an error in their judgement. Such stones would point out the double standards prevalent in society, repeated across cultures and regions for generations.

But stones don't speak and they don't feel. Their inertness stops them from rebelling, speaking up and breaking their silence. They continue to be silent spectators to the transgressions of the 'upholders of social norms', the learned, who are often the most illiterate when it comes to understanding the inner recesses of women's hearts.

Time wept silent tears upon witnessing this tragedy—the tragedy in which an innocent soul lost her existence. The tragedy of a woman who felt fulfilled for the first time in her life only for it to be the last time she ever felt anything at all! A tragedy where a woman was made the scapegoat in the fight for supremacy between two classes—the warriors and the sages. A tragedy where harsh punishments were meted out just to set an example for future generations and not once was the concerned individual asked about her wishes. A tragic event that would be told and retold for all the wrong reasons for generations to come.

However, time was happy about one thing—the woman was beyond all feelings now, for stones don't feel. Thank God for small mercies, as they say!

The Heartbreak

Indra reached his cottage in the middle of the night. He had been feeling sick and weak on the way. In the darkness of the night, he quaffed a few goblets of soma and tried to sleep but it evaded him. His body was crying for rest while his heart was crying for Ahalya. He wasn't sure if what had happened between them was right or wrong, but he knew one thing—that both of them had responded to their emotions, which had been true and heartfelt.

The tiredness of his body took over the grief in his heart. Indra slept off without realizing it.

The next morning, he woke up with immense body ache. He was burning up with fever and had broken out in hives all over his body. He was terrified of what was happening to him. Soon, the Ashwins were summoned and so were the other elders of the community. Mitra was the first to respond.

The Ashwins diagnosed that this was a debilitating disease and a cure would have to be found soon, before it consumed Indra's body. They also mentioned that this was more of an unnatural condition and less of an ailment that could be cured with their usual concoctions. However, they were unable, or rather unwilling, to say how this condition was different.

Mitra asked everybody to leave the cottage, so that he could spend some time alone with Indra to understand if he had anything to say. When everybody had left, Indra told Mitra everything that had happened the previous day at the gurukul. Mitra was both shocked and angry at Indra but decided to keep quiet and not add to his woes. Besides, he had to think of a way out of this, and soon, as Indra was in real pain.

The Ashwins were called in and Mitra shared some part of what he had heard. They immediately confessed that they had suspected that it was a sage's curse. They felt that the only cure for such a condition would be with Sage Gautama himself. Just as an antidote is made out of the poison itself, in this case, too, only the sage who had cursed Indra could cure him. However, they added that something had to be done soon, as the hives were spreading fast. Indra was also likely to take time to heal because he seemed mentally disturbed about something as well.

Mitra decided to go and meet Sage Gautama in his gurukul. He took Vayu with him, who could be trusted to keep matters to himself. Mitra also remembered Vishnu, who had been with Indra at the gurukul, and sent word to him to meet them at the gurukul. Leaving Indra in the charge of the Ashwins, the two of them left immediately to meet Sage Gautama.

Mitra and Vayu met Vishnu and apprised him about Indra. Vishnu felt responsible for what had happened, as he had given Indra the news of Ahalya. While Mitra was angry, he also understood that Vishnu couldn't be blamed for the same. All three of them decided to meet the sage at his cottage and convince him to help Indra.

When Sage Gautama saw the three of them, he knew why they were there. The sage was boiling in rage and, initially, he didn't want to listen to anything any of them had to say. On being egged on by Mitra, Vishnu managed to convince the sage to listen to them. Mitra narrated Indra's condition, which obviously didn't come as a surprise to the sage. He had meant for Indra to be in pain and had no regrets whatsoever.

'Guruji, while I do understand that what Indra did was

sinful, but you know him—how impulsive and hot-headed he is. He didn't mean to do what he did. Besides, he regrets his act and has sent his apologies,' lied Mitra.

Sage Gautama looked straight at Mitra and said, 'You are right, I know him well. Rather too well to know that he would never apologize. He doesn't know that language.'

Mitra looked embarrassed. 'Guruji, he is your student and, thus, a son. As a father, I am sure you will overlook his behaviour. He is in immense pain—'

'He ought to be,' the sage cut Mitra off, 'after the pain and insult inflicted on me. The sin! It's unmentionable. I wouldn't pardon my own for this!'

Mitra tried again, 'Guruji, he is our chief and we can't afford to lose him at this stage, when our society is going through so much change. He is dear to all and our community needs him right now. You can't punish an entire community for a personal transgression. Please, Guruji, help him.'

Vishnu pleaded, 'Guruji, he was your favourite student. For old times' sake, please...'

'Exactly! He *was* my favourite student and that is why the hurt is more. Besides, what he has committed is a sin, it's not just a mistake, and sins cannot go unpunished or else this will become commonplace and every man on the streets will resort to such acts. It's *my* duty, to stop this and nip it in the bud before such loose behaviour becomes endemic!' prophesied the sage.

Sage Gautama had clearly taken it upon himself to uphold the morals of society. 'People like me must sacrifice our own to uphold the morals of society. It's not that only he has been punished. It pained me as well to take such a severe step. For his sins, I, too, am paying a price. I am being judged by his misdemeanour. For times to come, people will judge this act, and Indra's and Ahalya's punishments will be a stark reminder of what happens when one transgresses this way.'

There was a silence and Mitra could see that the old man was venting both his anger and frustration about what had happened. The matter had already spread all around and they were being viewed with suspicion while they were on their way to the gurukul. He had also observed a number of other sages in the vicinity. This was no longer a matter of personal transgression, it was a transgression of mankind and an example was being made out of Indra and Ahalya. It had gone beyond the gurukul and the ramifications were enormous.

Mitra realized that it was time to go beyond cajoling, 'Guruji, while we do understand that what has happened has deep ramifications for the society at large, we want you to reconsider your curse, as it would become extremely untenable for us to stay together and be of help to each other henceforth if you don't.'

Guruji looked at Mitra sharply and said, 'Are you threatening me?'

Vishnu, too, was surprised by Mitra's statement.

'No, Guruji, I am not threatening, I would never do that,' but his stern tone did seem threatening.

Vishnu added, 'No, Guruji, I think he is trying to say that in a changing society, such things have no precedence, so, while it is definitely sinful, you might want to reconsider the punishment.'

Guruji was angry at Mitra, but looked at Vishnu and said, 'While your explanation is not the same as that of Mitra, you should both know that I don't like being threatened. Besides, if there is anybody who can cure him, it's me. So, such arrogance will take you nowhere.'

Mitra replied, 'It's not arrogance, Guruji. I only suggested that you reconsider, as the punishment is not in anybody's interest, although we do realize that the act was sinful.'

'But it is, Mitra, it is,' the sage refuted. 'This punishment is in the interest of mankind and future generations. It will be a norm-setter for the ages,' he argued.

Mitra realized that Sage Gautama was thinking far into the future and concluded that he had communicated enough. He would allow the silence to do the talking now. He wanted the sage to reconsider his curse, else, he was very sure that this would lead to a conflict and he would be left with no choice, but to... but to...

Vishnu could see Mitra's stance toughening, which worried him. Besides, he could see a growing schism between the two and he wasn't sure if that was good. But he felt that the best thing was to allow things to move as they did. The silence in the cottage showed the hardened stance of both the sides. Neither was budging nor withdrawing.

Mitra was very sure that he was not leaving without a cure. However, he decided to soften the expressions on his face and tried to plead once more. 'Guruji, please, we need your help...' what he did not add this time was, *just as much as you need us!*

This shift in tone made the sage take stock and realize that while Mitra was being a rebel, he could not jeopardize the future of his lot, who would need the protection offered by the likes of Mitra and Indra. What he had done to Indra would be a reminder of what the sage and his lot could do—it had been a strong display of their power, but it would be best to let it go, now that he had proved who was more powerful among them.

After a lull in the discussions, the sage got up and went inside and came back with a small bowl of a paste. 'Apply this over his hives a couple of times and he should be fine. But I can't do anything about the marks on his body, they will remain. They should remind him about his misdemeanour forever. It will also be a reminder to all mankind that sin will be punished.'

While Mitra did not like the last lines, better sense prevailed over him and he folded his hands in gratitude. The sage ignored the gesture and remained arrogantly aloof.

Having secured what they had come for, Mitra realized that they had not done enough. They had not been fair, as yet. He looked at the defiant sage and said, 'Guruji, while I must thank you for this, I have one more request.'

Vishnu looked at Mitra, wondering what more could they ask for. Vayu, too, looked at him, just as Guruji gave him a questioning look.

'Devi Ahalya, Guruji.' Mitra began feebly, 'I think you should reconsider her curse too.'

Guruji's nostrils flared, as he responded angrily, 'That's none of your problem. I don't think you have any right to speak about her.'

Vishnu realized the gravity of what Mitra had said. He folded his hands and added, 'Guruji, it would be unfair if only Indra is pardoned, when both were... I am sorry, I can't say it, but I hope you know what I mean,' fumbled Vishnu.

'Exactly!' retorted the sage, 'You can't even mention it and I have had to endure this for a lifetime!'

Vishnu offered his explanation, 'Guruji, while this is a serious offence on both their parts, not taking an impartial stance towards both would be unfair. In the future, women would blame you for being partial.'

'I don't care, Vishnu!' shouted the sage. 'I want women to be more careful than Ahalya. They are the gateways to the future and, thus, the onus of being responsible must be on them. Men will be men, but women? How can they give in to such behaviour? This single act should be a stark reminder for women to come that no matter what, they can't even let their gait slip, let alone falling to such levels!'

'Now, that is a bit unfair, Guruji,' Mitra intervened. 'For such sins both should be held equally responsible. The responsibility for this action falling only on Devi Ahalya is unfair to her. While your anger towards her is justifiable, punishing the woman more than the man seems very unfair and future generations will see this as…your…your transgression.'

Vishnu was shocked at what Mitra had just said. All eyes were on Mitra, who had matter-of-factly said what seemed to be true at that moment. Regardless, Guruji seemed adamant. However, on being further cajoled by Vishnu, his stance seemed to soften. After much contemplation, he said, 'My heart will never forgive her but, on your insistence, even if I try to reverse her curse, I can't do it. However, I can say that a time will come when a great person from your lineage, Vishnu, will bail her out of her stony inertness. He will be one of those who will right many a wrongs in his lifetime.'

Vishnu was rather taken aback to find him being made responsible, in a way, for the resurrection of his Gurupatni, which was both an honour and a serious responsibility. Although he did not know how, he thought that they had secured some relief for her and, in that moment, it seemed fair enough. He hoped the world would not judge them too badly for having tried to maintain a level of impartiality. Vishnu folded his hands and accepted the verdict.

Mitra and Vayu, who had been silent observers, got up with Vishnu to take their leave. Guruji stayed silent and did not even acknowledge their gestures. He just sat there, quietly staring at the ground. He kept wondering if he had been fair in granting some relief to his wife, Ahalya, well after they had left. He hoped that the world would be soft on him for his impartiality.

Indra after Ahalya

Indra's body healed after applying the sage's medicine a couple of times, though the scars remained and definitely affected his looks. However, he wore them with pride. What Sage Gautama might not have liked to learn was that the scars had not served their purpose. Indra never felt ashamed of what he had done, as he knew in his heart of hearts that he had not been wrong. The defiant look in Ahalya's face when they had been confronted had convinced him further that she, too, never felt sorry for what had happened.

However, Indra did feel sorry for what had happened to Ahalya and if there was one reason he still wanted to go back to the gurukul, notwithstanding Sage Gautama's ire, it was her. However, Mitra had forced him to swear that he would never go there again and that Mitra's word needed to be honoured. After all, Indra was aware that Mitra had personally gone there and secured his cure. He was also grateful to Vishnu, who had gone along with the others and tried to convince the old man. Indra wanted to make sure to thank him too.

This incident had ensured that Indra started disliking the sages in general. While Indra had never quite liked or respected them, as he felt that they took undue advantage of their knowledge of the scriptures, he was aware of the growing influence of these people on the populace. He wasn't comfortable with this, as he knew that they were misusing their knowledge. While some made good use of it, he felt that the majority were spreading fear through their awareness of the scriptures, which, of course, had been written by them or their ilk.

The society was growing oddly. While the sages were dependant on the ruling class for their sustenance and affairs, they seemed to think that they were superior to all. While it was obvious that they couldn't do without the ruling folks, they still tried to control the rulers. This unique position of the sages often ended up being the main cause of trouble between the two classes. It was neither possible to give in to them nor to let them be. Indra was aware that, with time, this conflict was only going to grow and his earlier hatred towards some of them was going to generalize to nearly all of them. After all, they had survived because of the protection and patronage of the ruling class and, yet, here they were, trying to control the rulers.

Indra often found it frustrating that some of them claimed that the wars had been won because of their yajnas and oblations. Such rumours had already been met with vehement opposition by Indra in quite a few forums where he had heard them, but then he couldn't be everywhere. Sage Brihaspati was being hailed for all the 'efforts' he had undertaken during the war with Vritra and paeans were being sung of Sage Dadhichi for sacrificing his life to give Indra the Vajra. While Indra sure acknowledged the sacrifice of Sage Dadhichi, giving all the credit of the victory to the dead sage was not something that was acceptable to Indra. The sages had been helpful because it was a part of their responsibility towards society, especially when they depended on the ruling class and the others, in general, to protect them.

Indra was also aware that his fame was spreading far and wide. He was being hailed as a hero and a saviour of the people and, in some places, people had even started worshipping him. While it was a great feeling to be loved and revered for all that he had done for his people, he was also aware that this hadn't quite happened before. With no precedence of such behaviour, he was often weary about this kind of hero-worship by his people who were simpletons. He worried about the responsibility that came with fame.

Indra's popularity was also something that made the sages uncomfortable. While he was brave and they needed his strength to sustain themselves, they were worried that worshipping Indra might not be to their advantage. The sages felt that people were simpletons, who fell for the display of Indra's physical strength. It was important to impress upon them that the strength of the scriptures was of prime importance. This needed to be done without letting people get too close to the secrets of the scriptures because this was fast becoming the sages' area of expertise. These sages, feeble and old, were a small, closed group that had mastered the scriptures and they knew one thing—knowledge was going to be key to long-lasting success in the changing society. Physical strength could be replaced and found in many but knowledge should be restricted to a few.

Indra was aware of the growing importance of these people, and while he hated it, he knew he couldn't be everywhere. He had to look after the expansion of his area since that was how his society would grow. He was aware of many more tribes trying to establish their reign across different parts of the world. Such competing tribes needed to be thwarted, lest they threaten him and his folks.

There were moments when he missed Ahalya and felt guilty about how little he could do about the state she was in—whatever and wherever she was. Indra had taken to excessive consumption of soma, leading to a significant dependence on it. He was often reminded that too much of anything, even if it be good, could be counterproductive. However, Indra had realized that he couldn't do without it, especially when memories overwhelmed him. Quaffing goblets of soma helped him overcome his increasingly frequent bouts of grief and gave him the strength to fight them.

Indra had moved to his capital city, Amravati, which was like an oasis of wonder in a desert. It was one of the most beautiful cities in the entire universe and many came from far and wide to witness its grandeur and opulence. Indra's palace was one of the most beautiful structures. He had hired musicians and dancers from across the world to entertain him. This helped him forget the past—which he wanted to shut in some inner recesses of his heart—overcome his inner sadness and revel in the present. He had the best of everything in his city and palace. The people, too, loved him and respected his power and the grandeur.

Indra was now Devendra, the king of all kings, and his new abode added to his grandeur. However, no king is complete without a queen. The sages would continuously remind him to find a wife because that was the norm for every individual and he, too, must take a wife and fulfil his individual role. Indra, too, had been feeling lonely and finally agreed to get married.

Shachi: The Indrani

The name and fame of Indra and his community had spread far and wide. The chief of a tribe without a queen was the target of many a father! Mitra and others, too, thought that it would be a good idea for Indra to settle down with a partner, put Ahalya behind and move on.

After the experience with Ahalya and its consequences, Indra had taken to drinking soma and was often found alone, staring blankly into space. His interest in matters pertaining to his people was often chequered. He was found missing, both physically and emotionally, even in crowds. While this was understood, it could not be sustained.

Many women vied for Indra's attention. Some were daughters of sages, were Danavas and Daityas. While none could hold Indra's interest for long, some were not even noticed, though many of them were quite beautiful. Unfortunately, Indra ended up comparing them all with Ahalya and, thus, every one of them faded in comparison. The incomparable beauty and simplicity of Ahalya was unmatched in the big world. But then she was gone and it made no sense to think of her all the time, reasoned many people who knew Indra's inner turmoil.

Indra, too, deep inside, had made peace with Ahalya's absence from his life and the sad predicament of her existence, or rather, non-existence. While the guilt did overwhelm him at times, soma came to the rescue. To avoid this dependency and excessive indulgence of soma, he would escape to his secret grove for some solitude; a place where no one judged him and he could be with himself.

It was during one such visit that he noticed a woman walking with a slow gait towards the mango grove. She seemed to be oblivious of anybody's presence and had never been sighted before. Indra was intrigued by this woman, who seemed to be strolling all by herself, with nobody in sight. She seemed to be humming to herself and her gait had something about it. He kept staring at her till she vanished deep inside the grove.

Indra decided to follow her. He walked softly and was soon inside the grove. He saw her sitting under the shade of a tree, still humming to herself, oblivious to the fact that she had been followed. Indra noticed her voluptuous figure and thick, long hair. She was quite big but nubile and she looked up at him.

When she noticed Indra, she got up in a huff and straightened her dress, which was barely staying on her. Indra couldn't help but stare at her. Her big eyes and dark skin, coupled with smell of ripe mangoes in the air, was intoxicating. He found her hesitation, mingled with fearlessness, attractive. She was constantly adjusting her dress, which when pulled from one end, revealed another.

Indra was standing right in front of the woman. There was silence and neither of them spoke. Both knew what they wanted in that moment. There was hunger in their eyes. Her luscious lips and voluptuous figure were inviting and she was making no moves to dispel any ideas Indra may have. There was no fear or resistance in her eyes and Indra read that correctly. She didn't seem unnecessarily coy nor was she willing to put up that pretence.

'I am Indra.'

'I know...rather, who doesn't?'

'What are you doing here, in *my* amra-kunj?'

'Yours? Oh! I am sorry, I didn't know it was yours...'

she responded with momentary concern. After regaining her composure, she added, 'I was pulled here by the aroma of the place...' She left the sentence unfinished.

A leaf moved, causing a thin ray of the sunlight to fall on her eyes, which twinkled in the light. The breeze blew strands of hair on her face.

Indra moved closer to her and pulled some of the strands away with his finger to get a good look at her face. She didn't object, but the touch of his finger made her shiver. She withdrew a few steps but was stopped by a tree trunk. She stood there, her eyes half closed. Indra advanced towards her, emboldened by the woman's acceptance of his move. A gush of wind blew her upper garment and she tripped while trying to stop it, landing in Indra's arms, who held her at the right time and stopped her from falling.

Shivers ran down her spine and she closed her eyes. Indra had had enough soma already and with the heady aroma in the air, he couldn't control himself. Rather, there was no need to, as the woman, yet unknown to him, also seemed to not want him to control himself.

Their lips met and, soon, so did their bodies. A few leaves fell on their bodies, as if trying to cover them as best as they could. The breeze blew away the heaving and moaning and no one knew what had happened in the grove.

After what seemed to be hours of passionate lovemaking, the woman tried to gather her clothes around her. Indra kept watching her every move. Adjusting her garments over her, she said, 'I am Shachi, the daughter of Daitya Puloman.'

Indra smiled and responded, 'Shachi, that's a beautiful name.'

Shachi smiled and looked straight at him. He liked her lack of coyness and her frank and bold attitude. 'Will Puloman be upset with...with what just happened?' he asked gesturing at both of them.

Shachi smiled. 'Will that matter to you? Besides, nothing happened by force.'

Indra was impressed by her forthrightness and honesty. And then, out of the blue, staring straight at her, he asked, 'Will you be my queen?'

Shachi seemed a trifle surprised. 'Your queen?'

'Yes, you heard me right, my queen,' said Indra without taking his eyes off her. He was observing every bit of her; clearly he hadn't had enough of her—not yet. He suddenly pulled her back to him. She barely managed to say 'yes', before their lips met again.

This time, the breeze had to blow harder to muffle the even louder heaving and moaning!

Elsewhere in the World

The world was growing and more and more people were being added to this ever-expanding, beautiful world. However, size begets differences, differences beget choices, choices beget preferences and preferences beget selection and rejection. The people of the world were getting increasingly used to choosing—choosing what suited them and choosing what was relevant to them.

While Indra was ruling the world, it was dependent on his benevolence. He took care of his people and they, in turn, celebrated life under him. All was well and people literally worshipped him for the bountiful rains and abundance of fertile growth everywhere. However, times were changing without anybody realizing it. As they say, while the sun sets somewhere, it rises elsewhere. This was natural but not many things were as natural as this.

Indra's queen, Shachi, also referred to as Indrani, was widely accepted and respected. Many felt that she had steadied Indra's restlessness and the edginess. She brought the much-needed stability and sincerity to him, something that was critical for a king who was ruling what seemed like the world.

Many things were happening at different places on earth. Births and deaths took place regularly. Once upon a time, Amravati, the abode of Indra, had been the world, but the earth had expanded far and wide, as had the reign of Indra. This vastness brought its own problems, so did the lack of wars.

While Indra had waged many wars, his fame and might had

spread far and wide. There were few who disagreed with him and, thus, accepted his supremacy. This meant that there had been no wars for long...rather too long now.

Indra's palace had been a subject of envy for everybody. It was rumoured that he had beautiful damsels entertaining him and his friends. They were beautiful maidens, who only existed for his entertainment—they were called apsaras, the women who excelled in entertainment, who belonged to no one in particular but to all! They were skilled in many art forms, which focussed on the sensuous pleasures of life. They were ably accompanied by the gandharvas, who were the best, most trained musicians in the world. Together, the apsaras and gandharvas were a class apart when it came to dance and music—the greatest entertainers ever known.

Indra's palace was a wonder of wonders. It was unimaginably large, spacious and airy. It had tall ceilings, numerous pillars and hundreds of rooms. It was something many had never seen. Many couldn't even imagine the luxury, opulence and the grandeur of the place. The central dance hall, which was also the court of Indra, was a space, or rather a region, in itself. Music was always playing in the court and soma flowed freely! The palace was surrounded by a garden, which housed the best, often unique, flora.

With the lack of wars and everything going well, Indra had taken to soma—rather, he had become dependent on it. Apsaras, music, dance and soma seemed to have become the centre of Indra's life. It seemed he could not do without any of them. But then, nobody was complaining either. If one prayed to him for anything, he was there to respond and take it up as his task—he would always oblige.

It was rumoured that a woman whose husband could not beget children had been obliged with Indra's child. It was the queen of Hastinapur, living in the foothills of the mountains, away from the kingdom and the queen, who had prayed to Indra for a child. Interestingly, the husband had been aware of this and had not objected to the liaison. The child, the sages said, would go on to become a very handsome and intelligent warrior when he grew up. Well, the woman was rumoured to have prayed to others, too, for more children, but then Indra was not jealous of the others. However, one day, he would be proud of this son of his.

Indra also had sons from his wife, Indrani. He was the proud father of Jayanta, Chitragupta and others. He was proud of them all. Along with a family, he had acquired new possessions as well. His horse had been replaced with a beautiful elephant, Airavat, the white elephant, who was the envy of many. Indra loved his new-found elephant and often stepped out astride it.

The society, too, was changing. People were now divided into groups and classes, based on their professions. The sages and the learned people were, of course, at the top and the most important in the society, followed by people who were entrusted with the security and administration of the society. They often worked hand in hand with the sages, though the latter felt that they were the first among equals. After these two was the business community, who took care of the trade, commerce and finances of society. They would often fund small wars and battles, if needed, besides employing ordinary people in various capacities. The fourth class included people that did the menial jobs of sanitation and cleaning the society. There were rumours that this segment of the society was beginning to feel oppressed. While this was being cited as a good way of life and segregation based on the division of labour, the fourth class, assigned menial jobs, felt discriminated against. A kind of power play was beginning to develop and the division of labour seemed to have become a hierarchy, where the power ran top-down.

Indra had started warming up to the importance the sages had acquired over a period of time, which he had detested earlier. There seemed to be an unsaid truce between the two. The sages wouldn't try to undermine Indra's position and he wouldn't overlook their significance in society, which was growing alarmingly quickly. Indra couldn't be everywhere for everybody. Besides, Indra understood that the sages needed attention and a regular supply of things for their yajnas and sacrifices. He would arrange for a regular supply of cattle and whatever else they needed and they would return the favour by not bothering him. The sages also continued to sing paeans to the glory and importance of Indra to mankind and impressed upon the ordinary mortals the relevance of Indra being at the helm of this kingdom.

So, things couldn't have been better. There was no trouble anywhere. But then, as they say, no trouble is always the beginning of trouble...

Far, far away, in the darkness of the night, a woman gave birth to a dark boy in a dungeon. Palace intrigues and matters unfathomable to many took him away from his parents across the river Yamuna, to a family of cowherds. This boy was being brought up as a cowherd and his name was Krishna. Strange stories were being heard about him—things like he had killed some demon by suckling her to death. He had also apparently thrown a many-headed serpent which had terrorized the region, out of a river. While it was hard to believe that a child had accomplished such feats, they were much spoken about. Besides all this, there was a certain charm about the child, which, too, was being discussed far and wide. However, none of these *insignificant stories* reached Indra, as he didn't have time for such fancies of life!

Part 3

The Fall

Indrotsav

Vasu was a king known for his bravery and benevolence towards his people. They loved him and he was in the good books of both the sages and Indra. Vasu, having won enough accolades and found happiness in life, wanted to renounce everything and embrace asceticism. With this, he started doing penance to please the gods.

When Indra learnt about his renunciation, he went down to meet Vasu. First, Indra wondered if he had thought of his succession—who would rule his kingdom in his absence? Vasu had not thought of it and was at a loss when Indra asked him this. Neither had he thought about it nor could he identify someone to replace him.

Indra went on to convince Vasu that renunciation was for ascetics and not for rulers. 'If rulers became ascetics, then who would undertake the great task of ruling?' asked Indra. Vasu seemed to have no answer to this. 'Remember one thing, Vasu,' continued Indra, 'we rulers have a task at hand and this task cannot be given to anybody else unless he is equipped and trained by us. I have been at this for I don't know how much time now, and I don't see why I must give it all up for asceticism.' He concluded with a sense of condescension, 'Such things are for the weak, and, of course, the sages, not for strong men like you and me!'

After convincing Vasu, Indra left for Amravati but not before giving him a chariot, which could speak to the winds, and a staff to ensure his allegiance to Indra. Vasu planted the staff at an elevated place in his kingdom and decided to honour this momentous event in his life by hosting the first Indrotsav—the festival of Indra!

Back in Indra's court, a messenger said, 'The large-scale celebrations of Indrotsav were a spectacle, My Lord! There were joy, happiness and celebrations galore!' Indra was warming up to the epithet that was being added to his name—My Lord! He had long stopped telling people not to use it, as they had been doing so voluntarily.

Sitting on his grand throne, which he had raised a little higher than the others—a far cry from the days when all the seats had been at the same level—Indra was listening to his messenger, who would bring news from far and wide of the happenings around his region and often further away too. The messenger was telling him about the Indrotsav that Vasu had organized to commemorate the completion of one year of Indra's visit to him and the gifts he had received.

'My Lord, the staff you gave Vasuji, who is now called Uparichara Vasu, has been placed on a high mound, which is visible from far and wide. For the festival, it was brought down from there, decorated with colourful flags and worshipped. It represented you in your absence.' The messenger paused before continuing, 'I am told that never has such an act been done before.'

Indra looked at the messenger quizzically.

Understanding the look, the messenger smiled. 'Never before, anywhere in the region, has anybody seen something representing someone. I mean this worshipping of the staff, as if it was you—I mean using an object like the staff is like a symbol, which represents you—it is something unique.' Indra understood while the messenger continued, 'This could just be the beginning of someone praying to you and using a symbol to communicate with you. Many appreciated the idea of using a symbol to communicate, as it made more sense to them than praying to a formless being.'

'Go ahead, my friend,' said Indra. 'This indeed seems to be a new form of praying. I am sure people will get used to the idea of using an object to represent me. Maybe that's how they are able to better concentrate and communicate in my absence. Quite obviously, I can't be everywhere!' there was a tinge of pride in the last sentence.

The messenger smiled. 'You are right, My Lord, that is exactly what many out there felt when the staff was brought out ceremonially. Another new activity was the community gathering for the said occasion. It was nice to see people coming together to celebrate this festival. Homes and streets were cleaned, people decked up their houses with lamps and colourful decorations, depicting different things of your choice outside their homes.' Looking at Indra's questioning look, the messenger smiled and clarified, 'Things like your Vajra, Airavat, thunder and lightning, cows, parijat—your favourite flower—and so on.'

Indra smiled. Seeing the Sakra pleased, the messenger continued, 'That and many other things were drawn on the ground. They were so beautiful and real. In other places, there were performances, which depicted scenes from your life, like your slaying of the mighty demon, Vritra. Vasuji felt that the current generation, which has not seen or heard about it, should learn about your efforts to rid the earth of the terrible demon. You should have seen the look on the children's faces! It was unbelievable! Some even felt as if such strength could only belong to someone who was from some other world altogether.'

Indra took a big swig of his drink and kept the goblet down with a thud. 'Tell me more, my friend. What else was happening?'

asked Indra, sipping on the newly filled goblet.

The messenger smiled. 'Of course, My Lord! There was music and dance everywhere. People gathered on the seashores and celebrated there. There were small, temporary altars made there with each of them hosting some event. For example, at some altars, there were beautiful women dancing; at others, some musicians were playing music; at still others, someone was singing. All this went on late into the night...nobody wanted to go back home! The music, the cool breeze and the sounds of the waves were all so intoxicating and joyous, you had to see it to believe it...'

At that, the messenger seemed to remember something. 'Oh yes, that reminds me. During the day, when Vasuji had brought out the staff and people had been worshipping it and songs praising you were being sung, a white swan had flown in from somewhere. Seeing it, Vasuji prostrated in front of it! He had then announced that the swan was you attending the celebrations! No sooner did he utter those words than everybody out there bowed down to the swan.'

Indra was smiling a weird smile, which said less and seemed to hide more!

The messenger waited for some response, but when none was forthcoming, he went on, 'Surprisingly, the swan sat through the entire event. It seemed remarkably at ease with the happenings around it. In the end, Vasuji made some offerings on a large plate. The swan just looked at it for some time, as if it had been eating with its eyes, then looked at Vasuji and flew away. Everybody present was awestruck. Nobody could explain the sudden presence and the subsequent absence of the swan. Vasuji, however, had been nonplussed. He was very happy and satisfied that *you* had attended his celebrations!' After pausing, the messenger continued, 'After the first day, every day something or the other was going on everywhere, yajnas, community meals, processions, performances—I can go on. It's a big, month-long celebration of everything you stand for. Your people are happy and proud of you, oh Lord.'

Indra was proud too! He was glad that he had managed to stop Vasu from asceticism, which would have been the wrong path for him and would have led to him never establishing a festival in Indra's honour. With this festival, people had been made aware of his deeds and fame, far and wide. This was, in a way, the first time that there had been celebrations in his name. Indra liked the idea and felt both proud and honoured to have people celebrate him.

Indra knew that when people were happy, his work was being done well. They were the ones for whom he toiled. They were the ones who needed to be happy and he ought to work for them. Unfortunately, a lot has changed in recent times, reminisced Indra. Unlike earlier, when only the people mattered, nowadays, the emerging say of the sages had become a bit of a menace. They would keep interfering with a lot of things and many of them constantly seemed to have their feelings hurt.

He remembered how, some time back, the irascible Sage Durvasa, had gotten angry with him. This had happened because, apparently, the garland he had given Indra had fallen on the ground, and Airavat, not knowing what it was, had trampled it under his feet. The old man had taken this as an insult and cursed that all of them would lose strength. Soon, many of his people started falling sick. Indra wondered how these old men did such things!

Everybody had rushed to the sage and he had suggested a concoction, which was available only at the bottom of the ocean.

To get it out, the oceans had to be churned. Unfortunately, they had to trick the Danavas, without whose might, the churning would have been impossible. However, quite obviously, the Danavas couldn't be given a part of the concoction, known as Amrita. This had led to animosity between the Devas and Danavas and they had become sworn enemies for life.

All this just because the garland, which anyway was not something Indra would have ever worn, had been trampled by mistake! What an unnecessarily heavy price for everyone to pay, Indra thought.

Much to Indra's dislike, these sages were getting an increasing say in matters beyond their domain. But, somehow, he felt that they did know a few things, and, thus, it had become a lot riskier to ignore them. While he didn't quite like their interference, he had begun caring less and less about certain things. He had heard that they would suggest all sorts of rituals to the common people, which the poor people would comply with. However, Indra couldn't be everywhere and stop everything. Besides, if this gave people mental satisfaction, then why bother at all? And anyway, no one was complaining! Why was he even thinking about it?

Indra gulped down the last few goblets of soma in one breath. Just then, he noticed another messenger standing in a corner, not looking very pleased. Indra looked at him and noticed that he was avoiding Indra's gaze. Now, what? Indra wondered but better sense prevailed and he didn't ask him anything in front of everybody, as he was a secret messenger.

Brahma-hatya

Indra dismissed the court and decided to take a stroll in his garden, famed to have the best flowers in the world. This was also an indication for the secret messenger to follow him. Soon, the messenger, who had been following him at a distance, was close behind him. From a distance, it seemed as if a guard was walking close to Indra.

'So, what is it that you have?' asked Indra.

'I have some strange news, My Lord,' answered the messenger with a glum face.

'Go ahead, tell me,' ordered Indra without looking at him.

Such messengers were told to relate things as they heard them. They were aware that they would not face any ire, no matter what they said. So, they were trained to relate any kind of news, however unpalatable. Nonetheless, such beginnings and the glum indication ensured that they couldn't speak in public, unlike the ones who brought good news.

'I heard a few sages saying that you need to atone for your sin,' the messenger blurted.

'Sin?' Indra asked, stopping in his tracks. 'What sin?'

'The sin of killing a Brahmin.'

Indra looked at him. 'Killing a *who*?'

'Brahmin, My Lord. According to them, you have killed a Brahmin. Vritra was a Brahmin and killing a Brahmin is a grave sin. If you don't atone for that, your kingdom will have to face the wrath of your sin.'

'This is sheer nonsense!' thundered Indra. 'I have never heard anything as preposterous as that. And, by the way, why is this being raised *now*, after so many years? Have they forgotten the trouble that he had unleashed? Or is the memory faint now and it doesn't seem as dangerous as it had been?' As an afterthought, Indra added, 'And since when did they become so big that killing them was a sin? Irrespective of what they did?'

'I heard a few of them mention this and the rest nodded their heads,' relayed the messenger. He knew that the news he had just conveyed made Indra angry, but he was only doing his job as a messenger. Besides, Indra had always given him, and some others like him, the freedom to say whatever they had heard or seen. After all, they were his eyes and ears on the ground and there was no turning away from the reality.

Indra decided to head back to his sabha—the place where everyone assembled. The messenger stayed back, lest the two be seen together. He would casually stroll into the sabha later to not arouse any suspicion.

As soon as Indra reached the sabha, he sent for Sage Brihaspati, who had acquired a great position in his kingdom by now. He was consulted on several matters, something that Indra didn't quite like but had come to accept. Sage Brihaspati now represented the growing power of the Brahmins, who had made deep inroads into the masses and suggested numerous, often meaningless, rituals to them. They literally had the masses eat out of their palms—something Indra detested, but then he couldn't be everywhere! Indra had found himself thinking that he couldn't be everywhere frequently and wondered if this had become an excuse or if it was, indeed, the reality. Sage Brihaspati was busy at some yajna, which were quite common. So, he sent word that he would be able to come only the next day. Indra was angry, as he needed this issue to be resolved and he hated waiting. Regardless, he decided to wait for Sage Brihaspati.

The next day, Sage Brihaspati was at the sabha. Indra met him in a separate enclosure to ensure privacy. He asked the sage if anything had been brewing against him among the sages. Brihaspati was taken aback and wondered what had prompted Indra to ask such a question. Besides, why him?

Indra did not have the patience for long discussions and that too with Sage Brihaspati, who had all the time for discourses, so, he directly came to the point, 'I have heard that your community is accusing me of *Brahma-hatya*, supposedly the grave sin of killing a Brahmin.'

'Oh, that!' said the sage.

'I mean, what exactly am I supposed to understand by that?' asked Indra, who found the sage's response quite irritating.

'Well, yes, that is true. There is a growing feeling among the Brahmins that your "crime" should be acknowledged and atoned for,' the sage stated matter-of-factly.

'Crime? Did you say crime?' Indra asked, his voice rising. 'Did you not tell them that it was a necessity? Could we have survived without killing him, given the circumstances?'

'Yes, I agree, but—'

The sage tried to explain feebly before Indra cut him off, 'But what, Rishivar? But what?'

'Well, no matter what the provocation, killing a Brahmin is a grave sin, indeed,' replied the sage.

'Irrespective of the gravity of *his sins*—I mean the Brahmin's sins?' Indra asked surprised. 'Besides,' he added, 'did you not tell them that you were party to it?'

Sage Brihaspati turned sharply to face Indra, 'Are you accusing me of this sin?'

'Well, I guess I am,' replied Indra. sipping soma. 'Can you

deny your role in helping me? For that matter, for quite some time to come, you even went on to say that Vritra was killed with your help.'

'You can't rope me in your sin. I, like the others, was only doing my duty,' the sage defended himself.

'And I was going on a killing spree to satiate my bloodlust, is it?' Indra demanded in rage. The sage was also seething in anger but decided to let Indra calm down. 'Sage Brihaspati, I can sense the change in the direction of the wind and I find you changing with it. Realities don't change and truths don't change, you might,' said Indra provocatively, infuriating the sage.

'Are you accusing me of conspiring against you?' the sage challenged.

'I am telling you that you are keeping quiet when you should not be. You should be telling those idiots who are spreading canards about this Brahma-hatya that it was no sin but the need of the hour. You should tell them about the grave conditions of that time,' Indra paused, 'and also that you were actively involved in that act.'

The sage did not like the tone of Indra's statements and hated his name being dragged into this. While it was true that he had also been involved in the battle, he was also sure that he had not been directly involved in the act of killing Vritra. To the sage, it was time to make one thing very clear: no matter how grave the sins of Brahmins may be, they can't be killed. With Vritra and his kind away, the recent sages were never going to rebel the way Vritra and his allies had. So, such a blanket rule would go a long way in ensuring the safety and significance of the Brahmins. Sage Brihaspati was going to fight for it and not leave any stone unturned, irrespective of the price he would have to pay. Needless to say, there weren't too many around to vouch for the fact that he had voluntarily participated in the battle, though not directly!

Sage Brihaspati looked at Indra and said, 'I will tell them what I want to tell them and I suggest you stop telling me what to do. You rule, but we make the rules for society. You rule over physical areas, we rule over the minds of the people. You make them fear your might and we make them fear for their destiny. You *try* telling them what to do and we tell them what to do and see the results.'

Indra was aghast. Since when did this sage grow those invisible fangs, which were being bared at him? Since when did this man become more dangerous than the evil Vritra? When did he and his ilk become so powerful? Since when did the sages become the new evil? Just what had he missed here?

'Be ready to atone, *My Lord*!' said the sage. 'What was just doing the rounds as a feeling is now going to be an overwhelming tide against you!' were his last words before he left without being dismissed.

Indra was left in the enclosure, shocked. He had never seen such strength of words emanating from such a weak-looking old man. There was something in the way he said what he did. There was a power of a different sort, which he had not witnessed or felt earlier. He knew this was dangerous. The evil power of Vritra had been defeatable, but this seemingly evil power was going to be tough to destroy.

Indra was left there, quaffing goblets after goblets of soma, unable to solve this menace or find a way out of it.

The Replacement

Vritra was history. Times had changed and Indra wasn't sure if they had changed for good or bad. Active combat was a part of the distant past—things were different now. Besides, Indra was beginning to think that some battles were just not worth fighting.

After much thought, Indra decided to atone for his sin of killing Vritra. After deliberating, it was decided that he would go away to some secluded place and repent till he was rid of the 'evil' of brahma-hatya, much to his and Indrani's displeasure. She had been shocked to hear about the new developments and was surprised to see how Indra had given in to the pressures of penance. She was beginning to feel that something was amiss if Indra had decided to 'atone' for something that had been laudable all this while. Just when and how did this change happen?

Indra's atonement led to another issue, which had not been reckoned with. If Indra left for the atonement, who would rule in his absence? How would the system run on its own? There wasn't a replacement for Indra. They needed another Indra! Just how was that possible? Whoever had heard of replacing Indra? Somebody would have to take charge, but who? This was the main issue.

It was the sages who suggested the name of a king—Nahush—who could replace Indra till he was back.

'Nahush? Just who on earth is Nahush?' asked Indra.

'Nahush? My Lord, he is a very brave and able king of a small kingdom,' said the representative sage who had suggested the name on the sages' behalf. 'He is a glowing symbol of the family of Chandravanshis, the race that traces its origins to Chandra, the moon!' added the sage.

'Oh really? The moon!' exclaimed Indra disdainfully. 'And what, may I ask, qualifies him to take my place?'

The sage did not like Indra's contempt for someone he had not even met yet, but he decided not to get provoked, as he had been adequately warned by Sage Brihaspati. 'Nahush, has many qualities to take your place, My Lord. To begin with, he is brave and his people love and respect him...much like you.' Indra noticed that the last words had been an afterthought, but he let it pass. The sage continued, 'Recently, he concluded the Rajasuya Yajna, a consecration ceremony organized for him, wherein he performed all the rituals that a king must perform. He has also been very careful and concerned about his people. What's more, his people are very happy and pleased with him. Above all, his people love and respect him.'

Somehow, Indra felt that all the praises for this man were being hurled as insults at him.

'So, you are telling me,' Indra asked the sage, 'that he is suitable to take my place because he has not "killed" a sage!'

The sage seemed to squirm in his place but didn't say anything, except, 'I was sent by Sage Brihaspati to inform you of our choice, My Lord. I don't know anything else.'

'You have done that, Rishivar. You may leave now,' replied Indra, resisting his terrible urge to physically drive him out of the court.

After everyone had left, Indrani said, 'What the sage did not tell you is that during the Rajasuya Yajna, this Nahush had distributed a lot of wealth, cows and land to the sages!'

Indra looked up astonished. 'How did you learn this, Shachi?'

'I am the queen of an efficient king, My Lord. I, too, have my eyes and ears to the ground!' Indrani responded with a smile.

Indra was proud of her. 'So, that is what makes him eligible to replace me! These...' Indra decided not to complete his statement.

Indrani noticed Indra's anger and frustration. While she was feeling bad about it, she didn't want to aggravate it. She had realized that she had to be the balancing factor in Indra's personality. She couldn't be the one to provoke him. Rather, she preferred to complement him and his behaviour. While it was going to be tough to live alone, if he atoned, it would be necessary to show a strong exterior instead of being sad.

Indrani put her hand on his shoulders. 'Can I say something?' asked Indrani. He smiled and looked at her while she continued, 'I think you should undergo this atonement and get rid of this accusation against you, even if you don't believe in it.'

Indra was wondering why she had said that. She recognized the look on his face and clarified, 'This is the first time anybody has cast aspersions on you. Your subjects need to see you want to clear yourself of this accusation. You must do this because it is important for your subjects, irrespective of whether you believe in the accusations.'

'But won't I be giving in to the unfair pressure of these people, who are now turning against me? Won't I be overlooking the fact that they had agreed to the thing that they are accusing me of?' Indra asked, taking a swig from the goblet. 'This is unfair and giving in once would also make it seem like I have bowed to their whims. It would prove me inferior to this bunch of—'

Indra felt the soft hand of his wife on his shoulders once again, 'Some battles are better not fought at all, especially when they don't matter.'

'That would be the response of a weakling,' Indra snapped.

'That would be the response of a flexible tree, which manages to weather storms by bending, rather than breaking by resisting,' countered Indrani.

Indra looked up at her. She seemed intent on urging him to undergo this atonement and get it over with. Indra was quiet and Indrani decided not to say anything, especially when she saw that he was willing to think about it.

Nahush

Soon, Indra decided to give in. The sages appointed Nahush to take over the administration of Amravati, as Indra had to be away for some time. Nahush was surprised with both the choice of the sages and the honour. The sages had promised him everything that Indra owned. He was going to be the other Indra in Amravati!

Nahush was not going to miss this opportunity to be the chosen one. He was glad that he was in the good books of the sages; his yajnas and offerings had clearly paid off, though this was not what he had ever hoped or wished for. If the sages could get him to replace Indra, even if it was for a short while, who knows, maybe they could even become the kingmakers of the future. While this was an unnerving thought, why bother now about it, when he was benefitting from their decision?

Soon, Nahush was Indra's replacement at Amravati. While Indra's decision to agree to atonement had surprised many, the idea of Indra's replacement was not very well-received by the immediate inhabitants of Amravati. However, if Indra himself was willing to give in, then who were they to resist? With the thought, soon, everyone fell in line and hoped that Nahush's time would end soon.

Nahush respected all the norms and rules of Amravati and took some time to absorb all that he was getting to know and learn. The ways of Amravati were different and he was impressed with the luxuries and joys that were at his beck and call. Soon, he was beginning to like the music and dance sessions and Indra's favourite drink, soma, was the highlight of his stay there. If this was life, then he simply didn't want to return to his region at all. He also started getting comfortable with the environment and every day was a revelation for him.

Not everyone can digest success, they say, especially those who don't deserve it. This was soon apparent when more and more people realized that Nahush used to get angry very soon and was quite rude. He would shout at people and often demean them in the court. While Indra had not been soft on people, they realized that he had seldom demeaned them. The difference between Indra and his replacement was beginning to be visible and the change was not being taken well by people around.

The taste of his misbehaviour was soon felt by those who had decided to make him replace Indra. One day, Sage Brihaspati visited the court only to find nobody there. He enquired about the absence of the court, only to be told that Nahush had decided not to hold court every day, as there was hardly any purpose for it. People were happy and everything was working fine under him and making people assemble for no reason was a waste of his time. So, he had decided that the court would be held only when necessary and that too if *he* found it necessary!

Sage Brihaspati was surprised at this new development. He asked a messenger to inform Nahush that he was waiting and wanted to speak immediately. The messenger was reluctant to do so but didn't have the courage to decline the sage's order, who was a respected visitor to the court of Indra.

The sage had to wait for an unduly long time for the messenger to return. When he did return, after the unnecessary delay, the sage was told that Nahush would not be able to come and that he should visit some other time.

'Why?' asked the rather surprised sage. When no answer was

forthcoming and the messenger decided to look at the ground rather than respond, the sage got angry and repeated, 'I asked why?'

'The Lord has said that he is resting, and...' the messenger began hesitatingly.

'And?' the sage asked loudly.

'And...' the messenger seemed to struggle with the sentence.

'Go ahead! And what?' the sage demanded, his voice reverberating across the empty court.

'And...and he has asked me to tell you that next time, please send a messenger before you come here...and not arrive unannounced. Also, it would be better if you could come on the days of the court...and not...' the messenger kept trailing off, making an effort to choose his words.

Sage Brihaspati was boiling with rage. He had never been insulted like this and that too by someone like Nahush. The nerve of that man to say whatever the messenger had just conveyed! The sage stood there, thinking for a few minutes, turned in a huff and left. The messenger stood there, alone, not knowing what was going to happen next. He just didn't want to be on the receiving end of the wrath of either parties and hoped that his Lord Indra would return soon. Things had definitely been way better when he had been around.

Nahush's Demand

While it had been quite some time since Nahush had kept Sage Brihaspati waiting and insulted him, the sage hadn't quite overcome the incident. Then, one day, the sage had a surprise visitor at his ashram.

He came out of his cottage and learnt that Indrani had come to meet him. He was both surprised and honoured by her arrival, as this was her first time visiting him. As he ushered her in with all the respect she deserved, he felt that something was amiss.

After she had settled inside the cottage, the sage noticed that she looked disturbed. She seemed worried and was hesitating to say something. The Sage asked the others to leave the cottage, looked at Indrani and said, 'What brings you here, Devi?'

Indrani looked at him and he noticed tears in her eyes. He immediately knew that it had to do with Nahush. 'Tell me, Devi. What has happened? Don't worry, nobody is listening to you other than me. What can I do for you?'

Indrani tried to regain her composure and said, 'Nahush, Rishivar, it is Nahush. I don't know how to say this...but he is quite a nuisance...'

Sage Brihaspati knew that he was right. 'What has he done?' he asked directly. He noticed some hesitation on the part of Indrani, so he egged her on, 'Go ahead, Devi, tell me what that... what has he done?'

Indrani wiped a tear from the corner of her eye and said, 'He...he wants me to...to marry him!'

'What?' the Sage nearly shouted. 'What did you say?'

'You heard me right, Rishivar; he wants me to marry him. He says, if everything of Indra's is his then why am I not his?' said Indrani breaking down.

The Sage was angry. He offered some water to Indrani, who could barely drink because she was crying bitterly now. He went close to Indrani and patted her head and tried to console her, 'Don't cry, my child, don't. I will do something soon.'

'When will My Lord return, Rishivar, when? This man is a nuisance. He shouts at everybody and does nothing else. Everybody at Amravati is tired and scared of him. He just roughs up anybody for no reason. The other day, he hurled a goblet at one of my maids for being a bit late in bringing something he had asked for. She is hurt and now the others don't want to serve him…and…' Indrani's voice trailed off.

'And? And what, my child?' the sage asked insistently.

'And the other day,' continued Indrani, feeling reassured, 'the other day, Urvashi and Menaka, the apsaras of My Lord's court, were saying that he tries to…he tries to touch them and…' she decided to leave the sentence incomplete.

'You don't have to tell me anything more, Devi. I have understood. It was indeed my mistake to even have suggested his name to replace Indra. Success and power need to be earned and not handed over on a platter,' the sage admitted. After what seemed to be a long silence, he said, 'You go back to Amravati, my child. I will do something immediately.' He called for some attendants waiting outside his cottage. As soon as someone came in, he instructed, 'Send someone to look for Lord Indra immediately and report to me. He should be near the rivers… just find him! Fast!'

Indrani was glad to hear her husband's name. The sage then told her, 'You go back, my child, and do as I say.' He then gave her some instructions. Indrani shuddered at the suggestions and stared at him, but the sage reassured her, 'Do as I say, my child, and trust me. He won't do anything. In the meanwhile, I will ensure that your husband is back. It's been a long while now.'

Indrani was unsure of the sage's suggestion, but she seemed to have no other option but to follow his instructions. She was scared and worried. Unmindfully, she went back to Amravati and decided to wait it out and hope that things would work out the way the sage had suggested.

No sooner had she sat under a tree than she heard the rude voice of Nahush ask, 'Where had you been, my dear?'

Indrani hated being addressed that way but decided to ignore it for the time being, 'I had gone down to the river.'

'So, what have you thought of my proposal?' demanded Nahush.

'What proposal, My Lo—?' she couldn't bring herself to complete the sentence.

'Of our wedding. Your husband will not return and I am Indra's replacement now…so—'

'I have heard that before,' Indrani interrupted him mid-sentence before he could repeat the unrepeatable.

Nahush smiled and asked, 'So, what have you thought? When can we get married?'

Indrani smiled at Nahush and said, 'I met a sage at the river. He said that nine days from today, we can get married, as it's a full moon day.'

Nahush was rather surprised at Indrani's acceptance. He immediately came closer to her. On seeing him advance towards her, Indrani quickly added, 'But till then, you should not touch me or, for that matter, any other woman, else…'

'Else what, my dear?' wondered Nahush.

'Else...else...it will not be good for you is what the sage told me. I didn't have the courage to ask the sage what would happen. I am sure you can do that for me and your well-being, can't you?' Indrani asked, looking at Nahush coyly.

Nahush withdrew immediately and said, 'Of course, my dear. Of course, I can.' He couldn't believe his luck! Nine days from that moment, he would be married to Indrani and would replace Indra in the truest sense.

'But I have a small condition,' Indrani added.

Nahush looked at her and asked, 'Condition? What condition, my dear?'

'When you come to marry me,' said Indrani, 'I don't want you to come to marry me sitting astride a mare or a bull.'

'Then how, my dear?' asked the impatient groom-to-be.

'I want you to come in a decorated palanquin, and...'

'And what?' asked an eager Nahush, who was already enjoying the very thought of it all.

'...and the palanquin should be carried by the Saptarishis, the seven sages.'

'Done!' announced Nahush, without even thinking of his promise. For the power-inebriated Nahush, nothing was impossible. Indrani was relieved that she had managed to buy nine days and put forth the condition for her marriage to Nahush, as had been suggested by Sage Brihaspati. She was rather surprised at Nahush's gullibility but was still unsure about how any of what she had done would help her. Her worries were far from over though. The only saving grace was that she had managed to push her problem nine days away. She was pinning her hopes on Sage Brihaspati's plan, whatever it was. She also prayed that her husband would be found. Once he came back, things would be fine. Too many dependants were at stake.

Nahush's Wedding

True to his promise, Nahush stayed away from Indrani and the other apsaras, who were surprised that she had agreed to give up on Indra so fast. While they were not happy about this, no one said anything to her. Indrani knew about the simmering disappointment towards her, but she decided not to react, lest Nahush also gets to know that this was all part of the sage's plan. Besides, even she had no idea how the plan was going to work.

When word was sent to the seven sages about the task at hand, they were shocked. They couldn't be reduced to palanquin bearers! They immediately landed at Nahush's court and raised their objection to the task.

'How dare you say no to me? It's an order and you might as well do so!' Nahush yelled angrily.

Sage Atri reasoned, 'Besides the disrespect of making us carry you in a palanquin, it is also unfair to marry a woman who is already married and has a husband. You can't do this.'

'Where is her husband? I am her husband! I am Indra. Do I need to tell you this, Rishivar?' Nahush responded, enraged.

'You are the original Indra's replacement. You are not *the* Indra. This is something you should never forget,' said Sage Kashyapa.

Nahush got up from his seat, 'Really? So you will decide who is Indra and for how long? If you thought you would decide on my "tenure", you are seriously mistaken, old man! You have got me till here but from here on out, I decide how long I stay and the way I stay here!'

The sages looked at each other, wondering what monster they had unleashed on the world. Sage Atri said, 'You are getting arrogant, Nahush.'

'Indra, Sage Atri! Lord Indra, to be precise. Please address me as I ought to be!' bellowed Nahush. 'I am your King and Indra and you will do as I say. Now, please prepare. I will see you seven days hence! You may leave now,' Nahush concluded, dismissing the sages.

The sages were both hurt and angry. They soon realized that they had unleashed a monster and it had come back to bite them. Indra had never misbehaved with them, ever. They realized their folly but had no option but to endure their creation!

On their way out, Sage Agastya said, 'I think we should confer with Brihaspati on this. He might have a way out of this nonsense.'

Sage Atri said, 'He knows. This is his creation. We shouldn't have fallen for his words of removing Indra in the first place. How can he help?'

'Besides, he is aware of everything,' mentioned Sage Kashyapa. 'I don't think he can be of much help. He is not even at the court.'

Dejected, they went on their way and, soon enough, the nine days were over and it was Nahush's wedding day! The sages arrived at his court. Nahush was ready and dressed in the full regalia of a groom, resplendent in fine clothes and ornaments, making every effort to be worthy of the woman he had fallen in love with, along with the power that had been bestowed on him.

The palanquin was decorated with flowers. He had an attendant carry a vat of soma, which he had grown addicted to, all the way to Indrani's chambers. Indrani's palace, too, had been decorated for the wedding. However, her heart was unhappy, as she was still not sure how long this charade was going to be and she desperately hoped that it did not become a reality. The apsaras and the gandharvas had all approached her and requested her not to give up on their Lord Indra, who was the most deserving king of Amravati. However, she had sworn to Sage Brihaspati that she would not speak to anybody about this supposed plan, as he did not trust Nahush and his means.

Nahush took his seat and the reluctant sages started lifting the palanquin with much effort. However, it dawned on them that seven was an odd number and there was an inequality of bearers; there was an extra bearer on one end. One of them tried to speak to Nahush about this, but he was too preoccupied with his dreams and did not even listen to them. He simply egged them on to hurry up and move.

The seven sages reluctantly lifted the palanquin and started to walk. Since the distance to Indrani's palace was not much, it ought not to have taken them too long to reach. However, the winding path and the unequal number of bearers made it very unwieldy. While the bearers constantly attempted to carry something they were not used to, an inebriated Nahush periodically shouted from inside, '*Sarpa, sarpa,* faster, faster!' However, he did not know that the other meaning of this word was serpent!

Occasionally, the palanquin would tilt towards Sage Agastya since he was the shortest of the lot. This would unsettle Nahush inside. A couple of times, Nahush spilled some soma on his dress and he yelled at Sage Agastya. The sage was unable to do anything about this and simply decided to keep quiet and bear it, as they had been left with no other option and people all around were watching them. It was both embarrassing and insulting.

Despite repeated warnings and insulting commands from Nahush, the short sage couldn't stop the palanquin from tilting.

Suddenly, to avoid a pit in the path, the sage tilted it more than usual. Unfortunately, a nearly full goblet of soma spilt all over Nahush and, in his anger, he kicked Sage Agastya, who was holding the palanquin closest to where Nahush's leg was. The sage was livid. He cursed him, '*Sarpa*! Did you say? By the powers of my penance, may you lead the life of a serpent! Go! Get out of this place and crawl all your life, as serpents do!'

The sages banged the palanquin down. Nahush fell out of the palanquin and rolled to the ground. He realized that he had exceeded his brief and should never have kicked Sage Agastya, someone who was revered. He sure had faltered. He tried to apologize, but it was of no use. The seven sages were staring at him in anger and they had already turned their backs on him. Nahush was shocked at his own behaviour and wondered what had gotten into him. But it was too late to think of all this now.

However, before he could even get up, he saw two looming figures walking towards him. It was Sage Brihaspati along with Indra! How had Indra come back? Nahush wondered.

As if reading his thoughts, Nahush heard Sage Brihaspati say, 'So, did you think that you would rule here forever? Didn't we tell you that this was for a short while, till our Indra returns from his atonement? But looks like power and fame are not for all to digest. Go your way, you imposter, and never come back here again. Go crawl back to where you came from.'

Indra stood there, wondering who was at fault in this situation. He felt sorry for Nahush, as he felt that first, the sages had made him dream and when this man had started to dream, they had thrown him on the floor. While Indra was aware of Nahush's evil intentions towards his wife, he didn't blame Nahush completely. Somewhere, he felt that while Nahush did err in looking at Indrani, the real malaise lay elsewhere.

Indra went to Nahush and tried to raise him, but he was too crestfallen to stand up. Indra looked at him pitifully and said, 'Go, my brother, go back to your place. While I bear no grudge against you, I guess you will have to endure the wrath of the sages. Farewell, my brother...'

Indra turned from there and headed for his palace. He was not quite feeling jubilant about returning. There was a sense of ominousness in his heart. Things were changing and he was not sure if the changes were good.

While Amravati rejoiced at having Indra back and getting a reprieve from Nahush, the same couldn't be said about Indra. His heart was heavy with how the events of the last few months had unfolded. He had begun to question his powers and his ability to weather the storms that his kingdom would face. Just when and how did he lose his ability to stand up against these old men, who were playing with fire? Just when did these people get stronger, even without any strength? Just how is it that they were getting away with all these ills, which they had recast as virtues? Why was he feeling so helpless? Just what had changed? And when? Yet again, these old men had managed to interpret right and wrong in their dubious way. First, they had used Indra to get rid of Vritra; then, they had used Indra's action to get rid of him for some time. What if Nahush wouldn't have insulted or become a problem for the sages? Would he have been remembered? If it had not been for Nahush's evil intentions towards Indrani, would they have even sought him out from his 'penance' at all?

Rumours About the Dark Boy

Once again, some rumours about the dark boy born in a dungeon started doing the rounds. His father was a *gopati*, owner of many cows, and quite influential in his region. This boy had somehow captured the imagination of his people and some rather strange stories about him were floating around.

While he was just a child, the ones who were spreading these rumours made him appear larger than life. Indra was often amused to hear some of them and thought people were naive to listen to them in strange, child-like awe. A particularly unbelievable rumour about him was that he had danced atop a strange, many-headed serpent.

Indra noticed his messenger did not just relate what he had heard but seemed to believe all that he heard. According to the messenger, this boy supposedly went deep down under the river and got rid of this strange serpent single-handedly along with the others. What Indra found odd was that his battle with Vritra had been forgotten and this new, fanciful tale was taking its place.

Indra smiled and wondered just how these gullible folks could believe this story. Who in his right mind would believe that a boy, rather, a child could go deep under a river, supposedly under the pretext of fetching some round object that it had been playing with, battle a huge, many-headed serpent and emerge from the waters, dancing atop the serpent and evict it and the other serpents from the dark waters of Yamuna! It was laced with fantasy, but what made it all the more unbelievable was that all this was being attributed to a *gopala*, a cowherd, who was still grazing cows!

Indra wondered if this was some kind of a conspiracy to undermine his encounter with the serpent Vritra with a story of another serpent, visibly more dangerous than Vritra. Where Indra had had to battle Vritra with an army, this boy, yes *boy*, had gotten rid of this many-headed beast all by himself. Besides, this time, there was no killing, just getting rid of him. *Was this story absolving the boy of the future atonement for the 'crime' of killing the serpent?*

Indra was growing increasingly uneasy about the reason for such a fantasy being woven. Was this a sinister move or was this just some fanciful story that would soon be forgotten? He was not sure it would be since he had been hearing it too often lately. Too many stories were being attributed to this boy and they all just kept coming back to him with alarming regularity.

Indra recollected a story he had been told some time back about this boy having upturned a cart when he could barely walk! Supposedly, the mother of the baby, while attending to some chore had left him under a cart that had been loaded with milk and butter, thinking that he had been fast asleep. Later, when everyone heard the cries of the baby, they found the cart smashed to pieces and a huge demon lying dead beside it. The people felt that the baby's uncle, a mighty king, had sent that huge demon to kill him. However, the baby boy had not only smashed the cart but also killed the demon. Just a baby!

However, it was not this piece of fiction that bothered Indra. What he couldn't understand was this incident being compared to Indra's smashing of Ushas's chariot. Just how were the two connected? Besides, why this comparison with Indra at all? First, the serpent and now the cart-chariot. Just how was this baby boy comparable to Indra? Had the people lost their sense of judgement or was there some conspiracy brewing? Just who was behind this and for what purpose?

While Indra was not keen on engaging in this kind of gossiping about this gopala who would barely reach his knees, the regularity with which some story or the other about this boy was brought to him was not only irritating but also worrying at times. Worrying because this boy, his antics and mischief seemed to be catching people's imagination in a rather silly manner. What seemed to be mischief of sorts was being eulogized as a prank and, as some called it, 'lovable' pranks! Just what was this kind of indulgence that seemed to be overlooking all the acts of this boy and enjoying the silliest things as matters of great interest and conversation? Surprisingly, the parents, all the villagers and the rest seemed to have nothing else to do but talk about the boy and his pranks and all the unbelievable feats attributed to him. Despite being aware that this might not be a matter of concern to Indra, his messengers kept bringing him such fantastic tales because they felt that such stories were doing the rounds among the people and, thus, he needed to know them.

While it was true that his instruction to his messengers was to bring matters of political, economic and social importance to him, he could hardly fault them for bringing in such fantastic stories about this boy. Further, Indra never told these people not to bring him certain kinds of information, as it was for him to sift out the irrelevant information. He did not want them to be sifting through such information, as he did not want them to be the judge of what was important and what wasn't. One needed a level of maturity and awareness to understand the importance of bits of information. Indra would rather have such decisions rest with him than his messengers.

With all this in mind, he would avoid showing his irritation and displeasure to the messengers who brought in such information. However, lately, it was becoming too regular and, quite often, unbearable to see the level of fictitious elements blended into bits of information. He was often worried about his messengers having started to believe in such rumours, much like the common people, who seemed to share the news with a sense of incredible belief!

Change of Lifestyle

Unknown to Indra, another change was sweeping through not all but a significant number of his subjects. More and more people were taking to grazing and rearing cattle. While this profession had been earmarked for people who were on the move, an increasing number of people in this profession were settling in one location, which was a new phenomenon. Earlier, this profession had been practised by people who used to be on the move but this was not so any more. The cattle-rearers had started settling down in one place for a long time, mostly grazing their cattle and making the area their home. This kind of settled pastoral life was a new phenomenon.

Due to the reduced need to grow their food, the people's dependency on the rains had started decreasing. While there was no denying that rains were still crucial for everybody, they had gone from being a must-have to avoid droughts and famines to something that was good to have—the rains had become more or less a given. Earlier, people used to offer sacrifices and engage the priests to conduct yajnas for the rains—they were celebrated as a divine gift. This mindset was changing. Suddenly, the rains were being taken for granted and the lack of it, though mostly there wasn't any, was met with indifference. Also, the society had become a lot more segmented. People who tilled the land were different from those who grazed animals and there was a good mode of exchange between the two communities. A sense of coexistence and a sort of bonhomie was visible, which, by itself, was good.

Some kings had smaller regions and were happy to rule them. Some were in peaceful coexistence with the others, while some kept trying to extend their areas through battles. Indra did not bother much as long as everyone owed their allegiance to him, which was kept well in check.

Several heroes had been emerging in different areas. Indra was glad to see that his old friend, Vishnu, seemed to be doing quite well. He was becoming quite well known among the people and more and more successes were being attributed to him. He had also heard about his marriage to a beautiful woman of wealth named Lakshmi. Those who had seen her praised her looks and her penchant for jewellery and finery in dressing. Many had said that the two looked very good together. Indra was glad for him and was happy that he and his diplomacy were often praised. What saddened him, though, was that they had lost touch. Vishnu did not come to meet Indra, like he used to before. Since he had gone missing from Indra's place long back, Indra had not even heard from him. However, Indra bore no hard feelings against Vishnu and wished him well. Occasionally, Indra would hear about him from his messengers and that would make him feel good.

While such changes were the signs of an emerging society, what was worrying were people's changing beliefs. Could one do away with one's past and past beliefs? While newness was attractive and often worth embracing, should that be done at the cost of the past? Could one's earlier lifestyle be abandoned at the first sign of change on the horizon? Were people so fickle? Or was that the hallmark of mankind? Such thoughts had started cropping up in Indra's mind a bit too often. Goblets of soma, too, didn't help him overcome these thoughts nor did the lovely apsaras of his sabha.

Far Away in Vrindavan

Like every year, the preparations for the Indrotsav had begun in Vrindavan. Paths were being cleared and animals were being washed and decorated. Even homes were being decked up, with ribbons of flowers being hung on doorways and colourful designs being made in the courtyards—suddenly the entire village was in the mood for celebration.

The little cowherd had been observing the preparations for the last few days and had been hearing about it in bits and pieces from his friends. There was excitement in the air and celebrations were something all children were happy about. Many homes were preparing different kinds of food that the children kept discussing.

However, something was bothering the little cowherd. While his life was full of fun and frolic, this time, he was a little worried. While his father, Nand, had been busy discussing and planning the festival with others, the boy had asked him, 'Father, what are all this celebrations about?'

The father was a bit elusive, as he knew getting into a discussion with his son could end up wasting some time. So, he answered hurriedly, 'Just the annual festival of Lord Indra, my son.'

'What festival, Father?' asked the boy, ignoring his father's hurry.

'It's the annual festival to thank Lord Indra for his benevolence on us, Krishna!' answered another man, before the father could respond.

'Benevolence? What benevolence, Uncle?' wondered the boy

aloud, much to the surprise of the others. But then, Krishna always had a lot of questions. So, everyone just smiled and, once again, before the father could answer, another old man who was sitting in the distance said, 'Benevolence of the rains, my boy, the benevolence of the rains! Lord Indra sends us the rains and, through this festival, we express our gratitude to him.'

'Krishna, please go and play with your friends, we have lots of work to do,' said the father, sensing that the boy had more questions and he would get all of them involved in some discussions. He was well aware that each of them would end up talking to him, wasting more time than necessary and there was still a lot of work left. Besides, people in his village wasted a lot of time after his child, but he did not have the heart to tell them so. If he allowed more discussions, soon, the children and the women would join in and then all hell would break loose.

'But, Father, I fail to understand this...' started the boy, ignoring his father's instructions, 'Why must we thank Indra—'

'*Lord* Indra, my son—Lord Indra,' the father corrected his son, mid-sentence.

The boy ignored his father and continued, 'I fail to understand! Why must we thank this Indra for the rains when they will arrive irrespective of him?'

There was a sudden hush at Krishna's words. All of them looked at him and then at each other.

The father was visibly embarrassed and commanded, 'Will you go inside or play with your friends?'

'Just what did you say, Krishna?' asked the old man sitting in the distance. 'Did you even hear yourself say that, my boy?'

'I asked a question, that's all I did,' replied Krishna, refusing to get the drift of the question, which was laced with more shock and disbelief than anything else. 'If you want to celebrate, at least celebrate for the right reasons.'

Nand was used to his son often speaking beyond his age and he had seldom considered this offensive, mostly because of Krishna's innocence and charm. However, that day, his words seemed neither innocent nor charming. Somewhere, he was trying to tell something to the elders, something that had started to worry Nand. Before things got out of hand, Nand shouted, 'Yashoda, will you please take Krishna inside?'

'Why are you trying to get rid of me, Father, instead of answering my questions?' asked the rather petulant Krishna.

Once again, before the father could say anything, the old man seated in the distance said, 'So what, according to you, are the right reasons to celebrate, *my dear*?' Everyone around started laughing at this.

Krishna responded, 'If you can explain the right reasons for this celebration, I will tell you what the right reasons for any celebration are. And, Father, let me explain, instead of shooing me inside.' There was a sense of authoritativeness in Krishna's voice, which was not missed by anybody. Just then, a servant came out to take the boy inside, but he looked at her and said, 'Stay there, I have something to discuss here.'

While the others were quite shocked at his command, the father decided to hear him out, not that there was ever an option with this little boy. Besides, the old man had stirred the hornets' nest! 'So, Uncle, could you explain the main reason for this celebration?' Krishna addressed the old man and all eyes moved towards him.

While the old man was feeling a little uncomfortable about the sudden shift in attention to him, he said, 'These celebrations are to thank Lord Indra for his benevolence. We thank him for the rains that he sends us, which help us grow crops and fodder for our cattle. The rains also replenish the rivers and bring all of us overall wealth around the year.' The old man felt that he had explained it quite comprehensively.

Krishna said, addressing everyone in general, 'If you think that your Indra sends us rains, then you are seriously mistaken. Rains are a natural phenomenon, to begin with. If at all anybody or anything needs to be credited for the rains, it is the great Govardhan giri, or the great mountain that all of us can see from here,' he said, pointing at the mammoth mountain at the back of the village. There was an air of disbelief among the gathering. The girl who had come to take Krishna away sensed trouble and ran inside to inform the mother. 'If the mountain was not there, then all of us would be in trouble. It stops the moving clouds and compels them to rain over our villages, besides providing fodder for our cattle. Our cattle find their sustenance from that mountain. Besides this, a lot of our herbs and food also come from the mountain. So, if it didn't exist, then, as I said before, we would be in trouble. Don't you think we should be worshipping the mountain, if anything at all?'

Nand was surprised at his son's impudence and so were the rest of them. His wife, too, had rushed in after she had been alerted by the girl. People were more shocked than surprised by now. Krishna, standing with his legs crossed over, was very much the man among all the grown-ups out there.

Finally, the old man found his voice and demanded, 'Where did you learn all this blasphemy, my boy?'

This also brought everyone else back to reality. Suddenly, there were murmurs all around. Nand indicated to his wife to take Krishna inside. But no sooner had she come close to Krishna than he raised his hand authoritatively to stop her. His action kind of disarmed her, much to her surprise.

Krishna then addressed everyone, 'You all have been organizing this festival for years now. Why don't you stop it this time and see what happens?'

'And who will bear the wrath of the Lord, my dear?' asked another person, who was beginning to get irritated with where this discussion was headed.

'I will!' replied Krishna, much to everybody's shock. 'I will take care of everything and if things go wrong, I will worship your Indra, on all your behalf, for the rest of my life!'

The challenge landed as a huge rock on all of them. Nand intervened, 'Krishna, you are unaware of what you are saying and that too among all the seniors who know what they are doing. I suggest you leave now and I don't want any more discussion on this matter. Please leave!'

Krishna had never seen his father get angry with him before, but he had been expecting it and responded, 'Trust me, Father. Nothing can go wrong, trust me!'

The confidence was not lost on anybody but subverting a tradition was also not quite palatable to anybody there. As if on cue, Krishna's mother rushed in, picked him up and went inside. All of them could hear Krishna being scolded by Yashoda, but Krishna knew that he had sowed the seeds of dissent.

After he had been taken away, the gathering did not discuss anything further. Everybody just left one by one, as if each wanted to digest what the child had just said to them, something that had never been uttered before. Some of them felt that the boy's argument had some merit to it. However, the majority was surprised or, rather, shocked at the appalling blasphemy.

Krishna Asserts

'What?' asked a rather surprised Nand, 'What the hell are you saying?'

'Yes, you heard me right,' said a rather sad Yashoda. 'He has declined all food since I brought him inside. He says he will not eat anything if the festival continues.'

'What nonsense is this? What's gotten into him?' wondered Nand.

One of his men standing behind him said, 'I think you should call for the Daai-ma. She is good with such matters.'

'In what matters?' asked Nand, looking around.

'He is possessed. Your son is possessed. I have never seen him like this before, especially the way he spoke in front of all of us,' said the rather scared attendant.

Hearing this, Yashoda started to cry. She immediately called for one of her maids and ordered her to get the Daai-ma, who was an expert in curing children with 'such' problems.

Nand protested and asked her to go inside. There was no need to call Daai-ma. 'He just needs some disciplining. Too much attention is his problem,' a rather angry Nand declared.

Suddenly, a woman rushed in and insisted that she wanted to speak to Yashoda. She was the mother of Krishna's friend, Vitanka. The two of them stood in a corner and whispered something. Nand could see that Yashoda was disturbed by the discussion. She came to Nand and said, 'Vitanka, too, has declined to have any food.'

Even as everyone was digesting this information, the mothers of Ujjvala, Pushpanka, Vidagdha and others rushed in. All the children had decided not to eat till Krishna's suggestions were taken seriously.

Nand was visibly angry at this rebellion and the pressure tactics being used by his son. Soon, more people rushed in, crowding Nand's courtyard. Nand decided to take matters into his hands. He called Krishna out in front of everybody and decided to reprimand him. As soon as Krishna was brought out, he said, 'Father, don't waste your time in saying anything to me. I will not eat till I am informed about the cancelling of this Indra festival of yours.'

'You have no right to stop a tradition that has been going on for ages. Besides, what do you know of life and its ways? You are a child, so you better act like one. And what is this organized rebellion?' Nand nearly shouted at his son.

'When elders behave like children, we have to step up' was Krishna's shocking response.

'What if the cancellation upsets Lord Indra? Who will save us from his wrath?' asked Pushpanka's father.

'I will! I have already said that,' Krishna replied nonchalantly.

'Really? May I ask how?' Pushpanka's father retorted.

'First, let Indra get angry!' Krishna said coldly.

Nand was aware of things starting to get out of hand. Something had to be done. However, as always, he was at a loss. Krishna was such a weakness for all of them that their fondness would often become a weapon in this boy's hands. He sometimes behaved much beyond his age. The gathering was only increasing in size, as more and more parents began walking in with the complaints that their children, too, had stopped eating. Nand was surprised that his son, who was used to eating at least eight times a day, had not taken even a morsel in the last several hours. Vidagdha, who was known to be a glutton and was seen eating the whole day to satiate his demonic hunger, too, had eaten nothing for many hours and his mother, who used to complain about his gluttony, was now inconsolable at his not eating anything!

'Nand, this is all because of you. You have spoilt your son—' Pushpanka's father began but was interrupted mid-sentence by Krishna, who firmly said, 'You don't have to shout at him, Uncle. This is my decision and my friends and I will stick to it till all of you decide against this festival.'

'You won't last another hour!' said Pushpanka's father.

'Did you even expect us to last this long? And if you are so sure, why have you rushed in here to complain to my parents?' retorted Krishna.

'Krishna! That's no way to speak to your elders!' shouted Yashoda at Krishna.

Ujjvala's father, who had not spoken a word till now and who had heard Krishna's arguments earlier in the day, said, 'What if we listen to this boy once? I did find some sense in what he had said during the day.'

'Are you crazy?' shouted Pushpanka's father, 'He has lost his mind!'

There were murmurs among the gathering. 'If we overlook the organized rebellion of the children and see this argument in isolation,' said Ujjvala's father, 'then what little Krishna has said is not quite incorrect. He is right when he says that it is indeed the mountain that sustains us. We should be worshipping the mountain and not Indra, I mean Lord Indra, if at all. I think we have been following this tradition for long—long enough to not realize that it might have lost its relevance or meaning.'

Soon, some heads started to nod and Krishna was smiling.

He knew he was on his way to success. Nand was rather surprised at the words of Ujjvala's father, who was seldom incorrect in his reasoning and, indeed, had a strong influence over people. What surprised Nand the most was his explanation and the subsequent reaction, where he found many nodding in agreement.

'And what if Lord Indra is upset with us for breaking this tradition?' asked Pushpanka's father sceptically.

'Have you ever seen him, Uncle?' asked Krishna. Once again, there was a commotion in the gathering at the impudent question. Even before Nand could say anything reprimanding him, Krishna raised his finger towards the towering mountain behind him and continued, 'That, at least, we can see!' There was a momentary hush at the unuttered logic of Krishna's argument. However, Krishna was not letting things be assumed, so, he clarified, 'You are scared of someone whom nobody has seen for ages but want to ignore the one that is right in front of you? How unfair and ungrateful can we be?'

'Yashoda, please take him inside,' ordered Nand.

'Wait,' requested Ujjvala's father, 'let him be. We are all discussing this because of him and he needs to be here, as he represents all the children, who have decided to support him. Maybe they are saying something that needs to be heard. Who knows, there might be some sense to it?'

'Or it is mere nonsense, maybe,' added Pushpanka's father, as a few giggled.

Ujjvala's father said, 'We could keep discussing this till the cows come home. However, I think we need to decide. I think we should call off the festival for once and see what happens.'

'While I can understand the boy and his foolishness,' said Pushpanka's father, 'I fail to understand your support for this boy! Looks like the girls and women of this village and now, some of the men, too, are losing their minds after this devil.'

Some of the women and the others took offence to the statement and that is what suddenly tipped the scales. Many of the women gathered there said that they, too, wanted to support Krishna and were willing to wait and watch.

Soon, Nand agreed to stop the celebrations because he saw more and more of the villagers agreeing to Krishna's views, and, suddenly, things were beginning to make sense. Instead of worshipping the *invisible*, it would make more sense to worship the Govardhan giri and the cattle, which were visible from any corner of the village.

The Wrath of Lord Indra

While the festival had been cancelled and all the arrangements had been put on hold, there were apprehensions and fear among many. The only redeeming aspect was that the children had started to eat again. Although Krishna and his supporting friends had made it very clear that if they found out that this move was only to get them to eat, the next time, they would go beyond just not eating food. While Vidagdha, the boy with a ravenous appetite, was scared to know what that would be, he had faith in Krishna and would do anything he said, much like the others.

All around Vrindavan, there were signs of the preparations for Indrotsav being left halfway. This is not to say that the usual share of the naysayers didn't exist, especially Pushpanka's father and others like him. They were worried that this crazy boy might lead them to an unknown catastrophe. They had rarely seen times when this festival had not been organized or Lord Indra had not been worshipped since Uparichara Vasu had started it and made it a ritual everywhere. Pushpanka's father, and many like him, were worried about the future. While his son had started eating again, which was a great relief, he was sure that there was something more ominous in store for them.

His worries were not unfounded. Within a few days of the festival being cancelled, dark clouds loomed over Vrindavan, the kind that were not normal for that time of the year. People started to look up at the sky with worry. Many of them started talking about the untimely clouds and what they might mean for the village. Nand, too, was beginning to get worried about them because he had never seen such dark clouds at this time of the year. Rather, the festival was always organized after the rains had receded, as a thanksgiving to Lord Indra for the bountiful rains. Seeing clouds now was odd.

The clouds hovered over Vrindavan for just a few days as a warning. When there was no reaction in terms of resuming the preparations for the festival, thunder and lightning lit up the sky. The sounds heralded the wrath of Lord Indra and old-timers from the village started seeing the folly of listening to a two-bit boy after whom the entire village had lost its mind. On the whim of the boy, an age-old tradition had been given a go-by. Many felt that they would have to bear the repercussions of such sin.

The thunder and lightning gave way to rains—untimely and incessant rains. The sky was dark and it seemed as if someone was pouring barrels of water from the skies. The rains were relentless, with thick curtains of water so dense that one could barely see the neighbouring house. The old people of Vrindavan swore that they had never seen such rains—they were not rains, they portended bad days! Lord Indra was sure to destroy them and their village for that silly boy, who had convinced them to commit such sacrilege.

It rained for the whole day and another day. The water levels started to rise and the lakes and ponds started overflowing—again, something that had never happened before. The fields started getting submerged in knee-deep water. It seemed to be pouring in from everywhere. People were visibly scared and worried.

Nand was surprised to see his son least worried about the sudden change. While that was less of his concern, he was sure that it had been a mistake to fall for his son's words. Why had they ever listened to a boy who was always up to some mischief?

Needless to say, this time, things had gone out of hand, but this was also their fault. Instead of giving in to his coercion, he should have stuck to his decision; at least the villagers would have been spared. Now, how on earth were they going to appease the Lord?

As if reading his thoughts, a group of people walked into his huge courtyard, led by Pushpanka's father. All of them had gathered to express their anger at the decision of cancelling Indrotsav. The crowd just went on swelling and their worries gave way to shouting and screaming. Nand knew that he had a rebellion at hand, though he could see some, like Ujjvala's father, trying to pacify the others. However, things were not getting any better. People were worried about the wrath of Indra spreading inside their homes, spoiling the crops and affecting the cattle. The rains were showing no signs of stopping and the villagers had been unable to do anything, except try to save themselves and all that was theirs from the rains.

The Unimaginable

'Tell me more!' said Indra, who was listening to his messenger. 'The people of Vrindavan were all gathered at Nand's house. It was nothing short of a rebellion. Many were angry, some were shouting and there was chaos. It was dark and the rains were just relentless...'

Indra took another goblet of soma and gulped it down. He was beginning to enjoy the narration. He smiled and looked at the messenger, who was so involved in what he had seen that he had forgotten that he was narrating it to Indra. He went on, 'There were thick curtains of ceaseless water—something that no one in the village had ever seen. Some said this was the *maha-pralay*, the great deluge, which would end the world. Many were worried about their cattle, often the only property they have. Parents were worried about their children's lives and futures if the cattle were to drown or be pulled away in the deluge. The water level had been rising at an alarming speed...'

Indra could see the sight in front of him. There was something magical about his messenger's narration, especially this one. He made it all seem so real that Indra felt that he had been there at that moment, amid all the chaos. Not for a moment did the messenger make one feel that this had happened in a distant land from the past.

'The gathering was blaming Nand for giving in to the whims of a child, especially one who was known for his pranks more than anything else. Some even suggested that they start praying and atoning for their sins,' the messenger continued.

Indra smiled and was glad that better sense was about to prevail. 'However, suddenly, someone realized that the boy was missing,' the messenger informed, staring into the distance.

Indra looked at him, holding his goblet halfway to his lips, wondering what had happened, 'What happened? Where was this boy?' asked Indra, but the messenger was not listening. He kept staring into the distance, as if in a trance.

'Something unbelievable happened. When all of them were looking for the boy, they heard some rumblings. The ground beneath them shook. Everything was trembling and right in front of them, things began to move. People were scared, the cattle were making weird sounds and many thought it was the end of the world,' the messenger described.

'So, what was happening?' demanded Indra.

The messenger, however, was not listening to anybody. He could hear no voices, no orders, no demands. He was staring into the distance, transported elsewhere—probably Vrindavan. Indra was rather surprised at the man's odd behaviour. Never had he seen anybody get so engrossed in relating what they had seen. This was rather unusual.

The messenger continued, 'While everyone was scared and wondering what was happening, someone shouted, "Look!", pointing towards the mountain behind. Everyone was shocked and overcome with disbelief. The mountain seemed to be rising! Yes! The mountain was rising and everyone was shocked to see that this little boy was lifting the mountain to create a giant umbrella.'

Indra was overcome with shock. A child lifted a mountain? 'Are you in your senses? Since when did you start telling such fanciful stories? Your job is to narrate what you saw, not tell me stories!' But the messenger could not hear Indra. He could only hear the rumblings of the mountain and the sound of the rains. He was only physically present in front of Indra. 'There were shrieks of horror from the people. Some noticed that the boy was holding the mountain on the tip of his *little finger*! The entire village was under the shade of the massive mountain. The village and its inhabitants were shielded from the terrible rains. People were shocked. Some bowed down to the boy and others were scared. Many felt that they were dreaming. Many who had opposed the boy bowed down to him. It was a sight to behold; never seen or heard of before,' the messenger paused.

Indra couldn't believe what he had just heard. He never had a reason to doubt his messengers, but today, he didn't know what to say. While it didn't seem as if he was lying, this was too much to believe. 'A child lifted the mountain?'

'Everybody took shelter under the mountain. The boy held it like that, without moving, for close to seven days and seven nights! The rains and their fury became meaningless. Soon, they stopped...' the messenger had barely managed to say those words when he swooned and fell. He had passed out.

Indra clapped his hands and immediately a few guards rushed inside. 'Call the Vaidya immediately. I want him treated now! Here!'

One of the guards rushed out to call the Vaidya, the physician, while the other lifted the messenger and placed him on the side. In no time, the Vaidya came. He examined the messenger and declared that he had passed out due to exhaustion. He needed to rest.

'Has he been smoking hemp?' demanded Indra.

The Vaidya examined the messenger and declared, 'No, he doesn't seem to have ever touched it.'

'And soma?' Indra asked again.

'No, My Lord, it doesn't seem like that. Looks like he was in some sort of daze before he passed out. I can't say anything at the moment. I will examine him once he is in his senses,' added the Vaidya.

'Take him away and let me know once he is able to speak,' said Indra.

The messenger was taken away and, soon, Indra was all alone. He had known this messenger and he was the most trustworthy among all his messengers. While he sure did not have any reason to lie or make up stories, what he had narrated was quite unbelievable too. Never had he heard of such imaginative stories. A boy lifting a mountain? Wasn't this too much to digest?

What was he to do? Trust him? Or verify it by himself? Why not? While he has never had the need to verify any of his messengers, this was unusual. Shouldn't he check for himself? Once maybe? Yes, why not? It has been a long time and a king has the right and the responsibility to visit his subjects. He would visit this village of cowherds...Yes, he would.

Back in Vrindavan

'Is it true that his boy, Nand's son, lifted a mountain?' asked Golaka, the cowherd from the neighbouring village to Ballabh, his regular supplier of milk products.

Ballabh beamed with pride, 'Of course, of course, *my* boy did.'

'Seriously? I mean you believe it?' asked Golaka, sceptical as ever.

'Do I believe it? Did you ask if I believe it? Of course, I do!' Ballabh exclaimed, 'I was there! It happened in front of me. Why me? All of us were there. Every living organism saw it. Why would anybody lie? We don't need to!'

Golaka was amazed. While he had no reason to distrust Ballabh, as he had always been very sensible, this sure was too much to take. But then, everybody in Vrindavan and the nearby villages had been talking only about this. It can't be a figment of everybody's imagination. Besides, this boy sure had a history of achieving the unachievable. He had done many such things before and if they were all believable, why not this? *But a mountain?*

'Will you stop staring at the mountain there? People like you would not believe it even if you were there! So, why bother?' reprimanded Ballabh. 'We saw it. I saw it. I saw this boy saving my home, my family, my cattle from that vengeful Indra. Had it not been for this son of Nand, my family and I would have perished.'

'Not if you had continued the festival,' added Golaka softly.

'Yes, you are right! But isn't that so unlike a father of a village?

Why did he turn vengeful? What kind of a king is he? Who simply takes revenge! I mean, we have been paying our respects to him for ages and all that was forgotten in one moment! After all, the boy was right. We need to worship the mountain, which actually sustains us, and not that Indra, who is too busy with his drinks, and...and...his women!'

Golaka was rather surprised at the venom being spewed by Ballabh. 'You shouldn't say things like that aloud. I have heard that he has his eyes and ears everywhere,' said Golaka in a hushed voice.

'No more,' laughed Ballabh loudly, 'he is much chastised now!'

'What do you mean "chastised"? Chastised by who?' asked a rather surprised Golaka.

'By our boy, Nand's son!' replied Ballabh.

'What are you saying?' asked a rather puzzled Golaka.

'Oh, haven't you heard what happened?' Ballabh asked. Golaka shook his head in ignorance. 'Oh, so you have heard nothing then,' Ballabh said. 'When this great *Lord* Indra of yours heard about our boy, Krishna, lifting the mountain, he came rushing to Vrindavan. He fell on his knees and sought pardon from Krishna.'

'What? You mean Lord Indra came and sought pardon from this boy? Have you lost your senses? Whoever has seen the Lord in recent times?' Golaka asked, summarily rejecting whatever Ballabh had to say.

'Exactly, *whoever has seen Lord Indra in recent times?* We have! We, the people of Vrindavan have, and that too as a much-humbled man!' said Ballabh with a lot of pride. 'All of us saw Indra go down on his knees and apologize to Krishna. It sure was a sight to behold. He realized that this boy of ours was no ordinary child. I mean, have you ever heard of a child lifting a mountain. While, after the event, it might seem quite unbelievable, but then can you distrust your own eyes?' Ballabh asked.

'Indra went down on his knees and apologized to this child? The mighty Indra, who slayed Vritra, went down on his knees to apologize to this boy?' Golaka asked, incredulously. This was becoming too much for him to digest. While he was willing to understand that this boy might have done something unimaginable, to think that Lord Indra would go down on his knees was too much to believe.

Ballabh was getting angry at Golaka's disbelief, 'Look, I don't have to make you believe it, that's not the point. Out there, everybody saw this. Ask anybody, man, woman or child, and you will get the same version of this incident, as all of us have seen it. It's for you to believe it or not, which is not very important for us because we know what is true.'

'I think you people of Vrindavan,' said Golaka, 'have been reeling under the shock of this rain and its aftermath and some of you haven't quite come out of this shock. Someone who is definitely against our Lord Indra is spreading these canards against him!'

'Canards? So you think we are making it all up?' shouted Ballabh. 'We are making stories up about our brave boy? Alright then, I am! I am making stories up about this boy. Stop me if you can. This boy of ours is a hero; he can do things that your old Indra can barely imagine. Sure, sure he slayed the mighty Vritra, but that's what we have been told. Have you seen him killing that serpent? We have seen our boy dancing atop this serpent in the Yamuna before driving it away from our village. We have seen our boy holding the Govardhan *parvat* on his little finger. We have seen *your* Indra kneel in front of *our* Krishna. We have seen it all. What do we believe now? The stories of the past that we have *heard* or the present that we have *seen*?' Ballabh demanded.

Golaka had no response, though he did not like Ballabh saying that since he had not seen Indra kill Vritra, he was not willing to believe it.

However, there was some sense in what he had asked—*what does one trust? What one has heard over the ages or what one has witnessed with one's own eyes?* Golaka had no answer.

Maybe posterity would be better able to answer this question.

Epilogue

At some point in history, Acharya Gyaneshwar ran his gurukul the way gurukuls used to be run in the times past when questions used to be an integral part of learning. He had not imbibed the no-questions-asked culture that many of the other gurukuls and their gurujis had started following. According to him, the best way to understand anything was by allowing questions to be asked, which were the natural responses of every seeking mind. Curtailing questions would be the biggest disservice to learning, which, according to him, was a process. While a teacher asked questions to gauge the understanding of the students, the students' questions reflected their curious minds that were seeking answers. Such an internal quest always led to greater knowledge, not blind acceptance.

Jignyasu, true to the meaning of his name—'curiosity', was a disciple full of questions. The other students would fret over his barrage of questions to Guruji. However, Guruji never deterred Jignyasu from asking questions. He had plenty of questions regarding Lord Indra and the other gods. He wasn't sure if he should worship Lord Indra at all. Guruji never quite suggested which God they should worship because he felt that this was a personal choice. Furthermore, the Supreme Creator, the one supreme energy, mattered more to him than individual gods. Nonetheless, he tried to help Jignyasu find his feet when it came to gods.

However, in this quest to understand which God to worship, Jignyasu had many queries, which inevitably centred on Lord

Indra. Since his queries would obstruct the classes, Guruji had once suggested that he keep them for his frequent evening strolls with Guruji. That way, the usual classroom deliberations would not be held up and the others would not get into personal discussions, as they often found no relevance in Jignyasu's questions.

On that breezy evening, Guruji could read Jignyasu's doubtful mind. Guruji knew that he wouldn't need too much prodding, though the child was also aware that Guruji had had a difficult day. However, what the child didn't know was that Guruji loved debating with his students, particularly this one!

'Anything bothering you, my son?' wondered Guruji aloud.

'Yes,' Jignyasu began the moment Guruji asked him, 'Is Lord Indra even worth worshipping?'

'Why do you ask that, my son?' asked Guruji as a response to the sudden outburst, which meant that Jignyasu had been grappling with this thought for quite some time. Besides, Guruji also knew that if any discourse had bothered Jignyasu the most, it had been when they had discussed Lord Indra.

'I mean a God who troubles his people and forces them to "worship" him cannot be a God, can he? What kind of a God has insecurities?' Jignyasu poured out his doubts.

Guruji smiled and allowed the import of the question to settle. 'All gods! All gods demand benevolence,' said Guruji. 'Gods that exude a sense of power insist on benevolence and often demand faith. Some do it directly, others subtly.' Jignyasu was kind of taken aback. He looked at Guruji, who was smiling benignly as he continued, 'Gods demand subservience, gods demand followers, gods demand faith and belief. All gods do.'

'What do you mean?' Jignyasu enquired.

'Choice was not a feature of primitive societies. Back then, a singular thought process was preferred to bind people together.

A growing society has too many issues to grapple with, so, the establishment of a society calls for the formation of a basic, cohesive group. This allows norms and rules to be set and once they have been established, anything that goes against the established norms is seen as an aberration. This is how rules are established,' Guruji paused, and then continued. 'Since a lot is happening in an emerging society, it can't tackle deviations from norms at an early stage. To avoid what you may call democratic thinking from frittering away the establishment of core values, the concept of God is established and strict adherence to his might and power is expected. At this stage, opposition to ideas is not warranted, as it would create more trouble. This is the first step to establishing a strong God. The fear of retribution is the core of this establishment.' Jignyasu was listening in amazement. Guruji had decided that the curiosity, so inherent in his student's name, had to be satiated once and for all! 'It is this thought process that creates a strict God. If gods are seen as soft and malleable, then society will scatter in different directions. Such strict adherence to rules, however unpalatable they might seem today—mark my words, Jignyasu: *today*—were necessary when they had been established. Nonconformity to the ways of God called for punishment, which would be a lesson for the wayward.'

Jignyasu looked more confused. 'While I am willing to understand that, why was only Indra so harsh, when the other gods, like Lord Vishnu, were not? He seemed to be quite a reasonable God; he never forced faith on people. He was quite benevolent.'

'Well, yes and no,' replied Guruji. 'Vishnu has been made to appear soft only in comparison to Indra. He had the growing influence of a different and new God who stood up against the authoritarian Indra. All gods, at some point in time, have expressed their dominance over people. As the Matsya avatar, Vishnu drowned the world because people were not following a moral life. Was that not a strong, destructive blow to mankind? Was that an act of benevolence?' Jignyasu nodded his head more in amazement than agreement. Guruji allowed the import of the statement to sink in. He knew that as a student, he had not connected the events and, like everybody, looked at them in abstract and individual terms. 'The might of any God,' continued Guruji, 'was often displayed at the cost of someone or something else.'

Guruji and Jignyasu stopped under a huge banyan tree, where they sat before heading back. Guruji sat on one of the massive roots, which had taken the shape of a small seating place with back support. Jignyasu sat a short distance away from where he could see Guruji's face and his expressions. The setting sun in the distance looked similar to the fading significance of Lord Indra!

'But why does this happen? I mean, why was there a need for a Lord Vishnu, when everything was going on well with Lord Indra? Was there a need to throw him off the pedestal and make him look mean and insecure? We read that Meghnad, the son of the Asura King Ravana, got the better of Lord Indra and even earned the epithet of Indrajeet, the one who was victorious over Indra. How sad could that be?' asked Jignyasu.

'Yes, it is sad, if you see it from Indra's perspective, but it is not so if you see it from the perspective of another God, like Vishnu,' replied Guruji. 'With times, our needs and perspectives change and it is this change that makes our gods look different to us,' Guruji elaborated with calm and composure.

Jignyasu had a frown on his face, 'How? I mean, how does a change in perspective give rise to the way we see our gods?'

'When we needed Indra, we found every aspect of Indra

venerable, but when our needs changed, we started finding faults with him. For example, we saw him as a vanquisher of the dreadful Vritra in the Vedic times. He was praised for this singular act, but as time passed, the same, venerable action came to be shunned as Brahma-hatya, the murder of a Brahmin, in our epics, and Indra was asked to atone for it. What if nobody had saved mankind from Vritra in the fear of being accused of Brahma-hatya and allowed our lakes and rivers to dry and our cattle to die? What if Indra had not come to rescue and allowed mankind to die of severe famine and drought, in fear of Brahma-hatya?' Jignyasu was beginning to see the point. 'Ethical qualms only started coming up after our basic need for safety and survival had been ensured!' Guruji added, smiling. 'Once Indra had ensured our security, he was sent to atone. Once his being at the helm of affairs was not considered significant, he was made to look silly and relegated to doing insignificant things, which were inconceivable in the earlier times!'

'Inconceivable? Like what?' wondered Jignyasu aloud.

'Like feeling insecure every time a sage was doing his penance, sending apsaras to disturb his penance, feeling threatened often and running to other gods for help, which made Indra feel dispensable,' Guruji explained. Jignyasu had questions on his face. Guruji understood that he needed an exact example. 'Let me narrate an incidence to make this clearer. At one point in time, Lord Indra, being proud of his achievements, decided to build a special palace for himself. He called the chief architect of the gods, Lord Vishwakarma, and asked him to build a unique, never-seen-before palace for him.

'Lord Vishwakarma started work and after some time, when he invited Lord Indra to see it, he was unimpressed and suggested some changes. Vishwakarma started working on these and soon, Indra was invited again to see it. Much to Vishwakarma's disappointment, Indra was still not happy with the palace. This went on for a while and Lord Vishwakarma was exasperated with the construction since Indra seemed impossible to satisfy.

'It was during this stage that Lord Vishwakarma met Vishnu. Vishwakarma told Vishnu his problem when he was asked. Vishnu told him not to worry and assured him that he would speak to Indra.

'Vishnu took the form of a dark, young boy and went to see Indra. On reaching the palace, he met Indra and expressed his desire to see the palace that had been constructed. Indra took him along and explained the structure but at one point, he said that, unfortunately, it was not yet ready, as Lord Vishwakarma was just not able to construct it the way he had conceived it. The boy responded to this by saying that the palace was big and, by far, the best palace made by *any Indra*. Indra was taken aback by the words *any Indra* and wondered what the boy meant by that. The boy repeated what he had said already: that it was, by far, the best palace built by *any Indra*. Indra was visibly upset and demanded that the boy explain himself.

'The boy said, frowning as if it was the most obvious thing in the world, that each time Lord Brahma wakes up, he creates the universe and a new Indra to rule over it. Every time Lord Brahma goes to sleep, the universe is destroyed with everything in it. Even Lord Brahma himself has a life cycle and after His time is over, another Brahma comes into existence. The dark boy looked at the puzzled Indra and added that he had seen all the Indras till date and asked the Indra in front of him how come he had not seen them.

'Meanwhile, a row of ants was marching inside Indra's palace. Looking at them, the boy started laughing. Indra was now feeling afraid. Hearing the boy laugh terrified him. He gulped and opened his mouth but no words came out. He then asked the boy why he was laughing.

'The boy pointed to the ants and said that the ants on the floor were all former Indras. Indra looked aghast since the boy added that they had all begun from the smallest creatures and become the most enlightened people. They destroy one monster and they suddenly think they are the King of the Universe and then they start from the beginning as ants.

'This perspective offered by Vishnu in the form of a boy is supposed to have had the most humbling effect on Lord Indra. He gave up the quest of making a never-seen-before palace!' Guruji paused and then added, 'Now, you see how Indra was made to feel small? And by who? By the same Vishnu, who had once been his friend and that too as a boy? These and many other such incidents were strong blows to Lord Indra's power by the new, emerging gods.'

'New, emerging gods? Why do we need new, emerging gods?' asked Jignyasu. Guruji smiled feebly, as he was tired of speaking. Jignyasu noticed that and felt sorry. He said, 'Oh, I am so sorry, Guruji. You seem tired. I think we should be heading back, it's getting dark.'

Guruji smiled, and said, 'No, my son Jignyasu, let me at least put an end to your *jignyasa*, your curiosity, about why we need new, emerging gods.'

After a deep breath, Guruji began, 'Every civilization has its own needs and concerns. The civilization where Indra was a hero had been a tribal society. People were constantly at war and the Brahmins were dependent on the warrior class. Tribal here means indigenous people, people who belonged to the land from the very beginning. Most importantly, these people were pastoral nomads, involved in cattle-rearing, cattle herding, breeding and capturing. A cattle raid was a common form of aggression, a form of warfare at that time. These people were skilled in working with alloys, like bronze, to make weapons and they went to battle in two-wheeled chariots. These tribes were patriarchal and were quite effective when it came to mobilizing support for wars or attacks.' Jignyasu was all ears and while he could sense that Guruji was visibly tired, he also knew that if he had decided to explain, he would. So, it was not worth trying to stop Guruji, besides it was important for Jignyasu to have clarity on matters that bothered him. Guruji continued, 'With an increase in wealth, society started getting divided into groups and sections. This seemed to be inevitable, as there were groups who wielded power based on their profession or power due to a certain alignment in society. This also led to the formation of power centres. With power came conflicts and conflicts required understanding or agreements to take care of each other. This led to the growth of a ruling class, which soon started to display their might.'

'While the society during Indra's time was primarily pastoral, it does not rule out the existence of agriculture, except that the society was not economically dependent on them. Pastoralism included livestock breeding and, particularly, cattle herding as the major activity. Cattle were wealth and cattle raids were a way of acquiring fresh stock. The winner of the cows was the hero of the times, as we have seen in the case of the Indra–Vritra conflict. Vritra had metaphorically held cows in captivity.

'When a king was successful in battle, he distributed the loot. The priests claimed that their rituals had helped the warrior succeed. For the warrior, who had won the battle, a display of generosity was important and he displayed it by distributing cattle along with other things from the loot. However, he kept the horses, gold, chariots and female slaves for himself. This also became important for winning loyalties and establishing the rights of lineages,' Guruji elaborated. Jignyasu was amazed at the clarity of Guruji's explanation. He was rather surprised to see that so much had been going on behind the otherwise fantastic stories of gods! He was not going to miss a word of what he was hearing. Guruji continued, 'With changing times, agriculture became important. The lord of the herd eventually gave way to the lord of men. The people gradually entered into agricultural production, adopting agriculture as an occupation along with cattle rearing. However, clearing land for agriculture was difficult for them because of the dense jungles and because iron had not been discovered until then. Copper and bronze implements were not effective to clear the land.

'As they gradually shifted to settled agriculture, they came to value land in a new way. Cattle had been the most important form of wealth to the pastoral nomads, but land came to be the prized possession with changing times. Control over land and its use was exercised by clans. With the increasing significance of agriculture and the growth of trade, power came to be based on greater control over tribes and their territories. The territories of tribes came to be named after their dominant lineage. Power started becoming key.

'Another important development was that agriculture had also started undergoing a sea of change. With an increase in the population and settlements, there was a need for more crops and one yield per year was not sufficient. People realized that they needed to grow more and this gave rise to two crops a year. Quite obviously, one of the crops had to be less dependent on the rains, as rains came only once a year!' There was a smile on Guruji's face as he noticed a visible change in Jignyasu's expression. He continued, 'A new approach to agriculture was needed to increase production, which also made the storage of water crucial. To address this requirement, some semblance of embankments, tanks, etc., were constructed. This facilitated the cultivation of a second crop, leading to less dependency on rains. This also became one of the main reasons for the fall of Indra, who had come to be associated with rains.

'Besides, while cattle remained a mark of wealth, land gained importance and land for grazing became significant. Soon, the dependency on rains began to diminish and, as we have seen, Krishna brought out the significance of mountains when he protested against the worshipping of Indra,' Guruji elaborated.

Jignyasu was amazed. He could now see the import of Guruji's earlier statement when he said, *new, emerging gods*! While Jignyasu was still putting the pieces together in his mind, Guruji added, 'However, it is important to understand one thing. This increase in other activities did not mean that agriculture did not continue being important. It did remain important and this was shown in the myths about Krishna too.'

Jignyasu was unsure about whether he had understood this part, so he asked, 'How? I mean how is Lord Krishna shown to have any allegiance to agriculture when he didn't quite represent it?'

Guruji smiled and responded, 'Our forefathers were very intelligent. They systematically ensured that they did not alienate this significant part of the new and emerging society. You will find the constant presence of the plough-bearing Balarama with Krishna! This close relationship of Krishna with his elder brother, Balarama—who, in a way personified agriculture—was an important element in the growing significance of Lord Krishna in those times. This ensured that no section felt left out!'

Jignyasu was rather impressed by this perspective, which, of course, he had never even thought about. The amazing clarity that Guruji brought was unfathomable and Jignyasu was rather happy that he had heard this reasoning. The sky was growing dark and Jignyasu was aware that Guruji's eyesight was weak. He got up and said, 'I think we should be heading back; it is getting dark.'

Guruji nodded in agreement and got up with the help of his staff. Soon, they were on their way back to the ashram. Jignyasu was unusually quiet. Guruji knew that he had been given much to think about, but he also knew that Jignyasu's curiosity had been satiated. He was glad that his student seemed content with understanding why certain gods suddenly don't do so well with changing times.

In the distance, the sky had turned orange. The sun had set. But tomorrow would be another day and the sun would rise again, bringing fresh light for a new tomorrow and a new hero—who knows?

Acknowledgements

This book has been in the making for a long time—long enough to forget that it had begun with the earnestness of a yajna! Like its protagonist, this book has weathered many a storm—opinions, doubts, the pandemic and more! But they say that fruits of labour are always sweet and I have a host of people to thank for believing in me and the idea that had been germinating in me for a while.

First and foremost, thanks to Rudra from Rupa Publications for going ahead with what was just an idea when we began. Second, thanks to his wonderful team, especially, the editor, Sneha, who was meticulous in her editing and the cover artist, Amith, who conceptualized the idea of what Indra ought to look like over just a few calls.

I am also grateful to all the researchers and scholars who have built a body of work for me to weave this final fictionalized product.

Last but not least, thanks to my family, Viki and Mallica, who have been my pillars of support in every initiative I decide to take on!

Bibliography

Bhattacharji, Sukumari, *The Indian Theogony : Brahmā, Viṣṇu and Śiva,* Penguin Books India, 2000.

Dandekar, R.N., *Vedic Mythological Tracts,* Ajanta Publications, Delhi, 1979.

Macdonell, A.A., Vedic Mythology, Strassburg K.J. Trübner, 1897.

Mohanty, Muralidhar, *Indra in Indian Mythology,* Punthi Pustak, 2008.

Thapar, Romila, *From Lineage to State: Social Formations of the Mid-First Millenium BC in the Ganga Valley,* Oxford University Press, 1984.

The Rig Veda, Translated by Wendy Doniger, Penguin Classics, 2005.

Tilak, Bal Gangadhar, *Arctic Home in the Vedas,* Tilak Brothers, Poona City, 1903.